Deploying and Managing Active Directory with Windows PowerShell

Tools for cloud-based and hybrid environments

Charlie Russel

PUBLISHED BY
Microsoft Press
A division of Microsoft Corporation
One Microsoft Way
Redmond, Washington 98052-6399

Library of Congress Control Number: 2015936016
ISBN: 978-1-5093-0065-5

Printed and bound in the United States of America.

First Printing

Microsoft Press books are available through booksellers and distributors worldwide. If you need support related to this book, email Microsoft Press Support at mspinput@microsoft.com. Please tell us what you think of this book at http://aka.ms/tellpress.

This book is provided "as-is" and expresses the author's views and opinions. The views, opinions and information expressed in this book, including URL and other Internet website references, may change without notice.

Some examples depicted herein are provided for illustration only and are fictitious. No real association or connection is intended or should be inferred.

Acquisitions and Developmental Editor: Karen Szall
Editorial Production: Online Training Solutions, Inc. (OTSI)
Technical Reviewer: David Coombes; Technical Review services provided by Content Master, a member of CM Group, Ltd.
Copyeditor: Kathy Krause (OTSI)
Indexer: Susie Carr (OTSI)
Cover: Twist Creative • Seattle

I'd like to dedicate this book to my users: David R. Guy; Trey, Lord Barksdale; Dame Priscilla Katz; Alfredo "Alfie No-Nose" Fettuccine; Stanley T. Behr; Harold Catz; Dr. M. Eep; Ms. G. Gusano; Ms. E. Boots; and, finally, the hardest-working Cavalier King Charles Spaniel ever, Sir William Wallace.

—CHARLIE RUSSEL

Contents

What do you think of this book? We want to hear from you!

Microsoft is interested in hearing your feedback so we can improve our books and learning resources
for you. To participate in a brief survey, please visit:

http://aka.ms/tellpress

What do you think of this book? We want to hear from you!

Microsoft is interested in hearing your feedback so we can improve our books and learning resources for you. To participate in a brief survey, please visit:

http://aka.ms/tellpress

Introduction

If you're a Windows system administrator who is tired of click, click, clicking your way through screen after screen of wizards to do the same job over and over again, this book is for you. If you've been told that Windows PowerShell is hard, this book is definitely for you, because it simply isn't true. Nearly all the commands in this book are a line or two of Windows PowerShell code—one, maybe two cmdlets, with their everyday options laid out in a way that makes them easy to read and understand.

The target audience for this book is the working Windows system administrator, whether your domain is totally on premises, totally in the cloud, or in a hybrid environment. I'm not trying to teach you everything you need to know about Active Directory Domain Services, nor am I pretending to teach you Windows PowerShell. I assume you have at least some familiarity with both but want to take your everyday tasks to the next level.

I've taken care in writing this book to format the Windows PowerShell commands to improve understanding, not obfuscate, and the Microsoft Press production team has done a superb job of maintaining that. We could easily give you the command to promote a server to domain controller as shown here.

```
Install-ADDSDomainController -SkipPreChecks -NoGlobalCatalog:$false -
CreateDnsDelegation:$false -CriticalReplicationOnly:$false -DatabasePath
"C:\Windows\NTDS" -DomainName "TreyResearch.net" -InstallDns:$true -LogPath
"C:\Windows\NTDS" -NoRebootOnCompletion:$false -SiteName "Default-First-Site-
Name" -SysvolPath "C:\Windows\SYSVOL" -Force:$true
```

But although that would be technically correct, and easy for me to create, it produces something that is at best daunting, and at worst useless. So, instead, I've chosen to format the Windows PowerShell commands to make them easier to read and follow. The same command, as you'll find it in Chapter 4, "Deploy additional domain controllers," is as shown here.

```
Install-ADDSDomainController `
    -SkipPreChecks `
    -NoGlobalCatalog:$false `
    -CreateDnsDelegation:$false `
    -CriticalReplicationOnly:$false `
    -DatabasePath "C:\Windows\NTDS" `
    -DomainName "TreyResearch.net" `
    -InstallDns:$true `
    -LogPath "C:\Windows\NTDS" `
```

```
-NoRebootOnCompletion:$false `
-SiteName "Default-First-Site-Name" `
-SysvolPath "C:\Windows\SYSVOL" `
-Force:$true
```

Both commands produce exactly the same results, but by breaking the command up into multiple lines and using the Windows PowerShell end-of-line escape character—the backtick character (`)—I've made the second command much easier to read and understand.

Throughout this book, we use shaded text to show the output of commands. This gives you the output of commands without using a graphical screen shot in most cases. The command is shown in a fixed-width font, with the output being in a shaded fixed-width font, as shown here.

```
Add-ADGroupMember `
    -Identity "Cloneable Domain Controllers" `
    -Members (Get-ADComputer -Identity trey-dc-04).SAMAccountName `
    -PassThru
```

```
DistinguishedName : CN=Cloneable Domain
Controllers,CN=Users,DC=TreyResearch,DC=net
GroupCategory     : Security
GroupScope        : Global
Name              : Cloneable Domain Controllers
ObjectClass       : group
ObjectGUID        : b12b23c1-499b-4dbe-8206-846a17cd2df2
SamAccountName    : Cloneable Domain Controllers
SID               : S-1-5-21-910751839-3601328731-670513855-522
```

Finally, I've included not just the actual scripts from this book, but also all of the commands used in each chapter. They're in the companion content that is available for download, as described in the next section.

About the companion content

The companion content for this book can be downloaded from the following page:

http://aka.ms/ADPS/files

The companion content includes the following:

- All scripts in the book
- The Windows PowerShell commands from each chapter
- A sample netcfg file for setting up the virtual network described in Chapter 10, "Deploy Active Directory in the cloud"

Acknowledgments

As only writers can fully appreciate, no book ever makes it into a reader's hands without the work of many, many people, some of whom I'll never know, but all of whose efforts I greatly appreciate. This is especially true with this book, which was written on a really tight schedule that stressed everyone in the process. I truly appreciate everything everyone did to make this book happen.

Of the people who worked on this book, or supported me during the process—those whom I do know—I'd like to sincerely thank Anne Hamilton, who has been a friend and an ally at Microsoft Press. My editor at Microsoft Press since at least Windows 2000 has been Karen Szall, and I couldn't possibly have a better editor or friend. Karen, you are the absolute best, full stop.

At Online Training Solutions, Inc. (OTSI), Kathy Krause has been a superb editor with a light but deft and accurate touch, and her team—including Jean Trenary, Jaime Odell, Jeanne Craver, and Kerin Forsyth—have excelled. My sincere thanks. My excellent tech reviewer has been David Coombes, who has carefully gone over every command in the book, and more than once put me back on the right track. Thank you for doing so gently, but firmly. The thorough and accurate index is the hard work of Susie Carr at OTSI.

I'd also like to thank Gaby Kaplan of Microsoft, who has patiently taken my Windows PowerShell documentation bug reports and either fixed them instantly or sent them off to the correct person. She's a perfect example of the dedication to perfection and community involvement that has made working with the Windows PowerShell team at Microsoft such a pleasure over the years.

From the wonderful group of Windows PowerShell MVPs at Microsoft that I've been so fortunate to know and work with over the years, I'd like to call out three names for special mention: Jeffrey Hicks, whose blog continues to provide useful answers and insights, and that specifically answered a conundrum that had me stumped; Richard Siddaway, for his amazing help with the problems of filtering in ADUser; and my friend Thomas Lee, whose blogs and script snippets have educated and enlightened me for years.

I'd also like to thank my co-workers at Kaseya, who have been supportive and understanding during the writing of this book. I'd especially like to thank my boss, Michael Duncan, who is a real pleasure to work for, and my fellow system administrators, Dan Lowry and Eugene Hoang. You guys do an amazing job and are great to know and work with.

Finally, my wife and frequent co-author, Sharon Crawford. Without you, this book would never have been completed. You make my life a joy.

Free ebooks from Microsoft Press

From technical overviews to in-depth information on special topics, the free ebooks from Microsoft Press cover a wide range of topics. These ebooks are available in PDF, EPUB, and Mobi for Kindle formats, ready for you to download at:

http://aka.ms/mspressfree

Check back often to see what is new!

Errata, updates, & book support

We've made every effort to ensure the accuracy of this book and its companion content. You can access updates to this book—in the form of a list of submitted errata and their related corrections—at:

http://aka.ms/ADPS/errata

If you discover an error that is not already listed, please submit it to us at the same page.

If you need additional support, email Microsoft Press Book Support at:

mspinput@microsoft.com

Please note that product support for Microsoft software and hardware is not offered through the previous addresses. For help with Microsoft software or hardware, go to:

http://support.microsoft.com

We want to hear from you

At Microsoft Press, your satisfaction is our top priority, and your feedback our most valuable asset. Please tell us what you think of this book at:

http://aka.ms/tellpress

The survey is short, and we read every one of your comments and ideas. Thanks in advance for your input!

Stay in touch

Let's keep the conversation going! We're on Twitter:

http://twitter.com/MicrosoftPress

CHAPTER 1

Deploy your first forest and domain

In this chapter, I cover how to create a new Active Directory Domain Services (AD DS) forest where one has never existed before. This is, in some ways, the easiest task you're likely to face, but it's also one where getting it right is *really* important. The decisions you make here will affect the entire organization for the life of this deployment.

Active Directory Windows PowerShell nouns used in this chapter:

- ADDSDomainController
- ADDSForestInstallation
- ADDSForest
- ADRootDSE
- ADObject

Other Windows PowerShell commands used in this chapter:

- Get-NetAdapter
- Get-Member
- Set-NetIPAddress
- New-NetIPAddress
- Set-DnsClientServerAddress
- Get-NetIPAddress
- Rename-Computer
- Install-WindowsFeature
- Get-Command
- Format-Table
- Update-Help
- ConvertTo-SecureString

Before you start

This section sets some expectations. And yes, much of this has been covered in the introduction of the book, but in my experience most people don't read that. So I'll take a bit of liberty and do it again.

Prerequisites

This book assumes that you know the basics of both Active Directory and Windows PowerShell. I won't attempt to teach you how to use either. But, that being said, I hope and expect you'll learn something about both of them.

Versions

This book is being written against Windows Server Technical Preview, Build 9841. This includes Windows PowerShell 5.0, but no changes to Active Directory Domain Services (AD DS) beyond those in Windows Server 2012 R2 that affect the examples in the book. If I use a feature beyond that built into Windows 8.1 and Windows Server 2012 R2, I'll call it out explicitly. Most examples will work with Windows Server 2008 R2 and Windows Server 2012.

Code

By its nature, this book includes a lot of code. Most is fairly basic—one or two lines of code, because most actions you need to do in AD DS are ones that lend themselves to a few commands in Windows PowerShell. Where the task requires a bit more, I give you a full script, complete with built-in comment-based help, as shown later in the Get-myADVersion script. Other scripts are a bit more casual and might not include full comment-based help. These scripts tend to be the kind of simple, one-off scripts that all Windows PowerShell users create to simplify their work. I don't include full and complex error-handling routines as part of the scripts—not that I don't think they're useful, but when performing actions against Active Directory, I really would prefer to have errors be errors and have the script fail, rather than hide any of that or try to recover and continue.

Deploy your first forest

Most Windows system administrators will probably never have to create a new forest in an environment where there has never been one before. Most of us join a company and an environment that has been up and running for some time, and our tasks are focused on maintaining that existing environment—adding users and groups, adding domain controllers to existing domains, and even adding new domains to an existing forest. I'll cover all of those tasks in this book, and you can certainly jump ahead to the chapter that covers what you want to accomplish. But for those who are tasked with creating a new environment, it's important to do the job right, and that means planning *first*.

This is not a book on how to plan a new namespace and Active Directory forest. Instead of covering that here, I suggest that you read Chapters 3 and 4 of *Windows Server 2008 Administrator's Companion* (Microsoft Press, 2008). Yes, it's been a while since I wrote those chapters, but they're still valid today and will give you a solid understanding of the process.

Before you begin, make sure you have identified all the elements you'll need to configure as you set up the server you'll use to create your new forest and domain, and what the values for those are. The exact list you'll need will vary depending on the results of the preliminary planning you've done, and your network configuration, but it will likely include at least the following:

- Server IP address
- Server name
- Domain Name System (DNS) namespace for the root domain of the new forest
- Domain name for the root domain of the new forest
- DNS server type (Active Directory–integrated, or stand-alone)

A comment here about the server IP address: your domain controllers should ideally all use static IP addresses, but definitely your first domain controller should be at a fixed IP address.

Configure the server IP address

You can configure the server's name before the IP address, but when you do, it costs an extra reboot because the name change requires a reboot, so I like to do the IP address first. Setting a fixed IP address for a computer requires four commands—one to get the name and index of the network adapter you're setting to a fixed IP address, and three to configure the settings for that adapter.

Get the adapter alias and index

Before you can configure new settings for a network adapter, you need to know either the adapter's *interface alias* (name) or *interface index*. The interface alias corresponds to the name shown in the Network Connections dialog box (ncpa.cpl). To determine the interface alias and interface index, use the Get-NetAdapter cmdlet.

```
Get-NetAdapter
```

Name	InterfaceDescription	ifIndex	Status	MacAddress	LinkSpeed
10 Network	Microsoft Hyper-V Network Adapter #2	4	Up	00-15-5D-32-10-02	10 Gbps
50 Network	Microsoft Hyper-V Network Adapter	3	Disabled	00-15-5D-32-50-02	1 Gbps

The default output from Get-NetAdapter uses the Name column for the InterfaceAlias property and the ifIndex column for the InterfaceIndex property. To view all the properties and the actions associated with Get-NetAdapter, use the following.

```
Get-NetAdapter | Get-Member
```

Set a fixed IP address

To set a fixed IP address for this first domain controller in the forest, you need to first disable Dynamic Host Configuration Protocol (DHCP) and then set the IPv4 and IPv6 addresses. For the lab network used in this book, I have chosen 192.168.10.0/24 as the IPv4 subnet, and 2001:db8:0:10::/64 as the IPv6 subnet.

To disable DHCP on the 10 Network adapter, use the following command.

```
Set-NetIPInterface -InterfaceAlias "10 Network" -DHCP Disabled -PassThru
```

The Set-NetIPInterface cmdlet is a quiet cmdlet that doesn't return anything by default, so I added the -PassThru parameter to have it report back on the status of the IP interface.

Next, set the static IPv4 address to 192.168.10.2 by using the following command.

```
New-NetIPAddress `
    -AddressFamily IPv4 `
    -InterfaceAlias "10 Network" `
    -IPAddress 192.168.10.2 `
    -PrefixLength 24 `
    -DefaultGateway 192.168.10.1
```

Now set the IPv6 address to 2001:db8:0:10::2 by using the following command.

```
New-NetIPAddress `
    -AddressFamily IPv6 `
    -InterfaceAlias "10 Network" `
    -IPAddress 2001:db8:0:10::2 `
    -PrefixLength 64 `
    -DefaultGateway 2001:db8:0:10::1
```

The New-NetIPAddress cmdlet automatically selects the IPv4 or IPv6 address family based on the settings in the command, so you can omit the -AddressFamily parameter from the preceding commands if you want.

Set the DNS server addresses

The last part of setting a fixed IP address is to set the DNS server addresses. Because your first domain controller in the new forest should also be your DNS server, that's pretty easy to do by using the Set-DnsClientServerAddress cmdlet.

```
Set-DnsClientServerAddress `
    -InterfaceAlias "10 Network" `
    -ServerAddresses 192.168.10.2,2001:db8:0:10::2
```

So, when you pull all that together and run it on the first domain controller in your new forest, you can then run Get-NetIPAddress and get something like the following.

```
Get-NetIPAddress -InterfaceAlias "10 Network"
```

```
IPAddress          : 2001:db8:0:10::2
InterfaceIndex     : 4
InterfaceAlias     : 10 Network
AddressFamily      : IPv6
Type               : Unicast
PrefixLength       : 64
PrefixOrigin       : Manual
SuffixOrigin       : Manual
AddressState       : Preferred
ValidLifetime      : Infinite ([TimeSpan]::MaxValue)
PreferredLifetime  : Infinite ([TimeSpan]::MaxValue)
SkipAsSource       : False
PolicyStore        : ActiveStore

IPAddress          : 192.168.10.2
InterfaceIndex     : 4
InterfaceAlias     : 10 Network
AddressFamily      : IPv4
Type               : Unicast
PrefixLength       : 24
PrefixOrigin       : Manual
SuffixOrigin       : Manual
AddressState       : Preferred
ValidLifetime      : Infinite ([TimeSpan]::MaxValue)
PreferredLifetime  : Infinite ([TimeSpan]::MaxValue)
SkipAsSource       : False
PolicyStore        : ActiveStore
```

Set the server name

Before you actually deploy your new forest, you should set the name of your domain controller to match your naming convention. Changing the name of a computer causes a reboot, which is why you should delay that change until after all the IP address setting is done. To change the name of the new server to trey-dc-02, use the Rename-Computer cmdlet by using the following syntax.

```
Rename-Computer -NewName trey-dc-02 -Restart -Force -PassThru
```

This changes the name of the server and automatically restarts it. The -Force parameter suppresses the confirmation prompt, and the -PassThru parameter returns the results of the command. After the server restarts, you're ready to actually deploy your forest.

Install Active Directory Domain Services

Before you can promote the server to be a domain controller, you need to install the Active Directory Domain Services role on the server. Installing a role or feature uses the Install-WindowsFeature cmdlet. This cmdlet replaces the Add-WindowsFeature cmdlet used in Windows Server 2008 R2. For compatibility, Add-WindowsFeature is an alias to Install-WindowsFeature. The command to install AD DS, including the management tools required, is as follows.

```
Install-WindowsFeature -Name AD-Domain-Services -IncludeManagementTools
```

This installs AD DS on the server and includes both the graphical and Windows PowerShell tools that are used to manage and deploy Active Directory. For the purposes of this book, this includes two Windows PowerShell modules—ActiveDirectory and ADDSDeployment.

> **NOTE** The Install-WindowsFeature cmdlet includes additional parameters not shown here. The ones of most interest are the -IncludeAllSubfeature, -Credential, -Computer-Name, and -Vhd parameters. The -Vhd parameter deserves some explanation. By using this parameter, you can use Install-WindowsFeature to add Windows Server roles and features to an offline VHD file, allowing you to "pre-load" features without having to bring the virtual machine (VM) online. The VHD file can be local or remote. If it is remote, the Universal Naming Convention (UNC) path to the VHD is the value of the parameter. When the -Vhd parameter is combined with the -ComputerName parameter, the VHD can actually be modified from the remote computer.

Create the forest (dcpromo)

Beginning with Windows Server 2000, and right up until Windows Server 2012, the command-line way to create a new domain controller was to use the dcpromo command. But beginning with Windows Server 2012, dcpromo has been replaced with the ADDSDeployment module. This module supports remoting so that you can promote a server to a domain controller, create a new domain, or even create a new forest, without logging on to the server that is being promoted. To view the cmdlets in this module, use the following syntax.

```
Get-Command -Module ADDSDeployment | Format-Table Name
```

```
Name
----
Add-ADDSReadOnlyDomainControllerAccount
Install-ADDSDomain
Install-ADDSDomainController
Install-ADDSForest
Test-ADDSDomainControllerInstallation
Test-ADDSDomainControllerUninstallation
Test-ADDSDomainInstallation
Test-ADDSForestInstallation
Test-ADDSReadOnlyDomainControllerAccountCreation
Uninstall-ADDSDomainController
```

As you can tell, almost all of the various promote/demote/test possibilities are included in the module. The five Test cmdlets need a bit of explanation. Each of these cmdlets allows you to actually test whether all prerequisites are met before you run the Install or Add cmdlet of the same noun. This way you can fully test your environment before committing. The Install and Add nouns actually perform these same tests and will error out if any of them fail. However, the time to find out that you've got a problem is not the weekend you're actually performing the installation, but well before, so that you can correct any deficiencies and be prepared for success.

Update Windows PowerShell help

Before you go any further, it's a good idea to update your Windows PowerShell help files. Unfortunately, there are only stub help files (man pages) included with Windows PowerShell. This allows Microsoft to update the help files on a regular basis, but it isn't terribly helpful if you're using an unfamiliar command. The only full help file included with Windows PowerShell is that for the Update-Help cmdlet.

You need to be running with Administrative privileges to update the help files. You can update directly from Microsoft (the default) or update from a network share. The basic command is the following.

```
Update-Help
```

Yes, it is just that simple. This downloads and installs help files for all modules in the current session and for any modules found in the $PSModulePath locations. If you run it on a computer that already has the help files installed, it will check the current version against the updated version and install only those that are new. You can install help files from a network share by using the -SourcePath parameter:

```
Update-Help -SourcePath \\trey-dc-02\PSHelp
```

It's a good idea to get in the habit of updating help files whenever you add new modules to a server. If you have servers that don't have Internet access, or if you just want to control your Internet bandwidth, you can use the Save-Help cmdlet to download and save the newest help files to a network share. The command to force an update to the current help files and then save them to the \\trey-dc-02\PSHelp share is the following.

```
Save-Help -DestinationPath \\trey-dc-02\PSHelp -force
```

Test the forest creation

Before you start your weekend forest creation, only to discover in the middle of the process that you don't have the necessary prerequisites, it's a good practice to use the appropriate Test cmdlet to verify your environment. For creating the first forest in this book, that means using the Test-ADDSForestInstallation cmdlet. To test the trey-dc-02 server, which is sitting in a completely isolated lab environment and has no DNS on the network, use the Test-myForestCreate.ps1 script.

Test-myForestCreate.ps1

```
Import-Module ADDSDeployment
Test-ADDSForestInstallation `
    -DomainName 'TreyResearch.net' `
    -DomainNetBiosName 'TREYRESEARCH' `
    -DomainMode 6 `
    -ForestMode 6 `
    -NoDnsOnNetwork `
    -NoRebootOnCompletion
```

This script imports the ADDSDeployment module into the current session and then tests the environment to find out whether installing the new forest will succeed. (And before I get comments—yes, I know that the Import-Module step is no longer required. But it's a good habit from the old days to explicitly load a nonstandard module when I know I'm going to need it.) The results of the test are shown in Figure 1-1.

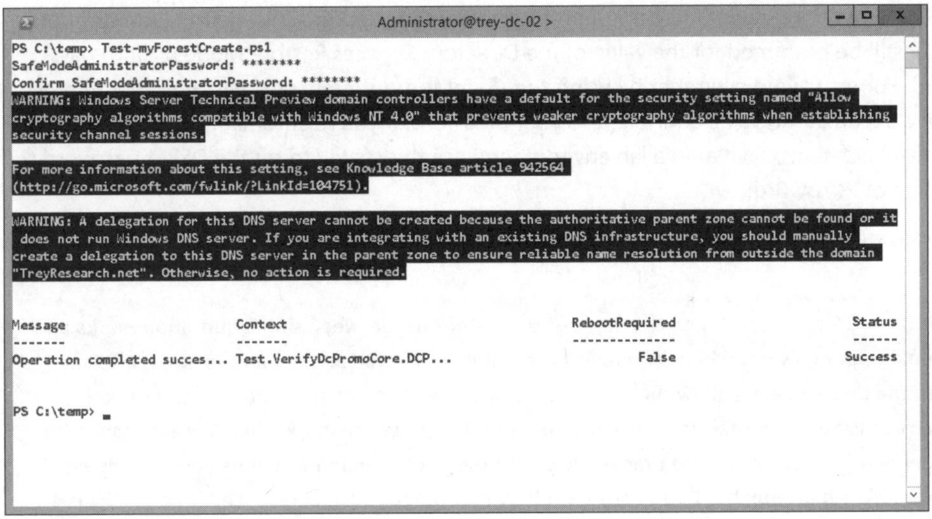

```
┌─────────────────────────────────────────────────────────────────────┐
│ ▦              Administrator@trey-dc-02 >               │ _ │ □ │ x │ │
├─────────────────────────────────────────────────────────────────────┤
│ PS C:\temp> Test-myForestCreate.ps1                                   │
│ SafeModeAdministratorPassword: ********                               │
│ Confirm SafeModeAdministratorPassword: ********                       │
│ WARNING: Windows Server Technical Preview domain controllers have a default for the security setting named "Allow │
│ cryptography algorithms compatible with Windows NT 4.0" that prevents weaker cryptography algorithms when establishing │
│ security channel sessions.                                            │
│                                                                       │
│ For more information about this setting, see Knowledge Base article 942564 │
│ (http://go.microsoft.com/fwlink/?LinkId=104751).                      │
│                                                                       │
│ WARNING: A delegation for this DNS server cannot be created because the authoritative parent zone cannot be found or it │
│  does not run Windows DNS server. If you are integrating with an existing DNS infrastructure, you should manually │
│ create a delegation to this DNS server in the parent zone to ensure reliable name resolution from outside the domain │
│ "TreyResearch.net". Otherwise, no action is required.                 │
│                                                                       │
│                                                                       │
│ Message              Context              RebootRequired        Status │
│ -------              -------              --------------        ------ │
│ Operation completed succes... Test.VerifyDcPromoCore.DCP...     False        Success │
│                                                                       │
│                                                                       │
│ PS C:\temp> _                                                         │
│                                                                       │
└─────────────────────────────────────────────────────────────────────┘
```

FIGURE 1-1 The results of Test-myForest.ps1

As you can tell, the Test-ADDSForestInstallation cmdlet returns two warnings. One is about the security settings; it warns about compatibility with some older versions of Windows NT due to a change in the cryptography. This is normal and expected, and it can be ignored unless you have computers or devices on your network that require settings that are compatible with Windows NT 4.0. The second is a delegation warning for DNS. This is also expected in most cases. Neither warning is sufficient to stop the installation or create problems, so you're ready to proceed.

Deploy the first domain controller and forest

At this point, you've configured your server, added the necessary Windows PowerShell modules and the Windows Server roles, and tested your environment. All is ready to do the actual initial deployment of your first domain controller and root AD DS forest.

The actual command to install the new forest and domain is nearly identical to the Test-ADDSForestInstallation command in the Test-myForest script. The main difference is that this time, you *do* want to reboot the server when the installation is finished, and because you just ran the tests, you can skip them.

```
Install-ADDSForest `
    -DomainName 'TreyResearch.net' `
    -DomainNetBiosName 'TREYRESEARCH' `
    -DomainMode 6 `
    -ForestMode 6 `
    -NoDnsOnNetwork `
    -SkipPreChecks `
    -Force
```

The other thing added here is a -Force parameter to suppress any confirmation prompts. You'll still be prompted for the value of the Directory Services Restore Mode (DSRM) password. You can avoid even that by using the -SafeModeAdministratorPassword parameter with a SecureString value equivalent to your password. If you're automating a lot of forest (or domain) creations, such as in a lab environment, use this syntax to set the DSRM password to a value of P@ssw0rd!.

```
$pwdSS = ConvertTo-SecureString -String 'P@ssw0rd!' -AsPlainText -Force
```

> **NOTE** This is a good time to point out the difference between single quotation marks and double quotation marks in Windows PowerShell. Both are used to identify strings, but a single quote doesn't allow the expansion or interpretation of special characters or variables inside the quotation marks, whereas double quotation marks do allow expansion. It's generally considered good practice to use single quotation marks unless you actually need variable expansion, but I don't always follow that practice. Here, however, it's a particularly good idea to use single quotation marks around a password string to avoid any interpretation of special characters.

The acceptable values for ForestMode and DomainMode are shown in Table 1-1.

TABLE 1-1 Acceptable DomainMode and ForestMode values

Functional level	Numeric	String
Windows Server 2003	2	Win2003
Windows Server 2008	3	Win2008
Windows Server 2008 R2	4	Win2008R2
Windows Server 2012	5	Win2012
Windows Server 2012 R2	6	Win2012R2

The default forest functional level for Windows Server is typically the same as the Windows Server version, with the exception that the default for Windows Server 2008 R2 is a forest functional level of Windows Server 2003.

The domain functional level can never be less than the forest functional level, but it can be higher. If the DomainMode isn't specified, it is computed from the environment.

> **MORE INFO** For more information about AD DS functional levels, see the "Understanding Active Directory Domain Services (AD DS) Functional Levels" TechNet article at *https://technet.microsoft.com/library/understanding-active-directory-functional-levels.aspx*.

When you create the new forest, the server is rebooted, and the only account active on the server is the TREYRESEARCH\Administrator account, which has the same password as the safe mode password you used with Install-ADDSForest.

To find out what Forest Mode, Domain Mode, and Schema Version you've just created, use the following.

Get-myADVersion.ps1

```
<#
.Synopsis
Get the current Schema version and Forest and Domain Modes
.Description
The Get-myADVersion script queries the AD to discover the current AD schema version,
and the forest mode and domain mode. If run without parameters, it will query the
current AD context, or if a Domain Controller is specified, it will query against
that DC's context. Must be run as a user with sufficient privileges to query AD DS.
.Example
Get-myADVersion
Queries against the current AD context.
.Example
Get-myADVersion -DomainController Trey-DC-02
Gets the AD versions for the Domain Controller "Trey-DC-02"
.Parameter DomainController
Specifies the domain controller to query. This will change the response to match
the AD context of the DC.
.Inputs
[string]
.Notes
    Author: Charlie Russel
 Copyright: 2015 by Charlie Russel
          : Permission to use is granted but attribution is appreciated
   Initial: 3/7/2015 (cpr)
   ModHist:
          :
#>
[CmdletBinding()]
Param(
    [Parameter(Mandatory=$False,Position=0)]
    [string]
    $DomainController
    )

if ($DomainController) {
   $AD = Get-ADRootDSE -Server $DomainController
   Get-ADObject $AD.SchemaNamingContext -Server $DomainController `
                              -Property ObjectVersion
```

```
} else {
    $AD = Get-ADRootDSE
    Get-ADObject $AD.SchemaNamingContext -Property ObjectVersion
}
$Forest = $AD.ForestFunctionality
$Domain = $AD.DomainFunctionality

# Use a Here-String to print out the result.
$VersionCodes = @"

Forest: $Forest
Domain: $Domain


Where the Schema version is:
72 = Windows Server Technical Preview Build 9841
69 = Windows Server 2012 R2
56 = Windows Server 2012
47 = Windows Server 2008 R2
44 = Windows Server 2008
31 = Windows Server 2003 R2
30 = Windows Server 2003
13 = Windows 2000
"@
$VersionCodes
```

The result of running Get-myADVersion is shown in Figure 1-2.

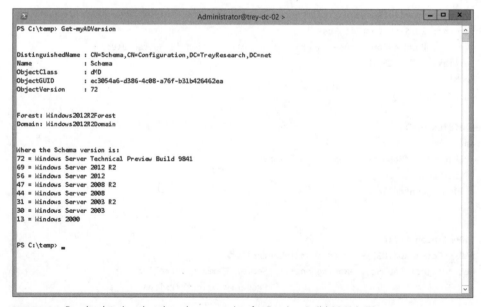

FIGURE 1-2 Results showing that the schema version for Preview Build 9841 is 72

Install-ADDSForest has some additional options that might be useful in your environment and that allow you to tweak the initial configuration. Table 1-2 shows a fuller list of the options for Install-ADDSForest.

TABLE 1-2 Key parameters for Install-ADDSForest

Parameter	Type	Description
-DomainName	String	The fully qualified domain name of the new domain (TreyResearch.net in this book's example).
[-CreateDnsDelegation]	Boolean	Attempts to create a DNS delegation to the new DNS server.
[-DatabasePath]	String	The location to store the domain database. Must be a local fixed disk.
[-DnsDelegationCredential]	PSCredential	A credential object with permission to create the DNS delegation.
[-DomainMode]	DomainMode	The AD DS domain functional level of the new domain.
[-DomainNetbiosName]	String	The NetBIOS name of the new domain (TREYRESEARCH in this book's example).
[-ForestMode]	ForestMode	The AD DS forest functional level of the new forest.
[-Force]	Boolean	Suppresses confirmation prompts.
[-InstallDns]	Boolean	Installs Active Directory Integrated DNS server. Default value is calculated based on the environment.
[-LogPath]	String	Path to the log of the install.
[-NoDnsOnNetwork]	Boolean	Specifies that there are no DNS servers present on the network. Active Directory Integrated DNS is installed, and the network adapter or adapters are configured to use 127.0.0.1 and ::1 as the DNS server.
[-NoRebootOnCompletion]	Boolean	Prevents the server from rebooting after the installation completes. Fair warning—the server is in an interim state and is not stable. Using this switch is really a bad idea.
[-SafeModeAdministratorPassword]	SecureString	Sets the DSRM password. If it is not specified, the user is prompted for the password and a confirming password.
[-SkipAutoConfigureDns]	Boolean	Skips automatic configuration of DNS settings. Used if the DNS Server service is already installed.
[-SkipPreChecks]	Boolean	Doesn't test the environment to find out whether the installation will succeed. Only recommended when you're separately running Test-ADDSForestInstallation.
[-SysvolPath]	String	Fully qualified local path to the fixed disk where the SYSVOL file is written.

Summary

In this chapter, you learned how to use Windows PowerShell to create a new Active Directory Domain Services deployment with a new Active Directory forest and root domain. You learned how to configure a network adapter to use a fixed IP address, including setting the DNS server address. You renamed the server to a more human-friendly name that fits with your organizational naming convention, and you installed additional roles and features on the server.

After configuring the networking on the server, you tested your environment to ensure that you were fully prepared to deploy the new forest, and when the test was successful, you promoted the server to be the root domain controller in your new forest.

In the next chapter, you'll learn how to configure your DNS server, adding DNS zones and resource records, and you'll also learn how to configure DHCP entirely with Windows PowerShell.

CHAPTER 2

Manage DNS and DHCP

I t's impossible to deploy and manage Active Directory Domain Services (AD DS) without also managing at least the Domain Name System (DNS), which is an integral part of Active Directory. And, if I'm going to cover DNS, I think it also makes sense to cover at least the basics of Dynamic Host Configuration Protocol (DHCP).

In this chapter, you'll learn how to create and manage DNS zones, including primary, secondary, and stub zones, and how to create and manage DNS records. You'll also learn basic DHCP setup and configuration.

Active Directory Windows PowerShell nouns used in this chapter:

None

Other Windows PowerShell commands used in this chapter:

- Add-DnsServerPrimaryZone
- Add-DnsServerSecondaryZone
- Get-DnsServerZone
- Format-Table
- Export-DnsServerZone
- Set-DnsServerPrimaryZone
- Set-DnsServerSecondaryZone
- Add-DnsServerStubZone
- Set-DnsServerStubZone
- Add-DnsServerConditionalForwarderZone
- Add-DnsServerZoneDelegation
- Set-DnsServerZoneDelegation
- Get-Help
- Add-DnsServerResourceRecord
- Add-DnsServerResourceRecordA
- Add-DnsServerResourceRecordAAAA
- Add-DnsServerResourceRecordCName
- Add-DnsServerResourceRecordDnsKey

- Add-DnsServerResourceRecordDS
- Add-DnsServerResourceRecordMX
- Add-DnsServerResourceRecordPtr
- Get-DnsServerResourceRecord
- Set-DnsServerResourceRecord
- Set-DnsServerScavenging
- Start-DnsServerScavenging
- Get-DnsServerScavenging
- Install-WindowsFeature
- Add-DhcpServerInDC
- Add-DhcpServerv4Scope
- Add-DhcpServerv4ExclusionRange
- Set-DhcpServerv4OptionValue
- Add-DhcpServerv6Scope
- Add-DhcpServerv6ExclusionRange
- Set-DhcpServerv6OptionValue

Manage DNS zones

A primary DNS zone provides authoritative name resolution for the zone. In traditional DNS, there is a single primary zone and as many secondary zones as needed to support the name resolution traffic for the zone. Windows Server supports traditional primary and secondary DNS zones and stub zones but uses an Active Directory–integrated, primary DNS zone by default. Because Active Directory integration is used, the zone can be stored on all AD DS domain controllers, providing a high level of fault tolerance and distributing the name resolution traffic across all domain controllers.

Secondary DNS zones are read-only zones that help distribute the network traffic and provide faster name resolution. They contain full copies of all DNS records for the zone. They are primarily useful with traditional primary DNS zones.

A stub DNS zone doesn't contain full DNS information for the zone, only the necessary information about which servers are authoritative for the zone. Stub zones are useful when you don't want to expose all the details of a particular zone but still need to provide name resolution. The stub zone has records only for the primary DNS servers for the zone. When a DNS request for the zone is received, the stub zone queries the name servers it has in the stub zone to answer the DNS request.

In Chapter 1, "Deploy your first forest and domain," when you deployed your initial AD DS domain and forest, an Active Directory–integrated primary DNS zone was created and configured for the new domain automatically. This was a *forward lookup zone*—that is, a zone that allows name lookups and returns IP addresses. The forest creation process does not, however, create *reverse lookup zones* that allow IP address lookups that return the machine name.

You can create additional DNS zones and configure them either as Active Directory–integrated or to use stand-alone zone files. Secondary DNS zones always use stand-alone zone files. When you configure a zone by using zone files, the zone is stored in those zone files. The default location for DNS zone files is %windir%\system32\dns, with a file name of *zonename*.dns, where *zonename* is the name of the zone, such as TreyResearch.net.

Manage primary zones

Primary DNS zones are the core of name resolution and are used for both forward lookup and reverse lookup zones. You can create new zones, change the settings of existing zones, convert zones from file-based to Active Directory–integrated, or even convert an Active Directory–integrated zone to a file-based zone by first exporting the zone, deleting it from AD DS, and then recreating the zone as a file-based zone with the LoadExisting parameter.

Create new primary zones

You can create new zones for both Active Directory–integrated and file-based zones. Use the Add-DnsServerPrimaryZone cmdlet to create new zones. To create an Active Directory–integrated primary forward lookup zone for TailspinToys.com, use the following command.

```
Add-DnsServerPrimaryZone -Name 'tailspintoys.com' `
                         -ComputerName 'trey-dc-02.treyresearch.net' `
                         -ReplicationScope 'Domain' `
                         -DynamicUpdate 'Secure' `
                         -PassThru
```

This creates an Active Directory–integrated zone that is replicated to the domain only. It accepts secure dynamic updates. The -PassThru parameter tells Windows PowerShell to report the results of the command, as shown in Figure 2-1.

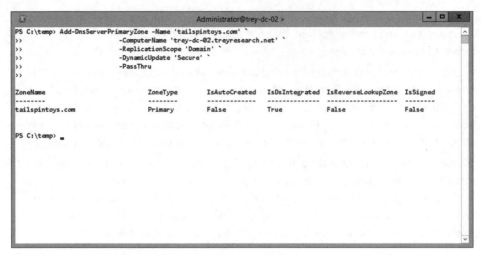

FIGURE 2-1 Adding a new Active Directory–integrated DNS zone

For those who only believe it when they see it in the graphical user interface (GUI), Figure 2-2 shows the DNS Manager after the zone for TailspinToys.com is added by using Windows PowerShell.

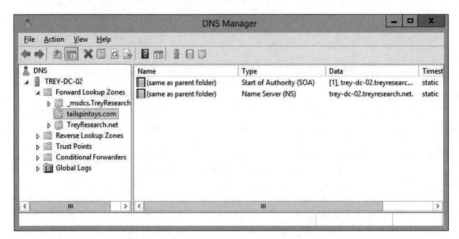

FIGURE 2-2 DNS Manager showing the new TailspinToys.com zone

Creating a reverse lookup zone is similar to creating a forward lookup zone. The difference is that instead of using the Name parameter, you use the NetworkID parameter. Thus, to create an Active Directory–integrated reverse lookup zone that is replicated across the entire forest and that accepts both secure and nonsecure dynamic updates, use the following command.

```
Add-DnsServerPrimaryZone -NetworkID 192.168.10.0/24 `
                         -ReplicationScope 'Forest' `
                         -DynamicUpdate 'NonsecureAndSecure' `
                         -PassThru
```

The NetworkID parameter deserves a bit more detail. The parameter expects an ID in the A.B.C.D/prefix format for IPv4 or the 1111:2222:3333:4444::/prefix format for IPv6. Only A, B, C, or D class zones can be created for IPv4; partial zones are not supported. For IPv6, zone prefixes of /16 to /128 in 4-bit increments are supported.

To create an IPv6 reverse lookup zone for TreyResearch.net's IPv6 range, use the following command.

```
Add-DnsServerPrimaryZone -NetworkID 2001:db8:0:10::/64 `
                         -ReplicationScope 'Forest' `
                         -DynamicUpdate 'Secure' `
                         -PassThru
```

The results of creating these two reverse lookup zones are shown in Figure 2-3.

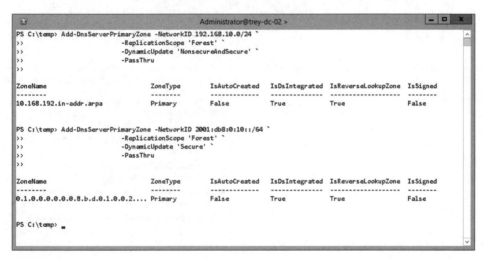

FIGURE 2-3 Creating primary reverse lookup zones

Creating file-based zones uses the -ZoneFile parameter. For example, see the following code.

```
Add-DnsServerPrimaryZone -Name 'tailspintoys.com' `
                         -ZoneFile 'tailspintoys.com.dns' `
                         -DynamicUpdate 'None'
```

Change the settings of a primary zone

When you create a new primary DNS zone, some settings are simply set to their default values, and there aren't specific parameters to Add-DnsServerPrimaryZone so that those values can be configured at creation. However, you can use the Set-DnsServerPrimaryZone cmdlet to configure those settings. Settings that can be configured after creation are shown in Table 2-1.

TABLE 2-1 DNS primary zone settings

Setting	Value	Description
AllowedDcForNsRecordsAutoCreation	String[]	An array of domain controller IP addresses as strings that can add themselves as name servers for the DNS domain.
Notify	String	The value of the Notify parameter specifies how secondary zone controllers are notified of changes to the zone. ■ **NoNotify** The domain does not notify secondary servers. ■ **Notify** The domain sends change notifications to all secondary servers. ■ **NotifyServers** The domain sends notifications only to listed name servers.
NotifyServers	IPAddress[]	An array of IP addresses of secondary zone controllers that are notified when a change to the zone is made and the Notify setting is set to NotifyServers.
SecondaryServers	IPAddress[]	An array of IP addresses of servers that are permitted to receive zone transfers for the zone.
SecureSecondaries	String	The value of the SecureSecondaries parameter specifies how the DNS master server allows zone transfers. The options are: ■ **NoTransfer** Transfers are not allowed from this zone. ■ **TransferAnyServer** Any server that requests a zone transfer receives it. ■ **TransferToZoneNameServer** Zone transfers are only allowed to listed name servers. ■ **TransferToSecureServers** Zone transfers are only allowed to listed secondary servers.

To set the TailspinToys.com DNS zone to send notifications to the secondary DNS servers at 192.168.10.201 and 192.168.10.202, use the following command.

```
Set-DnsServerPrimaryZone -Name 'TailspinToys.com' `
                -Notify 'NotifyServers' `
                -NotifyServers "192.168.10.201","192.168.10.202" `
                -PassThru
```

To view the details of the TailspinToys.com DNS zone, use the command Get-DnsServerZone -Name 'TailspinToys.com' | Format-List, as shown in Figure 2-4.

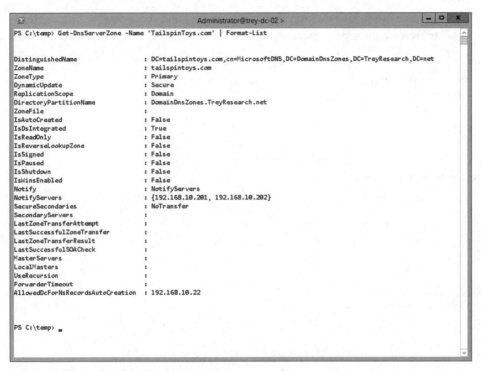

FIGURE 2-4 The results of the Get-DnsServerZone command

Export a primary zone

An Active Directory–integrated DNS zone is stored in AD DS and isn't typically stored as a file. However, it can be useful to have a file of the DNS zone for disaster recovery purposes or for building test environments, and this is easy with the Export-DnsServerZone cmdlet. To export the IPv6 reverse lookup zone created earlier, use the following command.

```
Export-DnsServerZone -Name '0.1.0.0.0.0.0.0.8.b.d.0.1.0.0.2.ip6.arpa' `
                -Filename '0.1.0.0.0.0.0.0.8.b.d.0.1.0.0.2.ip6.arpa.dns'
```

The file is saved in the %windir%\system32\dns directory and contains all the information necessary to recreate the zone as shown here.

```
;
;  Database file (null) for Default zone scope in zone
0.1.0.0.0.0.0.0.8.b.d.0.1.0.0.2.ip6.arpa.
;      Zone version:  1
;

@                    IN  SOA trey-dc-02.treyresearch.net.
hostmaster.treyresearch.net. (
                     1           ; serial number
                     900         ; refresh
                     600         ; retry
                     86400       ; expire
                     3600      ) ; default TTL

;
;  Zone NS records
;

@                    NS   trey-dc-02.treyresearch.net.

;
;  Zone records
;
```

Manage secondary zones

Secondary DNS zones are primarily used for providing distributed DNS resolution when you are using traditional file-based DNS zones. Secondary DNS zones are used for both forward lookup and reverse lookup zones. The DnsServerSecondaryZone set of cmdlets is used to deploy and manage secondary DNS zones.

A secondary DNS zone is a read-only zone and depends on transferring the data for the zone from another DNS server. That other server must be configured to allow zone transfers.

Create secondary zones

Use the Add-DnsServerSecondaryZone cmdlet to create a new secondary DNS zone. You can use this command to create either forward lookup or reverse lookup zones. To create a secondary reverse lookup zone for the IPv6 zone created and exported earlier, copy the exported DNS file to %windir%\system32\dns on the server you want to add a secondary DNS zone to, and then use the following command.

```
Add-DnsServerSecondaryZone -Name 0.1.0.0.0.0.0.0.8.b.d.0.1.0.0.2.ip6.arpa `
                           -ZoneFile "0.1.0.0.0.0.0.0.8.b.d.0.1.0.0.2.ip6.arpa.dns" `
                           -LoadExisting `
                           -MasterServers 192.168.10.2,2001:db8:0:10::2 `
                           -PassThru
```

The results of the command are shown in Figure 2-5.

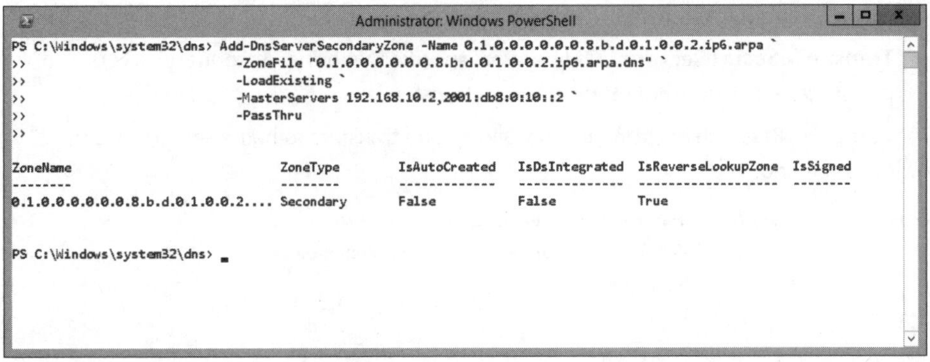

FIGURE 2-5 Creating a secondary DNS zone

Change the settings of a secondary zone

Secondary DNS zones have few settings because they are read-only zones dependent on their master servers. When you create a new secondary DNS zone, all of the settings for the zone can be set as part of the Add-DnsServerSecondaryZone cmdlet. However, if you later need to change those values (to change the master servers, for example), you can use the Set-DnsServerSecondaryZone cmdlet to modify the zone settings. To modify the same IPv6 reverse lookup secondary zone to use a different array of master servers, use the command.

```
Set-DnsServerSecondaryZone -Name 0.1.0.0.0.0.0.0.8.b.d.0.1.0.0.2.ip6.arpa `
                           -MasterServers 192.168.10.3,2001:db8:0:10::3 `
                           -PassThru
```

> **TIP** When setting the properties of a reverse lookup zone, you can use either the Name parameter or the NetworkID parameter.

Configure zone transfer settings

A secondary zone can only transfer the zone from a primary zone that allows the transfer, preventing unauthorized zone transfers. The setting of zone transfer permissions is done at the primary zone, not at the secondary zone. To set the zone transfer permissions, use the

Set-DnsServerPrimaryZone cmdlet. The SecureSecondaries parameter controls the servers to which transfers are allowed. The SecureSecondaries parameter accepts the following values:

- **NoTransfer**   No transfers are allowed for this zone from this server.
- **TransferAnyServer**   Any server can request a zone transfer, including servers that you know nothing about and don't manage or control.
- **TransferToZoneNameServer**   Only servers in the NS records for this zone are allowed to request transfers.
- **TransferToSecureServers**   Only servers specified with the -SecondaryServers parameter are allowed to request a zone transfer.

To set the TreyResearch.net zone to only allow zone transfers to name servers, use the following command.

```
Set-DnsServerPrimaryZone -Name 'treyresearch.net' `
                         -SecureSecondaries TransferToZoneNameServer `
                         -PassThru
```

Manage stub zones

Stub DNS zones contain the necessary records to locate a zone's name servers *only*. They do not maintain the records of other devices or computers in the zone. They're a useful way to keep track of which servers are currently authoritative for a child zone, without maintaining full records for that child zone. Stub zones can be file-based or Active Directory–integrated and can be used for both forward lookup zones and reverse lookup zones.

Secondary zones are a significant security concern, because they expose all of the records of the zone, potentially providing an attacker with important information that would facilitate further attack. With stub zones, the only exposure is the names and IP addresses of the designated name servers. Further, stub DNS zones don't require that the primary zone allow zone transfers. The DnsServerStubZone pair of cmdlets is used to deploy and manage stub zones. To add a new stub zone for TailspinToys.com, whose master server is 192.168.10.4, and replicate that stub zone across the domain, use the following.

```
Add-DnsServerStubZone -Name TailspinToys.com `
                      -MasterServers 192.168.10.4 `
                      -ReplicationScope Domain `
                      -PassThru
```

To change the properties of the DNS stub zone for TailspinToys.com to use a local array of master servers (stored in the Windows registry), use the following.

```
Set-DnsServerStubZone -Name TailspinToys.com `
                      -LocalMasters 192.168.10.201,192.168.10.202 `
                      -PassThru
```

Configure conditional forwards

Use conditional forwards to specify where to forward DNS requests for a specific DNS domain. When you have multiple internal DNS domains (such as after a merger or acquisition, for example), you might need to resolve DNS names from another internal domain. You could maintain a stub zone for that domain, but you can also use conditional forwards. For example, if your DNS domain is TailspinToys.com, and your DNS server at 192.168.10.201 receives a request for connection to trey-rdsh-06.treyresearch.net, the DNS server would first look to find out whether it hosted the domain, either as a primary or secondary zone, or as a stub zone. Failing that, it would check the DNS cache to find out whether it had recently looked up the address for it. If it still didn't have an address for trey-rdsh-06.treyresearch.net, it would forward the address to another server. The first server it would forward the request to is any configured conditional forwards for TreyResearch.net. If it didn't have any, however, the address would be forwarded to the Internet, either to a configured forwarding address or the root servers. If TreyResearch.net is on your internal network, you don't want to be resolving addresses on the Internet. By setting a conditional forward, you ensure that your internal traffic stays internal.

To add a conditional forward for TreyResearch.net, use the following command.

```
Add-DnsServerConditionalForwarderZone -Name treyresearch.net `
                             -MasterServers 192.168.10.2,2001:db8::10:2 `
                             -ForwarderTimeout 5 `
                             -ReplicationScope "Forest" `
                             -Recursion $False `
                             -PassThru
```

This command creates a conditional forwarder for TreyResearch.net. Each server in the MasterServers is queried in turn. If a server hasn't answered in five seconds (the value of ForwarderTimeout), the next server is queried. Because the Recursion parameter is specified as $False, if none of the master servers specified answers the request, the DNS lookup fails. To change the settings of an existing DNS conditional forward, use the Set-DnsServer-ConditionalForwarderZone cmdlet. For example, to change the conditional forward for TreyResearch.net to specify new master servers, use the following syntax.

```
Add-DnsServerConditionalForwarderZone -Name treyresearch.net `
                             -MasterServers 192.168.10.3,2001:db8::10:3 `
                             -PassThru
```

Conditional forwards are stored as zones and can be stored either in the Windows registry or as Active Directory–integrated zones. If the ReplicationScope or DirectoryPartition are specified, the zone is stored in the registry. To remove a conditional forward, use the Remove-DnsServerZone cmdlet.

Manage zone delegation

DNS zone delegation delegates the administration of a DNS zone. With this you can divide a large zone into smaller subzones to distribute the load and improve performance. So, for example, if TreyResearch.net has several subzones (engineering.treyresearch.net, corp.treyresearch.net, lab.treyresearch.net, and administration.treyresearch.net), you can delegate a subzone to a different DNS server to distribute the load and administrative overhead. To add a delegation for the engineering subzone to server trey-engdc-12, use the following command.

```
Add-DnsServerZoneDelegation -Name TreyResearch.net `
                    -ChildZoneName Engineering `
                    -IPAddress 192.168.10.12,2001:db8:0:10::c `
                    -NameServer trey-engdc-12.engineering.treyresearch.net `
                    -PassThru
```

The DnsServerZoneDelegation group of cmdlets includes the verbs Add, Get, Remove, and Set. Use the Set-DnsServerZoneDelegation cmdlet to change the IP address or addresses to which to delegate the zone. This doesn't add to the existing delegation IP address but replaces it. So, for example, to change the delegation of the Engineering subzone of TreyResearch.net to the DNS server trey-engdc-13, use the following.

```
Set-DnsServerZoneDelegation -Name TreyResearch.net `
                    -ChildZoneName Engineering `
                    -IPAddress 192.168.10.13,2001:db8:0:10::d `
                    -NameServer trey-engdc-13.engineering.treyresearch.net `
                    -PassThru
```

Manage DNS records

DNS servers do more than simply translate a computer name into an IP address, though that's certainly their first and primary duty. They also provide the information that other services and servers need to know which server hosts a particular service. So, for example, Internet mail servers need to know which server in TreyResearch.net is the mail server for all of TreyResearch.net's email. And other clients and servers on the TreyResearch network need to know which servers are official name servers for the zone.

Each of these services is designated by a specific type of DNS *resource record*. The basic A or AAAA resource record translates a DNS name into an IPv4 or IPv6 address, respectively. An MX resource record specifies a mail server for the domain, and NS resource records are used to specify which servers are name servers for the domain.

Windows DNS supports a wide variety of DNS records, but the core resource records are the following:

- **A**   An IPv4 host address record. The A record is a forward lookup record that translates a host name into an IPv4 address.

- **AAAA**   An IPv6 host address record. The AAAA record is a forward lookup record that translates a host name into an IPv6 address.

- **CNAME** A canonical name record. The CNAME record facilitates the use of more than one resource record to refer to a single host.

- **DS** A Delegated Signer record. The DS record is used with Domain Name System Security Extensions (DNSSEC) to designate the subzone signing key.

- **DNSKey** The public key record for a DNSSEC signed zone.

- **MX** A Mail Exchanger record. The MX record identifies the email server for a domain. There can be multiple MX records for a domain; they are used in order of precedence.

- **NS** A Name Server record. The NS record identifies a name server for the domain. There can be multiple NS records in a domain.

- **PTR** A pointer record. The PTR record is a reverse lookup record that translates an IP address into a host name. PTR records can be IPv4 or IPv6 addresses.

- **TXT** A text record. The TXT record is used to assign unformatted text to a host in DNS. A common use of TXT records is for Sender Policy Framework (SPF) records used to identify legitimate email senders.

- **SOA** A Start of Authority record. The SOA record is a version number record identifying the version number of the DNS zone.

- **SRV** A Service record. The SRV record identifies the host name and port number of servers for the specified service.

All of the resource records listed here can be created or changed by using the Windows PowerShell DnsServerResourceRecord cmdlets with the exception of the SOA record. SOA records are automatically updated whenever a change is made to the DNS zone. In addition to the general Add-DnsServerResourceRecord cmdlet, which can be used to make all supported resource records, there are specific Add- cmdlets for the A, AAAA, CNAME, DS, DNSKey, MX, and PTR resource records.

```
Get-Help Add-DnsServerResourceRecord* | ft -auto Name,Synopsis
```

Name	Synopsis
Add-DnsServerResourceRecord	Adds a resource record of a specified type to…
Add-DnsServerResourceRecordA	Adds a type A resource record to a DNS zone.
Add-DnsServerResourceRecordAAAA	Adds a type AAAA resource record to a DNS server.
Add-DnsServerResourceRecordCName	Adds a type CNAME resource record to a DNS zone.
Add-DnsServerResourceRecordDnsKey	Adds a type DNSKEY resource record to a DNS zone.
Add-DnsServerResourceRecordDS	Adds a type DS resource record to a DNS zone.
Add-DnsServerResourceRecordMX	Adds an MX resource record to a DNS server.
Add-DnsServerResourceRecordPtr	Adds a type PTR resource record to a DNS server.

Create name (A and AAAA) resource records

The process for creating any DNS resource record is essentially the same, though each record type has settings appropriate to the type. So, for example, to create an A record for the server trey-wds-11, use the following command.

```
Add-DnsServerResourceRecord  -ZoneName "TreyResearch.net" `
                             -A `
                             -Name trey-wds-11 `
                             -IPv4Address 192.168.10.11 `
                             -CreatePtr `
                             -PassThru
```

This uses the general Add-DnsServerResourceRecord cmdlet, therefore I need to specify the record type (-A). And because I'm also running a reverse-lookup zone, I added the CreatePtr parameter to automatically create the PTR resource record for this server. The results are displayed back to the console because I used the PassThru parameter, otherwise this is a completely silent command. Figure 2-6 shows the command and the result.

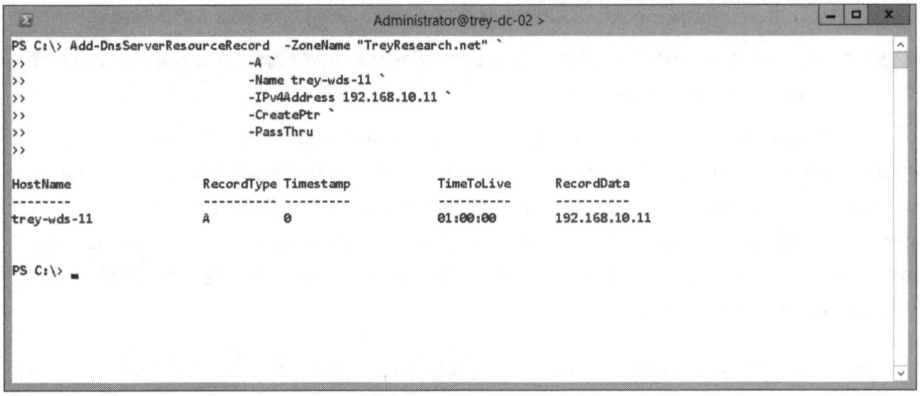

FIGURE 2-6 Creating a new A record for trey-wds-11

Using the specific Add-DnsServerResourceRecordA cmdlet to create the same DNS A record would use the following command.

```
Add-DnsServerResourceRecordA -ZoneName "TreyResearch.net" `
                             -Name trey-wds-11 `
                             -IPv4Address 192.168.10.11 `
                             -CreatePtr `
                             -PassThru
```

I'm not quite sure why there are specific cmdlets for some record types. It just makes one more thing to remember. I prefer using the general Add-DnsServerResourceRecord cmdlet, and adding the appropriate switch type to it. But it does make for an ugly looking syntax for the cmdlet.

syntax Add-DnsServerResourceRecord

```
Syntax for Add-DnsServerResourceRecord is:

Add-DnsServerResourceRecord [-ZoneName] <string> -InputObject
<CimInstance#DnsServerResourceRecord> [-ComputerName <string>]
[-PassThru] [-AllowUpdateAny] [-Force] [-CimSession <CimSession[]>]
[-ThrottleLimit <int>] [-AsJob]
[-WhatIf] [-Confirm] [<CommonParameters>]


Add-DnsServerResourceRecord [-ZoneName] <string> [-Name] <string> -X25 -PsdnAddress
<string> [-ComputerName <string>]
[-PassThru] [-TimeToLive <timespan>] [-AgeRecord] [-AllowUpdateAny]
[-CimSession <CimSession[]>] [-ThrottleLimit
<int>] [-AsJob] [-WhatIf] [-Confirm] [<CommonParameters>]


Add-DnsServerResourceRecord [-ZoneName] <string> [-Name] <string> -Wks
-InternetAddress <ipaddress> -InternetProtocol <string>
-Service <string[]> [-ComputerName <string>] [-PassThru] [-TimeToLive
<timespan>] [-AgeRecord]
[-AllowUpdateAny] [-CimSession <CimSession[]>] [-ThrottleLimit <int>] [-AsJob]
[-WhatIf] [-Confirm] [<CommonParameters>]


Add-DnsServerResourceRecord [-ZoneName] <string> -WinsR -LookupTimeout <timespan>
-CacheTimeout <timespan>
-ResultDomain <string> [-ComputerName <string>] [-PassThru] [-Force] [-Replicate]
[-CimSession <CimSession[]>]
[-ThrottleLimit <int>] [-AsJob] [-WhatIf] [-Confirm] [<CommonParameters>]


Add-DnsServerResourceRecord [-ZoneName] <string> -Wins -LookupTimeout <timespan>
-WinsServers <ipaddress[]>
-CacheTimeout <timespan> [-ComputerName <string>] [-PassThru] [-Force] [-Replicate]
[-CimSession <CimSession[]>]
[-ThrottleLimit <int>] [-AsJob] [-WhatIf] [-Confirm] [<CommonParameters>]
```

```
Add-DnsServerResourceRecord [-ZoneName] <string> [-Name] <string> -Txt
-DescriptiveText <string> [-ComputerName
<string>] [-PassThru] [-TimeToLive <timespan>] [-AgeRecord] [-AllowUpdateAny]
[-CimSession <CimSession[]>]
[-ThrottleLimit <int>] [-AsJob] [-WhatIf] [-Confirm] [<CommonParameters>]


Add-DnsServerResourceRecord [-ZoneName] <string> [-Name] <string> -Srv
-DomainName <string> -Priority <uint16> -Weight <uint16>
-Port <uint16> [-ComputerName <string>] [-PassThru] [-TimeToLive <timespan>]
[-AgeRecord] [-AllowUpdateAny]
[-CimSession <CimSession[]>] [-ThrottleLimit <int>] [-AsJob] [-WhatIf] [-Confirm]
[<CommonParameters>]


Add-DnsServerResourceRecord [-ZoneName] <string> [-Name] <string> -RT
-Preference <uint16> -IntermediateHost <string>
[-ComputerName <string>] [-PassThru] [-TimeToLive <timespan>] [-AgeRecord]
[-AllowUpdateAny] [-CimSession <CimSession[]>]
[-ThrottleLimit <int>] [-AsJob] [-WhatIf] [-Confirm] [<CommonParameters>]


Add-DnsServerResourceRecord [-ZoneName] <string> [-Name] <string> -RP -
ResponsiblePerson <string> -Description <string>
[-ComputerName <string>] [-PassThru] [-TimeToLive <timespan>] [-AgeRecord]
[-AllowUpdateAny] [-CimSession <CimSession[]>]
[-ThrottleLimit <int>] [-AsJob] [-WhatIf] [-Confirm] [<CommonParameters>]


Add-DnsServerResourceRecord [-ZoneName] <string> [-Name] <string> -Ptr
-PtrDomainName <string> [-ComputerName <string>]
[-PassThru] [-TimeToLive <timespan>] [-AgeRecord] [-AllowUpdateAny]
[-CimSession <CimSession[]>]
[-ThrottleLimit <int>] [-AsJob] [-WhatIf] [-Confirm] [<CommonParameters>]


Add-DnsServerResourceRecord [-ZoneName] <string> [-Name] <string> -NS
-NameServer <string> [-ComputerName <string>]
[-PassThru] [-TimeToLive <timespan>] [-AgeRecord] [-AllowUpdateAny] [-CimSession
<CimSession[]>] [-ThrottleLimit <int>]
[-AsJob] [-WhatIf] [-Confirm] [<CommonParameters>]


Add-DnsServerResourceRecord [-ZoneName] <string> [-Name] <string> -MX -MailExchange
<string> -Preference <uint16>
[-ComputerName <string>] [-PassThru] [-TimeToLive <timespan>] [-AgeRecord]
[-AllowUpdateAny] [-CimSession <CimSession[]>]
[-ThrottleLimit <int>] [-AsJob] [-WhatIf] [-Confirm] [<CommonParameters>]
```

```
Add-DnsServerResourceRecord [-ZoneName] <string> [-Name] <string> -Isdn
-IsdnNumber <string> -IsdnSubAddress <string>
[-ComputerName <string>] [-PassThru] [-TimeToLive <timespan>] [-AgeRecord]
[-AllowUpdateAny] [-CimSession <CimSession[]>]
[-ThrottleLimit <int>] [-AsJob] [-WhatIf] [-Confirm] [<CommonParameters>]

Add-DnsServerResourceRecord [-ZoneName] <string> [-Name] <string> -HInfo -Cpu <string>
-OperatingSystem <string>
[-ComputerName <string>] [-PassThru] [-TimeToLive <timespan>] [-AgeRecord]
[-AllowUpdateAny] [-CimSession <CimSession[]>]
[-ThrottleLimit <int>] [-AsJob] [-WhatIf] [-Confirm] [<CommonParameters>]

Add-DnsServerResourceRecord [-ZoneName] <string> [-Name] <string> -DName
-DomainNameAlias <string> [-ComputerName <string>]
[-PassThru] [-TimeToLive <timespan>] [-AgeRecord] [-AllowUpdateAny]
[-CimSession <CimSession[]>]
[-ThrottleLimit <int>] [-AsJob] [-WhatIf] [-Confirm] [<CommonParameters>]

Add-DnsServerResourceRecord [-ZoneName] <string> [-Name] <string> -DhcId
-DhcpIdentifier <string> [-ComputerName <string>]
[-PassThru] [-TimeToLive <timespan>] [-AgeRecord] [-AllowUpdateAny]
[-CimSession <CimSession[]>]
[-ThrottleLimit <int>] [-AsJob] [-WhatIf] [-Confirm] [<CommonParameters>]

Add-DnsServerResourceRecord [-ZoneName] <string> [-Name] <string> -CName
-HostNameAlias <string> [-ComputerName
<string>] [-PassThru] [-TimeToLive <timespan>] [-AgeRecord] [-AllowUpdateAny]
[-CimSession <CimSession[]>]
[-ThrottleLimit <int>] [-AsJob] [-WhatIf] [-Confirm] [<CommonParameters>]

Add-DnsServerResourceRecord [-ZoneName] <string> [-Name] <string> -Atma
-Address <string> -AddressType <string>
[-ComputerName <string>] [-PassThru] [-TimeToLive <timespan>] [-AgeRecord]
[-AllowUpdateAny] [-CimSession <CimSession[]>]
[-ThrottleLimit <int>] [-AsJob] [-WhatIf] [-Confirm] [<CommonParameters>]

Add-DnsServerResourceRecord [-ZoneName] <string> [-Name] <string> -Afsdb -SubType
<uint16> -ServerName <string>
[-ComputerName <string>] [-PassThru] [-TimeToLive <timespan>] [-AgeRecord]
[-AllowUpdateAny] [-CimSession <CimSession[]>]
[-ThrottleLimit <int>] [-AsJob] [-WhatIf] [-Confirm] [<CommonParameters>]
```

```
Add-DnsServerResourceRecord [-ZoneName] <string> [-Name] <string> -AAAA
-IPv6Address <ipaddress> [-ComputerName
<string>] [-PassThru] [-CreatePtr] [-TimeToLive <timespan>] [-AgeRecord]
[-AllowUpdateAny] [-CimSession <CimSession[]>]
[-ThrottleLimit <int>] [-AsJob] [-WhatIf] [-Confirm] [<CommonParameters>]

Add-DnsServerResourceRecord [-ZoneName] <string> [-Name] <string> -A
-IPv4Address <ipaddress> [-ComputerName <string>]
[-PassThru] [-CreatePtr] [-TimeToLive <timespan>] [-AgeRecord] [-AllowUpdateAny]
[-CimSession <CimSession[]>]
[-ThrottleLimit <int>] [-AsJob] [-WhatIf] [-Confirm] [<CommonParameters>]
```

TIP The Windows PowerShell Get-Help cmdlet is a quick way to get help on a specific cmdlet, but often it gives you more than you really need or want—all you really need is a reminder of the syntax. Here's a quick script to print out the syntax from one or more cmdlets. Add an alias to it in your $profile and you're in business.

```
Get-Syntax.ps1

<#
.Synopsis
Get the syntax for a cmdlet or cmdlets
.Description
The Get-Syntax script is a wrapper script to run
Get-Command <cmdlet name> -Syntax against one
or more cmdlets. This allows a quick read on the syntax expected.
.Example
Get-Syntax Get-Help
Returns the only the syntax for the Get-Help command.
.Example
Get-Syntax Get-Help,Get-Alias,New-Item
Returns the syntax for each of the specified commands.
.Parameter cmdlet[]
An array of cmdlets to return the syntax for.
.Inputs
[string[]]
.Outputs
[string]
.NOTES
    Author: Charlie Russel
 Copyright: 2015 by Charlie Russel
         : Permission to use is granted but attribution is appreciated
   Initial: 3/13/2015 (cpr)
   ModHist:
```

```
#>
[CmdletBinding()]
Param(
    [Parameter(Mandatory=$True,Position=0)]
    [string[]]
    $Cmdlet
    )
ForEach ($cmd in $cmdlet) {
    "Syntax for $cmd is:"
    Get-Command $cmd -Syntax
}
```

Creating an AAAA record (IPv6 name record) uses the same basic syntax as creating an A record. So, for the same trey-wds-11 server, with an IPv6 address of 2001:db8:0:10::b, the command is as follows.

```
Add-DnsServerResourceRecord  -ZoneName "TreyResearch.net" `
                             -AAAA `
                             -Name trey-wds-11 `
                             -IPv6Address 2001:db8:0:10::b `
                             -CreatePtr `
                             -PassThru
```

Create CNAME resource records

The CNAME record, sometimes called an *alias*, is a canonical record you can use to add an additional host name to a server. The CNAME record points to an existing host name record. When the DNS server receives a name query for the name in the CNAME record, it looks up the A record for the host name that the CNAME points to and returns the IPv4 address for that host name. To create a CNAME record for server WDS that points to the A record for trey-wds-11, use the following command.

```
Add-DnsServerResourceRecord -ZoneName "TreyResearch.net" `
                            -CName `
                            -Name wds `
                            -HostNameAlias trey-wds-11.treyresearch.net `
                            -PassThru
```

You can, of course, use the CNAME-specific cmdlet. Both produce exactly the same record and produce no visible output unless you specify the PassThru parameter, as I did in this example. With this parameter, you get the following simple output.

```
HostName RecordType Timestamp TimeToLive RecordData
-------- ---------- --------- ---------- ----------
wds      CNAME      0         01:00:00   trey-wds-11.treyresearch.net.
```

Create MX resource records

The MX resource record is a Mail Exchanger record that is used by Simple Mail Transfer Protocol (SMTP) servers to identify which host or hosts in a domain handle email for the domain. The MX record includes a Mail Server Priority field that enables you to have backup mail servers. The email is always delivered to the server with the lowest value in the Mail Server Priority field in the server's MX record. So, for example, if TreyResearch.net has a primary mail server named mail.treyresearch.net, hosted on premises, and a backup mail server named mail2.treyresearch.net, hosted in Microsoft Azure, you would create two MX records for the domain.

```
Add-DnsServerResourceRecord -ZoneName "TreyResearch.net" `
                            -Name "." `
                            -MX `
                            -MailExchange mail.treyresearch.net `
                            -Preference 10

Add-DnsServerResourceRecord -ZoneName "TreyResearch.net" `
                            -Name "." `
                            -MX `
                            -MailExchange mail2.treyresearch.net `
                            -Preference 20
```

Create additional resource records

The basic syntax for creating any DNS resource record by using the Add-DnsServerResource-Record cmdlet is the same. What varies is the specific parameters for the resource type. Use the Get-Help pages (or the Get-Syntax.ps1 script I provided earlier) to get the specific parameters for the record type you're creating. For example, the SRV record type supports the parameters shown in Table 2-2.

TABLE 2-2 The Add-DnsServerResourceRecord Parameters for SRV records

Parameter	Type	Description
[-ZoneName]	String	The name of the DNS zone.
[-Name]	String	The name of the resource record object.
[-AgeRecord]	Switch	When present, use a time stamp to allow record scavenging.
[-AllowUpdateAny]	Switch	When present, any authorized user can update the record.
[-PassThru]	Switch	When present, produce output to the console.
[-TimeToLive]	TimeSpan	The time (in seconds) that other servers should cache the record.
-DomainName	String	FQDN of the server providing the resource.
-Port	Uint16	The port the server listens on for this service.

Parameter	Type	Description
-Priority	Uint16	The priority of this DNS server. Clients attempt to contact the server with the lowest priority.
-Weight	Uint16	The weighting value of the target host for this resource. If there are multiple hosts, the resource use is proportional to the weights of the hosts.

To create an SRV record for a Network News Transfer Protocol (NNTP) server (trey-edge-1. treyresearch.net), listening on port 119, use the following command.

```
Add-DnsServerResourceRecord -ZoneName "TreyResearch.net" `
                            -Name _nntp._tcp `
                            -SRV `
                            -DomainName "trey-edge-1.treyresearch.net" `
                            -Port 119 `
                            -Priority 0 `
                            -Weight 0 `
                            -PassThru
```

```
HostName    RecordType Timestamp TimeToLive RecordData
--------    ---------- --------- ---------- ----------
_nntp._tcp SRV         0         01:00:00   [0][0][119][trey-edge-1.treyresearch.net.]
```

For complete details on the parameters supported for a particular resource record type, use the Windows PowerShell Get-Help cmdlet. And for the most up-to-date version of the help, use Get-Help with the -Online parameter.

> **TIP** The NS record uses different parameters than other resource records. The Name field for an NS record is entered as "." which equates to "(same as parent folder)".

Configure zone scavenging and aging

Use the Set-DnsServerScavenging cmdlet to configure and enable DNS zone scavenging. This cmdlet accepts parameters related to scavenging intervals, refresh times, and which zones to apply the scavenging to. Use the Start-DnsServerScavenging cmdlet to start the scavenging. However, scavenging will not actually happen unless:

- Scavenging is enabled for the server and the zone.
- The zone is started.
- Resource records have a time stamp.

Use the Get-DnsServerScavenging cmdlet to get information on the current state of scavenging.

To configure the settings for all zones and set a scavenging interval of four days, a refresh interval of three days, and a no-refresh interval of zero, use the following command.

```
Set-DnsServerScavenging -ScavengingState:$True `
                        -ScavengingInterval 4:00:00:00 `
                        -RefreshInterval 3:00:00:00 `
                        -NoRefreshInterval 0 `
                        -ApplyOnAllZones `
                        -PassThru
```

Because I used the -PassThru parameter, the command returns the current state of scavenging.

```
NoRefreshInterval   : 00:00:00
RefreshInterval     : 3.00:00:00
ScavengingInterval  : 4.00:00:00
ScavengingState     : True
LastScavengeTime    : 3/25/2015 6:07:39 PM
```

This is the same result as if I'd used the Get-DnsServerScavenging cmdlet.

Configure record options including Time To Live (TTL) and weight

You can configure the options of resource records without deleting them and re-creating them. Use the Set-DnsServerResourceRecord cmdlet to set the value of resource records. You can't change either the name or the type of the resource record, and you have to use Get-DnsServerResourceRecord to get an object to work on before you can make the change. So, for example, to change the weight of the SRV record created earlier for the NNTP server to 20, we can do the following.

```
$NewDNSObj = $OrigDNSObj = Get-DnsServerResourceRecord -Name _nntp._tcp `
                                                       -ZoneName TreyResearch.net `
                                                       -RRType SRV
$NewDNSObj.RecordData.Weight = 20
Set-DnsServerResourceRecord -NewInputObject $NewDNSObj `
                            -OldInputObject $OrigDNSObj `
                            -ZoneName 'treyresearch.net' `
                            -PassThru
```

Manage DHCP

DHCP is the method used to dynamically assign IP addresses to computers and devices on a Windows network. DHCP can be deployed on servers running Windows Server, or on other devices or servers on the network, but for most Windows AD DS domains, a server running Windows Server and the DHCP service is preferred. Plus, that lets us use Windows PowerShell to deploy and configure the DHCP.

Deploy DHCP

Depending on the size and complexity of your Windows network, you might have a single DHCP server or many, and they can be stand-alone or clustered. But this isn't a book about DHCP, so I'm going to cover just the basics of setting up a single DHCP server on a lab-sized 192.168.10.0/24 network, and on the corresponding 2001:db8::10:0/64 network.

To deploy DHCP, you need to first install the role. For this, use the server trey-dns-03 at 192.168.10.3 as the target.

```
Install-WindowsFeature -ComputerName trey-dns-03 `
                       -Name DHCP `
                       -IncludeAllSubFeature `
                       -IncludeManagementTools
```

No surprises there, and actually the IncludeAllSubFeature parameter isn't really needed, because DHCP doesn't have any subfeatures. But it's a good habit to get into, and it won't complain or throw an error if there aren't any subfeatures. Notice here that I'm running this as a remote command. I'm actually running the command from an elevated Windows PowerShell window on trey-dc-02, but I want the DHCP to be on a different server. As you can tell from Figure 2-7, the installation was a success. But that's just barely the start. Now you need to actually do the initial setup of the server and activate it in AD DS.

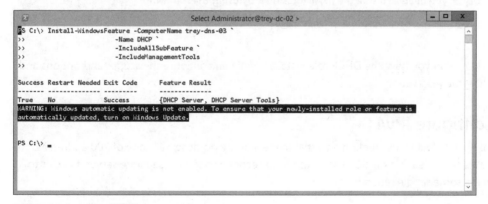

FIGURE 2-7 Installing DHCP on a remote server

Next, you need to create two local groups on the DHCP server, DHCP Administrators and DHCP Users. You can do this by using lusrmgr.msc or by using the following commands.

```
#The WinNT in the following IS CASE SENSITIVE
$connection = [ADSI]"WinNT://trey-dns-03"
$lGroup = $connection.Create("Group","DHCP Administrators")
$lGroup.SetInfo()
$lGroup = $connection.Create("Group","DHCP Users")
$lGroup.SetInfo()
```

> **NOTE** Creating a local group uses the Windows PowerShell [ADSI] adapter because there aren't any native Windows PowerShell cmdlets for manipulating local users or groups. Creating local users is covered in more detail in Chapter 7, "Configure service authentication and account policies."

The final step before you start configuring the DHCP server is to activate it in AD DS as an authorized server. To do this, use the Add-DhcpServerInDC cmdlet. Because you're still running remotely, you need to specify which server to add. You could use either the DNS name or the IP address. The command is.

```
Add-DhcpServerInDC -DnsName 'trey-dns-03' -PassThru
```

```
IPAddress          DnsName
---------          -------
192.168.10.3       trey-dns-03
```

> **NOTE** If you want to use cmdlets in the DHCP module on a computer that is not running DHCP, you need to install the RSAT tools first, by using the following.
>
> ```
> Install-WindowsFeature -Name RSAT-DHCP
> ```

Now that you have the DHCP role installed, you can configure the scopes and options and add some reservations.

Configure IPv4

For IPv4, let's start by creating an initial scope. For my purposes, a scope of 200 addresses makes sense, leaving me 50 or so to use for a second scope on a separate server if I want to create some simple redundancy.

The command to create an IPv4 scope is Add-DhcpServerv4Scope, and again, you can run it from a remote computer. You need to assign a start for the scope and an end point, set the subnet mask, and set the scope to active. The command is as follows.

```
Add-DhcpServerv4Scope -Name "Trey-Default" `
                      -ComputerName "trey-dns-03" `
                      -Description "Default IPv4 Scope for Lab" `
                      -StartRange "192.168.10.1" `
                      -EndRange   "192.168.10.200" `
                      -SubNetMask "255.255.255.0" `
                      -State Active `
                      -Type DHCP `
                      -PassThru
```

The result is echoed back to the console by using the PassThru parameter.

ScopeId	SubnetMask	Name	State	StartRange	EndRange	
LeaseDuration						
192.168.10.0	255.255.255.0	Trey-Default	Active	192.168.10.1	192.168.10.200	
8.00:00:00						

Next, let's set an exclusion range so that we can have some fixed IP address servers. For this, use the Add-DhcpServerv4ExclusionRange cmdlet. This uses the ScopeID to identify which scope is being configured. The command to exclude addresses from 192.168.10.1 through 192.168.10.20 is as follows.

```
Add-DhcpServerv4ExclusionRange -ScopeID "192.168.10.0" `
                               -ComputerName "trey-dns-03" `
                               -StartRange "192.168.10.1" `
                               -EndRange   "192.168.10.20" `
                               -PassThru
```

The result is echoed back to the console by using the PassThru parameter.

ScopeId	StartRange	EndRange
192.168.10.0	192.168.10.1	192.168.10.20

Next, set the options on your scope, by using the Set-DhcpServerv4OptionValue cmdlet. Then you should be good to go for IPv4.

```
Set-DhcpServerv4OptionValue -ScopeID 192.168.10.0 `
                            -ComputerName "trey-dns-03" `
                            -DnsDomain "TreyResearch.net" `
                            -DnsServer "192.168.10.2" `
                            -Router "192.168.10.1" `
                            -PassThru
```

The result is echoed back to the console by using the PassThru parameter.

```
OptionId Name             Type          Value
-------- ----             ----          -----
15       DNS Domain Name  String        {TreyResearch.net}
3        Router           IPv4Add...    {192.168.10.1}
6        DNS Servers      IPv4Add...    {192.168.10.2}
```

Configure IPv6

To configure the IPv6 scope, use the Add-DhcpServerv6Scope cmdlet. You need to assign a start for the scope and an end point, set the Prefix (subnet mask), and set the scope to active. The command is as follows.

```
Add-DhcpServerv6Scope -Name "Trey-IPv6-Default" `
                      -ComputerName "trey-dns-03" `
                      -Description "Default IPv6 Scope for Lab" `
                      -Prefix 2001:db8:0:10:: `
                      -State Active `
                      -PassThru
```

The result is echoed back to the console by using the PassThru parameter.

```
Prefix           PrefixLength    Name               State
------           ------------    ----               -----
2001:db8:0:10::  64              Trey-IPv6-Default  Active
```

Next, set an exclusion range for the servers. Here, we're carving out 32 addresses.

```
Add-DhcpServerv6ExclusionRange -ComputerName trey-dns-03 `
                               -Prefix 2001:db8:0:10:: `
                               -StartRange 2001:db8:0:10::1 `
                               -EndRange   2001:db8:0:10::20 `
                               -PassThru
```

The result is echoed back to the console by using the PassThru parameter.

```
Prefix                StartRange            EndRange
------                ----------            --------
2001:db8:0:10::       2001:db8:0:10::1      2001:db8:0:10::20
```

Next, set the options on your scope by using the Set-DhcpServerv6OptionValue cmdlet to set the Scope options for IPv6.

```
Set-DhcpServerv6OptionValue -Prefix 2001:db8:0:10:: `
                            -ComputerName "trey-dns-03" `
                            -DnsServer 2001:db8:0:10::2 `
                            -DomainSearchList "TreyResearch.net" `
                            -PassThru
```

The result is echoed back to the console by using the PassThru parameter.

```
OptionId  Name              Type         VendorClass    Value
--------  ----              ----         -----------    -----
24        Domain Search Lis String                      {TreyResearch.net}
23        DNS Recursive Nam... IPv6Address              {2001:db8:0:10::2}
```

And we're done with a basic DHCP setup. There's lots more you can configure for the DHCP server role. Use the Set-DhcpServer set of cmdlets to configure the additional options.

Summary

In this chapter, you learned how to manage and deploy DNS zones to support your Active Directory deployment, and you learned how to create and manage many different kinds of DNS records. Finally, you learned the basics of setting up a DHCP server and configuring simple IPv4 and IPv6 scopes for that DHCP server.

In the next chapter, I cover how to start populating your Active Directory with users and groups, and how to set the properties for those users and groups. You'll learn how to add individual users and how to use a simple comma-separated text file (CSV file) to add users in batches.

CHAPTER 3

Create and manage users and groups

Now that we have a forest and domain, and we've got the basics of networking and name resolution sorted, the next step is to add some users to our domain. We'll start with adding a simple user, interactively, and then create a bunch of users by using a script and a comma-separated values (CSV) file. We'll create a new group and then add a group of users into that group, using a filter to ensure that we add the correct set of users. Then we'll create a new organizational unit (OU) and move users and computers into the OU. Pretty basic stuff, really, but essential for any domain administrator.

Active Directory Windows PowerShell nouns used in this chapter:

- ADUser
- ADGroup
- ADGroupMember
- ADAccountPassword
- ADPrincipalGroupMembership
- ADObject
- ADComputer

Other Windows PowerShell commands used in this chapter:

- Import-CSV
- ConvertTo-SecureString
- Get-Command
- Test-Path
- Read-Host
- Write-Host

Create users

Use the New-ADUser cmdlet to create new users. Most user properties can be directly added by using the parameters of New-ADUser detailed in Table 3-1, shown later in this section. Those user attributes not explicitly available as direct parameters to New-ADUser can be added by using the OtherAttributes parameter, which accepts a hashtable of attribute names and values.

Create a single user

The first thing you'll want to do for your new domain is create an administrative user that isn't "Administrator." That first Administrator account is sometimes referred to as the 500 account because the last three digits of its security identifier (SID) are 500, as we can tell from a quick Get-ADUser.

```
Get-ADUser -Identity Administrator
```

```
DistinguishedName : CN=Administrator,CN=Users,DC=TreyResearch,DC=net
Enabled           : True
GivenName         :
Name              : Administrator
ObjectClass       : user
ObjectGUID        : a196f5de-343f-48d5-8aab-5289bfa6fabc
SamAccountName    : Administrator
SID               : S-1-5-21-910751839-3601328731-670513855-500
Surname           :
UserPrincipalName :
```

The 500 account is a bit too well known to use for everyday administration and should be given a really long and onerous password that is locked away somewhere very secure and then left alone except in dire emergencies. So let's give ourselves a working administrative account, and then we'll change the password on the 500 account and retire it from everyday use.

To add a new user, use the New-ADUser cmdlet. There are three basic ways to use New-ADUser:

1. Create a user by specifying all details on the command line.
2. Create a user from a template object—either one you create or an existing user.
3. Use a CSV file to create multiple users from a list of users and properties.

We're going to use option #1 to create our first administrative user. We need to specify the settings for the new user at the command line. Then we need to add the user to the appropriate Active Directory Domain Services (AD DS) security groups. First, to create the user, "Charlie," use the following commands.

```
$SecurePW = Read-Host -Prompt "Enter a password" -asSecureString
New-ADUser -Name "Charlie Russel" `
           -AccountPassword $SecurePW `
           -SamAccountName 'Charlie' `
           -DisplayName 'Charlie Russel' `
           -EmailAddress 'Charlie@TreyResearch.net' `
           -Enabled $True `
           -GivenName 'Charlie' `
           -PassThru `
           -PasswordNeverExpires $True `
           -Surname 'Russel' `
           -UserPrincipalName 'Charlie'
```

The Read-Host in the previous code prompts for a password and masks what the user enters, and the result of the New-ADUser command is displayed at the console because I used the -PassThru parameter, as shown in Figure 3-1.

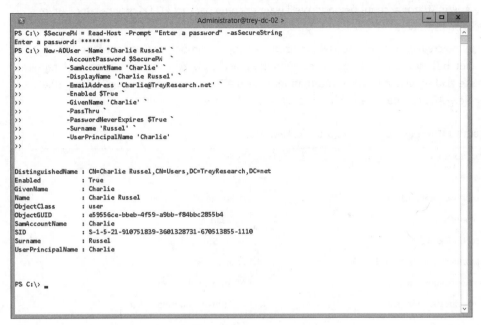

```
Administrator@trey-dc-02 >
PS C:\> $SecurePW = Read-Host -Prompt "Enter a password" -asSecureString
Enter a password: ********
PS C:\> New-ADUser -Name "Charlie Russel" `
>>          -AccountPassword $SecurePW `
>>          -SamAccountName 'Charlie' `
>>          -DisplayName 'Charlie Russel' `
>>          -EmailAddress 'Charlie@TreyResearch.net' `
>>          -Enabled $True `
>>          -GivenName 'Charlie' `
>>          -PassThru `
>>          -PasswordNeverExpires $True `
>>          -Surname 'Russel' `
>>          -UserPrincipalName 'Charlie'
>>


DistinguishedName : CN=Charlie Russel,CN=Users,DC=TreyResearch,DC=net
Enabled           : True
GivenName         : Charlie
Name              : Charlie Russel
ObjectClass       : user
ObjectGUID        : e59556ce-bbeb-4f59-a9bb-f84bbc2855b4
SamAccountName    : Charlie
SID               : S-1-5-21-910751839-3601328731-670513855-1110
Surname           : Russel
UserPrincipalName : Charlie



PS C:\>
```

FIGURE 3-1 Creating a new user by using New-ADUser

This creates our first user but doesn't make the user a member of any domain security groups except Domain Users, the default. To add the user to security groups, we need to use the Add-ADGroupMember cmdlet. And because the goal is to give Charlie the same set of security groups as the Administrator account, we'll use Windows PowerShell to get the list of security groups that the Administrator is a member of, and then loop through the list and add Charlie to each of the groups.

```
$SuperUserGroups = @()
$SuperUserGroups = (Get-ADUser -Identity "Administrator" -Properties * ).MemberOf

ForEach ($Group in $SuperUserGroups ) {
    Add-ADGroupMember -Identity $Group -Members "Charlie"
}

(Get-ADUser -Identity Charlie -Properties *).MemberOf
```

```
CN=Group Policy Creator Owners,CN=Users,DC=TreyResearch,DC=net
CN=Domain Admins,CN=Users,DC=TreyResearch,DC=net
CN=Enterprise Admins,CN=Users,DC=TreyResearch,DC=net
CN=Schema Admins,CN=Users,DC=TreyResearch,DC=net
CN=Administrators,CN=Builtin,DC=TreyResearch,DC=net
```

As we can tell from the Get-ADUser command in the previous code, the account Charlie is now a member of five security groups: Group Policy Creator Owners, Domain Admins, Enterprise Admins, Schema Admins, and Administrators. These are the same security groups to which the Administrator account belongs. We'll want to come back to AD DS groups later, but let's focus on users first.

In the creation of this first user, we used the most common parameters of the New-ADUser cmdlet, but they're only a fraction of the options available. Your situation might well require you to add significantly more information to each AD DS account. The available parameters for New-ADUser that relate to users are listed in Table 3-1.

TABLE 3-1 The user property parameters of New-ADUser

Parameter	Type
Name	String
AccountExpirationDate	Datetime
AccountNotDelegated	Boolean
AccountPassword	SecureString
AllowReversiblePasswordEncryption	Boolean
AuthenticationPolicy	ADAuthenticationPolicy
AuthenticationPolicySilo	ADAuthenticationPolicySilo
AuthType	ADAuthType
CannotChangePassword	Boolean
Certificates	X509Certificate[]
ChangePasswordAtLogon	Boolean
City	String
Company	String
CompoundIdentitySupported	Boolean
Country	String
Credential	PSCredential
Department	String
Description	String
DisplayName	String
Division	String
EmailAddress	String
EmployeeID	String
EmployeeNumber	String

Parameter	Type
Enabled	Boolean
Fax	String
GivenName	String
HomeDirectory	String
HomeDrive	String
HomePage	String
HomePhone	String
Initials	String
Instance	ADUser
KerberosEncryptionType	ADKerberosEncryptionType
LogonWorkstations	String
Manager	ADUser
MobilePhone	String
Office	String
OfficePhone	String
Organization	String
OtherAttributes	Hashtable
OtherName	String
PassThru	Switch
PasswordNeverExpires	Boolean
PasswordNotRequired	Boolean
Path	String
POBox	String
PostalCode	String
PrincipalsAllowedToDelegateToAccount	ADPrincipal[]
ProfilePath	String
SamAccountName	String
ScriptPath	String
Server	String
ServicePrincipalNames	String[]
SmartcardLogonRequired	Boolean

Parameter	Type
State	String
StreetAddress	String
Surname	String
Title	String
TrustedForDelegation	Boolean
Type	String
UserPrincipalName	String

> **NOTE** In this table of parameters, and in others throughout the book, I've deliberately ignored the parameters that don't directly relate to the object we're working with. This means I haven't included Common Parameters, nor have I included Confirm or WhatIf parameters.

Add users in a batch

There are multiple ways to add users in a batch, but probably the simplest is to use a CSV file. You can easily create the CSV file in Microsoft Excel or any plain text editor, and then use Windows PowerShell to read the values in the CSV file and add the users. In my lab, all my animals have their own domain accounts, so I'll use them to show how to quickly and easily create new users. All are initially created as Domain Users, with a default password, and then one account gets elevated and prompts for a password. The list of users and their basic properties are in the following code.

TreyUsers.csv

```
Name,GivenName,Surname,DisplayName,SAMAccountName,Description
David Guy,David,Guy,Dave R. Guy,Dave,Customer Appreciation Manager
Alfredo Fettucine,Alfredo,Fettuccine,Alfie NoNose,Alfie,Shop Foreman
Stanley Behr,Stanley,Behr,Stanley T. Behr, Stanley,WebMaster
Priscilla Catz,Priscilla,Catz,Dame Priscilla,Priscilla,Shop Steward
Harold Catz,Harold,Catz,Harold S. Catz,Harold,Engineering Manager
William Wallace,William,Wallace,Sir William Wallace,Wally,Marketing Manager
Trey Barksdale,Trey,Barksdale,Lord Barksalot,Trey,Sales Manager
Charlie Russel,Charlie,Russel,Charlie Russel,Charlie,SuperUser Account
```

As you can tell, I've only used the most basic information for each new user. To read the CSV file, use the Import-CSV cmdlet, and then loop through each user from the CSV file and create the user with New-ADUser by using a basic ForEach loop.

Create-TreyUsers.ps1

```
<#
.Synopsis
Creates the TreyResearch.net users
.Description
Create-TreyUsers reads a CSV file to create an array of users. The users are then added
to the users container in Active Directory. Additionally, Create-TreyUsers adds the
user Charlie to the same AD DS Groups as the Administrator account.
.Example
Create-TreyUsers
Creates AD Accounts for the users in the default "TreyUsers.csv" source file
.Example
Create-TreyUsers -Path "C:\temp\NewUsers.txt"
Creates AD accounts for the users listed in the file C:\temp\NewUsers.txt"
.Parameter Path
The path to the input CSV file. The default value is ".\TreyUsers.csv".
.Inputs
[string]
.Notes
    Author: Charlie Russel
 Copyright: 2015 by Charlie Russel
         : Permission to use is granted but attribution is appreciated
   Initial: 3/26/2015 (cpr)
   ModHist:
         :
#>
[CmdletBinding()]
Param(
    [Parameter(Mandatory=$False,Position=0)]
    [string]
    $Path = ".\TreyUsers.csv"
    )


$TreyUsers = @()
If (Test-Path $Path ) {
   $TreyUsers = Import-CSV $Path
} else {
   Throw  "This script requires a CSV file with user names and properties."
}

ForEach ($user in $TreyUsers ) {
   New-AdUser -DisplayName $User.DisplayName `
            -GivenName $user.GivenName `
            -Name $User.Name `
            -SurName $User.SurName `
            -SAMAccountName $User.SAMAccountName `
```

```
                    -Enabled $True `
                    -PasswordNeverExpires $true `
                    -UserPrincipalName $user.SAMAccountName `
                    -AccountPassword (ConvertTo-SecureString -AsPlainText -Force -String
"P@ssw0rd!" )
    If ($User.SAMAccountName -eq "Charlie" ) {
        $cprpwd = Read-Host -Prompt 'Enter Password for account: Charlie' -AsSecureString
        Set-ADAccountPassword -Identity Charlie -NewPassword $cprpwd -Reset
        $SuperUserGroups = @()
        $SuperUserGroups = (Get-ADUser -Identity "Administrator" -Properties * ).MemberOf

        ForEach ($Group in $SuperUserGroups ) {
            Add-ADGroupMember -Identity $Group -Members "Charlie"
        }
        Write-Host "The user $user.SAMAccountName has been added to the following AD
Groups: "
        (Get-ADUser -Identity $user.SAMAccountName -Properties * ).MemberOf
    }
}
```

> **NOTE** As you'll notice, I've included the same superuser account as in the previous sec-
> tion. If you've already added that account, just change the account name and details or
> remove the account from the list.

When we run the Create-TreyUsers script, we get output only about the superuser account
that was created, as shown in Figure 3-2.

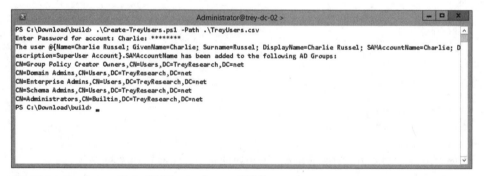

FIGURE 3-2 Creating multiple AD DS users from a CSV file

If you want more detail about the individual accounts that you created, modify the New-
ADUser command in the script to include the PassThru parameter. With that change, though,
you'll get a lot more detail than you likely want. Instead, try a quick one-line search to find
the users.

```
(Get-ADUser -Filter {Enabled -eq "True"} -Properties DisplayName).DisplayName
```

```
Dave R. Guy
Alfie NoNose
Stanley T. Behr
Dame Priscilla
Harold S. Catz
Sir William Wallace
Lord Barksalot
Charlie Russel
```

Now that's just introduced a whole new set of issues with the Filter parameter. I'll cover filters, both traditional Windows PowerShell filters as we used here and LDAP filters, later in the "Manage groups" section, but for the moment let's examine this particular one-line search. The goal of the search is to get a list of the users we just created. Get-ADUser is the cmdlet to use to get users, but we only want to get a list of users that are actually enabled, to avoid accounts like the Guest account and some other special accounts. To get the DisplayName value, we need to add that property to the list of properties returned by Get-ADUser because it isn't part of the default properties.

Create and manage groups

Use the ADGroup set of cmdlets to create, delete, modify, or list Active Directory groups, and either the ADGroupMember set of cmdlets or the ADPrincipalGroupMembership set of cmdlets to add, remove, and list the members of an Active Directory group. By using the ADGroupMember cmdlets, you add or remove one or more users, groups, service accounts, or computers to or from a group, whereas with the ADPrincipalGroupMembership cmdlets you add or remove a user, group, service account, or computer to or from one or more groups. Or, to try to make that a little clearer—if you want to add many objects into one group, use Add-ADGroupMember, but if you want to add one object into many groups, use Add-ADPrincipalGroupMembership. Or you can ignore one or the other set of cmdlets and use looping to accomplish the same thing, as I did earlier when I added the user Charlie into multiple groups by using the Add-ADGroupMember cmdlet and a ForEach loop.

In AD DS, two types of groups are supported: security groups and distribution groups. And there are three scope levels for each: Domain Local, Global, and Universal. To demonstrate how these cmdlets work, let's create a new group, Accounting Users, as a security group with Universal scope, and add a couple of users to the group. Then we'll search to get a list of users in the group, by using both standard Windows PowerShell filtering and LDAP filtering.

Create a new group

Creating a new group is easy and uses the same basic techniques as creating a new user. The difference is that there are far fewer properties and parameters to creating a new group. For example, use the following command to create a new security group called Accounting Users and give that group Universal scope.

```
New-ADGroup -Name 'Accounting Users' `
            -Description 'Security Group for all accounting users' `
            -DisplayName 'Accounting Users' `
            -GroupCategory Security `
            -GroupScope Universal `
            -SAMAccountName 'AccountingUsers' `
            -PassThru
```

The results of this command are shown in Figure 3-3. Notice that even though we didn't specify the full path where we wanted to create the Accounting Users group, Windows PowerShell defaulted to putting the group in the Users container. To override that default, specify the Path parameter. Windows PowerShell will use the default container for your domain if you don't specify a path.

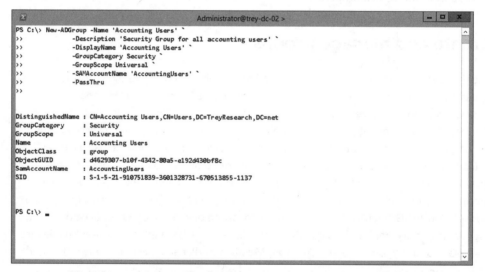

FIGURE 3-3 Adding a new AD DS security group

Add users to a group

Let's start by adding a couple of members to the Accounting Users group we just created. For this, because we're adding multiple users to a single group, we'll use the Add-ADGroupMember cmdlet.

Add-ADGroupMember has the following syntax.

```
Add-ADGroupMember [-Identity] <ADGroup> [-Members] <ADPrincipal[]>
[-AuthType {Negotiate | Basic}] [-Credential PSCredential>]
[-Partition <String>] [-PassThru] [-Server <String>]
[-Confirm] [-WhatIf] [<CommonParameters>]
```

The Identity parameter accepts a Distinguished Name (DN), GUID, security identifier (SID) or SAM account name to identify which group you want to add members to. The Members parameter accepts an *array* of new members that you want to add to the group. The new members can be identified by the same methods as the group identifier, but the parameter also accepts user, computer, and group object variables that identify the members to be added. You *cannot*, however, pass objects to Add-ADGroupMember through the pipeline.

To add Dave R. Guy and Stanley T. Behr to the Accounting Users group, use the following command.

```
Add-ADGroupMember -Identity AccountingUsers -Members Dave,Stanley -PassThru
```

```
DistinguishedName : CN=Accounting Users,CN=Users,DC=TreyResearch,DC=net
GroupCategory     : Security
GroupScope        : Universal
Name              : Accounting Users
ObjectClass       : group
ObjectGUID        : d4629307-b10f-4342-80a5-e192d430bf8c
SamAccountName    : AccountingUsers
SID               : S-1-5-21-910751839-3601328731-670513855-1137
```

To verify that the members were added, because the PassThru parameter doesn't really help with that, use the Get-ADGroupMember cmdlet.

```
Get-ADGroupMember -Identity AccountingUsers
```

```
distinguishedName : CN=Stanley Behr,CN=Users,DC=TreyResearch,DC=net
name              : Stanley Behr
objectClass       : user
objectGUID        : 17527a2f-2710-49d7-ad6d-ce6342bb8c63
SamAccountName    : Stanley
SID               : S-1-5-21-910751839-3601328731-670513855-1131

distinguishedName : CN=David Guy,CN=Users,DC=TreyResearch,DC=net
name              : David Guy
objectClass       : user
objectGUID        : 93534ac0-bbd4-4a29-aae0-470b8e604b18
SamAccountName    : Dave
SID               : S-1-5-21-910751839-3601328731-670513855-1129
```

Manage groups

Now, let's take this a bit further. Let's create another new security group for management. We'll call the group Managers, and we'll use the Description property to add members to the group. So, first create the group by using New-ADGroup.

```
New-ADGroup -Name 'Managers' `
            -Description 'Security Group for all Managers' `
            -DisplayName 'Managers' `
            -GroupCategory Security `
            -GroupScope Universal `
            -SAMAccountName 'Managers' `
            -PassThru
```

```
DistinguishedName : CN=Managers,CN=Users,DC=TreyResearch,DC=net
GroupCategory     : Security
GroupScope        : Universal
Name              : Managers
ObjectClass       : group
ObjectGUID        : 625b4911-301a-4249-8c39-40b88734a124
SamAccountName    : Managers
SID               : S-1-5-21-910751839-3601328731-670513855-1138
```

Now we need to select just the users who are managers to add to the group. We can do that by using the Description property, because we populated that when we created the users, and we know it includes "Manager" in the description for those who are managers. This would be easy if we could just pass the results of Get-ADUser directly through the pipeline to Add-ADGroupMember, but we can't. So, instead, we'll create an array of SAM account names from the results of Get-ADUser.

```
$ManagerArray = (Get-ADUser -Filter {Description -like "*Manager*" } `
                            -Properties Description).SAMAccountName
```

Now we'll use the $ManagerArray variable with Add-ADGroupMember.

```
Add-ADGroupMember -Identity "Managers" -Members $ManagerArray -PassThru
```

And finally, to confirm the identity of who we added, use this.

```
Get-ADGroupMember -Identity Managers | ft -auto SAMAccountName,Name
```

```
SAMAccountName Name
-------------- ----
Trey           Trey Barksdale
Wally          William Wallace
Harold         Harold Catz
Dave           David Guy
```

But there's a problem with that—it really doesn't confirm that the users we added were managers. We could try changing that Format-Table command to the following.

```
ft -auto SAMAccountName,Name,Description
```

Unfortunately, that just yields an empty column for the Description field. And we can understand why with this.

```
Get-ADGroupMember -Identity Managers | Get-Member
```

```
   TypeName: Microsoft.ActiveDirectory.Management.ADPrincipal

Name              MemberType            Definition
----              ----------            ----------
Contains          Method                bool Contains(string propertyName)
Equals            Method                bool Equals(System.Object obj)
GetEnumerator     Method                System.Collections.IDictionaryEnumerator
GetEnumerator()
GetHashCode       Method                int GetHashCode()
GetType           Method                type GetType()
ToString          Method                string ToString()
Item              ParameterizedProperty
Microsoft.ActiveDirectory.Management.ADPropertyValueCollection Item(string p...
distinguishedName Property              System.String distinguishedName {get;set;}
name              Property              System.String name {get;}
objectClass       Property              System.String objectClass {get;set;}
objectGUID        Property              System.Nullable`1[[System.Guid, mscorlib,
Version=4.0.0.0, Culture=neutral, ...
SamAccountName    Property              System.String SamAccountName {get;set;}
SID               Property              System.Security.Principal.SecurityIdentifier
SID {get;set;}
```

We can't add a -Properties Description to the Get-ADGroupMember, because it doesn't support that parameter, so instead, we pass the results through Get-ADUser, which does support the Properties parameter, and now we get the following.

```
Get-ADGroupMember -Identity Managers `
                | Get-ADUser -Properties Description `
                | Format-Table -auto SAMAccountName,Name,Description
```

```
SAMAccountName Name            Description
-------------- ----            -----------
Trey           Trey Barksdale  Sales Manager
Wally          William Wallace Marketing Manager
Harold         Harold Catz     Engineering Manager
Dave           David Guy       Customer Appreciation Manager
```

That worked. Now we can clearly tell that each of the members of the Managers group is described as a manager in Active Directory.

How about adding a user to multiple groups at a time? We saw earlier in the "Create users" section that we could do that with a loop, but wouldn't it be more efficient to just do it in a single command? Let's give Alfie the power he's always wanted and make him a superuser, just like Charlie. And, instead of looping, we'll use the Add-ADPrincipalGroupMembership cmdlet.

```
$Groups = (Get-ADUser -Identity Charlie -Properties *).MemberOf
Add-ADPrincipalGroupMembership -Identity Alfie -MemberOf $Groups


(Get-ADUser -Identity Alfie -Properties MemberOf).MemberOf
```

```
CN=Group Policy Creator Owners,CN=Users,DC=TreyResearch,DC=net
CN=Domain Admins,CN=Users,DC=TreyResearch,DC=net
CN=Enterprise Admins,CN=Users,DC=TreyResearch,DC=net
CN=Schema Admins,CN=Users,DC=TreyResearch,DC=net
CN=Administrators,CN=Builtin,DC=TreyResearch,DC=net
```

Now Alfie has his wish; he's a superuser. But really, that's more than we think he should have, so instead, we'll just give him basic Domain Admins membership by removing him from the groups he really shouldn't be in.

```
Remove-ADPrincipalGroupMembership -Identity Alfie `
                             -MemberOf "Enterprise Admins",`
                                   "Schema Admins",`
                                   "Group Policy Creator Owners" `
                             -PassThru
```

And after we confirm that we really want to do it, Alfie has been reduced to a more reasonable level, as shown with the following.

```
(Get-ADUser -Identity Alfie -Properties MemberOf).MemberOf
```

```
CN=Domain Admins,CN=Users,DC=TreyResearch,DC=net
CN=Administrators,CN=Builtin,DC=TreyResearch,DC=net
```

Create and manage OUs

Organizational units, or OUs, are used to segregate groups of users, computers, or other objects in Active Directory without the overhead of creating a whole new domain for them. You can apply different group policies to different OUs and have different password requirements.

Create an OU

Use the New-ADOrganizationalUnit cmdlet to create a new OU. The cmdlet parameters can be used to set commonly used properties of OUs, such as DisplayName, Description, and ProtectedFromAccidentalDeletion. The only required parameter is the Name parameter.

For properties that aren't covered by the cmdlet parameters shown in Table 3-2, use the OtherAttributes parameter. The OtherAttributes parameter accepts a hashtable with property name and property value pairs.

TABLE 3-2 The parameters of New-ADOrganizationalUnit

Parameter	Type
Name	String
City	String
Country	String
Credential	PSCredential
Description	String
DisplayName	String
Instance	ADOrganizationalUnit
ManagedBy	ADPrincipal
OtherAttributes	Hashtable
PassThru	Toggle
Path	String
PostalCode	String
ProtectedFromAccidentalDeletion	Boolean
Server	String
State	String
StreetAddress	String
Name	String

There are three basic ways to use New-ADOrganizationalUnit:

1. Create an OU by specifying all details on the command line.

2. Create an OU from a template object—either one you create or an existing OU.

3. Use a CSV file to create multiple OUs from a list of OUs and properties.

To create a new Engineering OU for our TreyResearch.net domain, use the following command.

```
New-ADOrganizationalUnit -Name Engineering `
                         -Description 'Engineering department users and computers' `
                         -DisplayName 'Engineering Department' `
                         -ProtectedFromAccidentalDeletion $True `
                         -Path "DC=TreyResearch,DC=NET" `
                         -PassThru
```

Note that the path specified is actually the default path, so we could have skipped that parameter, and the same is true for the ProtectedFromAccidentalDeletion parameter, which defaults to True. Because we used the -PassThru parameter, the command returned the following.

```
City                      :
Country                   :
DistinguishedName         : OU=Engineering,DC=TreyResearch,DC=NET
LinkedGroupPolicyObjects  : {}
ManagedBy                 :
Name                      : Engineering
ObjectClass               : organizationalUnit
ObjectGUID                : c2b42af8-a80b-48c1-949d-c8dbd6d60ee9
PostalCode                :
State                     :
StreetAddress             :
```

And, as we can tell in Figure 3-4, the new Engineering OU is created in the root of the TreyResearch.net domain tree.

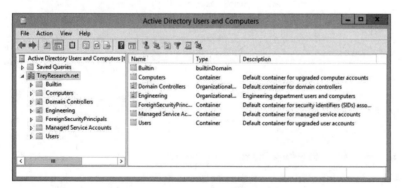

FIGURE 3-4 The TreyResearch.net domain, showing the new Engineering OU

Add computers and users to an OU

Now that we have an Engineering OU, we should move our engineering users and computers into that OU. You might expect that there would be a Move-ADUser cmdlet, but there isn't, and you might even quite reasonably expect that you could use Set-ADUser with a Path parameter to do the job. But no, there isn't a Path parameter and you can't move users that way either. After poking around a bit, however, it occurred to me to use Windows PowerShell to help me find the solution.

```
Get-Command -Module ActiveDirectory -Verb Move | ft -auto CommandType,Name
```

```
CommandType     Name
-----------     ----
Cmdlet          Move-ADDirectoryServer
Cmdlet          Move-ADDirectoryServerOperationMasterRole
Cmdlet          Move-ADObject
```

Well, I don't want to move the directory server, nor the Flexible Single Master Operation (FSMO) roles, at least not right now, so those won't help. But users and computers are just a form of Active Directory object, so that last item looks promising. Let's find out what its syntax is.

```
syntax Move-ADObject
```

```
Syntax for Move-ADObject is:

Move-ADObject [-Identity] <ADObject> [-TargetPath] <string> [-WhatIf]
[-Confirm] [-AuthType ADAuthType>] [-Credential <pscredential>]
[-Partition <string>] [-PassThru] [-Server <string>]
[-TargetServer <string>] [<CommonParameters>]
```

That looks like it should do what we want. We need to specify the identity of the object we want to move, and the target path we want to move it to. And it supports a WhatIf parameter to make sure it's going to do what we expect. So, I remember that one of my users is an engineering manager, but which one? Well, let's find out.

```
Get-ADUser -Filter {Description -like "*Engineering*" }
```

```
DistinguishedName : CN=Harold Catz,CN=Users,DC=TreyResearch,DC=net
Enabled           : True
GivenName         : Harold
Name              : Harold Catz
ObjectClass       : user
ObjectGUID        : 944bb855-0342-4875-a8d2-8447ab6f93e5
SamAccountName    : Harold
SID               : S-1-5-21-910751839-3601328731-670513855-1133
Surname           : Catz
UserPrincipalName : Harold
```

Ah, yes, Harold. Of course. So, now that we know who we want to move, let's verify where we want to move him to.

```
Get-ADOrganizationalUnit -Filter {Name -eq "Engineering" }
```

```
City                      :
Country                   :
DistinguishedName         : OU=Engineering,DC=TreyResearch,DC=net
LinkedGroupPolicyObjects  : {}
ManagedBy                 :
Name                      : Engineering
ObjectClass               : organizationalUnit
ObjectGUID                : c2b42af8-a80b-48c1-949d-c8dbd6d60ee9
PostalCode                :
State                     :
StreetAddress             :
```

The Distinguished Name is the target path for our move, so let's check that we've got everything as we want it.

```
Get-ADUser -Filter {Description -like "*Engineering*" } | Move-ADObject `
        -TargetPath (Get-ADOrganizationalUnit -Filter {Name -eq "Engineering" }) `
        -WhatIf
```

```
What if: Performing the operation "Move" on target "CN=Harold
Catz,CN=Users,DC=TreyResearch,DC=net".
```

That looks like we're moving Harold, which was the plan, so we remove the WhatIf, and issue the command again.

```
Get-ADUser -Filter {Description -like "*Engineering*" } | Move-ADObject `
        -TargetPath (Get-ADOrganizationalUnit -Filter {Name -eq "Engineering" })
```

Oops, we forgot to include the -PassThru parameter, so our move happened silently. No problem, let's just verify that the user Harold is in the correct OU.

```
Get-ADUser -Identity Harold
```

```
DistinguishedName : CN=Harold Catz,OU=Engineering,DC=TreyResearch,DC=net
Enabled           : True
GivenName         : Harold
Name              : Harold Catz
ObjectClass       : user
ObjectGUID        : 944bb855-0342-4875-a8d2-8447ab6f93e5
SamAccountName    : Harold
SID               : S-1-5-21-910751839-3601328731-670513855-1133
Surname           : Catz
UserPrincipalName : Harold
```

And the DistinguishedName property shows that he is in the Engineering OU. Good. Now, let's just move Harold's desktop over to the same OU. A quick check finds that TREY-DESK-22 is assigned to Harold.

```
Get-ADComputer -Filter {Description -like "*Harold*" }
```

```
DistinguishedName : CN=TREY-DESK-22,CN=Computers,DC=TreyResearch,DC=net
DNSHostName       : trey-desk-22.TreyResearch.net
Enabled           : True
Name              : TREY-DESK-22
ObjectClass       : computer
ObjectGUID        : 46df71bd-ba88-4b26-9091-b8db6e07261a
SamAccountName    : TREY-DESK-22$
SID               : S-1-5-21-910751839-3601328731-670513855-1141
UserPrincipalName :
```

Looks like Harold only has one computer, so let's do it by simply specifying the identity of the computer we want to move. Move-ADObject accepts the DN or the GUID for the Identity parameter, or the result of Get-ADUser, Get-ADGroup, Get-ADComputer, Get-ADServiceAccount, Get-ADOrganizationalUnit, or Get-ADFineGrainedPasswordPolicy. We've got both the DN and the GUID in the output from your Get-ADComputer, so after a bit of copy and paste we get the following.

```
Move-ADObject -Identity "46df71bd-ba88-4b26-9091-b8db6e07261a" `
              -TargetPath " OU=Engineering,DC=TreyResearch,DC=net" `
              -PassThru
```

```
DistinguishedName          Name          ObjectClass  ObjectGUID
-----------------          ----          -----------  ----------
CN=TREY-DESK-22, OU=Engine... TREY-DESK-22  computer     46df71bd-ba88-4b26-9091-
b8db6e07261a
```

Even though we only moved a single computer and a single user, the same methods can be used to move hundreds or even thousands of users. Of course, making a mistake when moving one user is a nuisance, for both you and the user, but it's fairly easily corrected. Making a mistake by moving thousands of users is still easily corrected but is likely to cause somewhat more annoyance. Therefore, always check your work before committing to large changes that will affect many users.

Summary

In this chapter, you learned how to create and manage users, groups, and OUs. You learned how to filter against the properties of users, groups, and computers to selectively act on the results of that filter. You also learned how to add users to groups and move users and computers into an OU.

In the next chapter, you'll learn how to deploy additional domain controllers into your existing domain and how to manage the FSMO roles in your domain.

CHAPTER 4

Deploy additional domain controllers

Now that we've got our first domain set up, with basic networking configured, and we've added some users and computers, it's time to add an additional domain controller or two. In the process, we'll deploy domain controllers, clone domain controllers, transfer operations master (FSMO) roles the polite way, and finally we'll seize the FSMO roles for those situations that require brute force.

Active Directory Windows PowerShell nouns used in this chapter:

- ADDSDomainController
- ADDSDomainControllerInstallation
- ADDCCloningExclusionApplicationList
- ADComputer
- ADGroupMember
- ADDCCloningExcludedApplicationList
- ADDCCloneConfigFile
- ADComputerServiceAccount
- ADServiceAccount
- ADDirectoryServerOperationMasterRole
- ADDomain
- ADForest
- ADDomainController

Other Windows PowerShell commands used in this chapter:

- Get-NetAdapter
- Set-NetIPInterface
- New-NetIPAddress
- Set-DnsClientServerAddress
- Get-WindowsFeature
- Install-WindowsFeature
- Get-Credential

- Add-Computer
- Rename-Computer
- Import-Module
- Restart-Computer
- Stop-Computer
- Stop-VM

Deploy domain controllers

Deploying domain controllers into an existing domain doesn't require you to think about many options as long as the domain controllers are reliably connected with high-speed network links. When you have domain controllers that are only intermittently connected, or whose connections are slower, such as remote sites, there are specific considerations you need to take into account. I'll cover those in Chapter 9, "Manage sites and replication."

Converting a server to a domain controller is a four-step process:

1. Configure networking appropriate to a domain controller. This means assigning a fixed IP address to the server and configuring Domain Name System (DNS) to point to an existing domain controller (if you are using Active Directory–integrated DNS) or to an authoritative DNS server (if you are using stand-alone DNS).

2. Install the Active Directory role on the server.

3. Join the server to the domain if it isn't already domain-joined. If this is a new server, now is also the time to change the name of the server to match your organizational standard.

4. Promote the server to a domain controller.

Configure networking

A domain controller in a Windows Server domain is typically configured with a fixed IPv4 address and a fixed IPv6 address (and I strongly recommend you set yours accordingly). If you're using Active Directory–integrated DNS, configure the networking adapter used to join the server to the domain and to promote it to domain controller. This network adapter should point to an existing domain controller as its primary DNS server. If you are using stand-alone DNS, you should configure the DNS setting to point to an authoritative DNS server for the domain.

To configure your adapter, use the Set-NetIPInterface and New-NetIPAddress cmdlets, along with the Set-DnsClientServerAddress cmdlet, to set the DNS server address. The server I'm working with here is trey-dc-09, though it's only a bare-bones new Windows Server Technical Preview server at this point.

First, make sure you're configuring the correct network adapter by using the following command.

```
Get-NetAdapter
```

```
Name     InterfaceDescription        ifIndex Status MacAddress        LinkSpeed
----     --------------------        ------- ------ ----------        ---------
Ethernet Microsoft Hyper-V Network...    3      Up 00-15-5D-32-10-09 10 Gbps
```

We can tell that we have only one network adapter, named "Ethernet," in this server. That makes it easy. Let's capture that adapter into a variable we can work with.

```
$Nic = Get-NetAdapter -Name Ethernet
```

Now we need to reconfigure $Nic to disable the DHCP.

```
$Nic | Set-NetIPInterface -DHCP Disabled
```

Then we configure the IPv4 address.

```
$Nic | New-NetIPAddress -AddressFamily IPv4 `
                        -IPAddress 192.168.10.9 `
                        -PrefixLength 24 `
                        -type Unicast `
                        -DefaultGateway 192.168.10.1
```

Next, let's configure the DNS setting for $Nic. We can't just pass $Nic through the pipeline, so we use the following.

```
Set-DnsClientServerAddress -InterfaceAlias $Nic.Name `
                           -ServerAddresses 192.168.10.2,2001:db8:0:10::2 `
                           -PassThru
```

This command returns the following output.

```
InterfaceAlias           Interface Address ServerAddresses
                         Index     Family
--------------           --------- ------- ---------------
Ethernet                     3 IPv6   {2001:db8:0:10::2}
Ethernet                     3 IPv4   {192.168.10.2}
```

This is good, but we haven't configured an IPv6 address yet. To do so, use the following command.

```
$NIC | New-NetIPAddress -AddressFamily IPv6 `
                        -IPAddress 2001:db8:0:10::9 `
                        -PrefixLength 64 `
                        -type Unicast `
                        -DefaultGateway 2001:db8:0:10::1
```

This returns a detailed output of IPv6-related properties of $Nic. But I'm old-fashioned, and as much as I love Windows PowerShell, I still find the output from Ipconfig more useful.

```
ipconfig
```

```
Windows IP Configuration

Ethernet adapter Ethernet:

   Connection-specific DNS Suffix  . : TreyResearch.net
   IPv6 Address. . . . . . . . . . . : 2001:db8:0:10::9
   IPv6 Address. . . . . . . . . . . : 2001:db8:0:10:a5d5:3f5d:ba64:6eee
   Link-local IPv6 Address . . . . . : fe80::1d74:4bcb:bb10:240d%3
   IPv4 Address. . . . . . . . . . . : 192.168.10.9
   Subnet Mask . . . . . . . . . . . : 255.255.255.0
   Default Gateway . . . . . . . . . : 2001:db8:0:10::1
                                       192.168.10.1

Tunnel adapter isatap.{27307BC2-FF3A-4EDE-B1AD-F6ED9AD7FEE9}:

   Media State . . . . . . . . . . . : Media disconnected
   Connection-specific DNS Suffix  . : TreyResearch.net
```

Here's a quick-and-dirty script to do all of this configuration in a single pass. It assumes that your IPv4 network is 192.168.10.0/24 and your IPv6 network is 2001:db8:0:10::0/64. Change those static variables to suit your environment. Also set the $Gateway4 and $Gateway6 variables, and adjust the hard-coded DNS server addresses as required. Like I said, it's a quick–and-dirty script.

Set-myIP.ps1

```
# Quick and dirty IP address setter

Param ($IP4,$IP6)

$Network = "192.168.10."
$Network6 = "2001:db8:0:10::"
$IPv4 = $Network + "$IP4"
$IPv6 = $Network6 + "$IP6"
$Gateway4 = $Network + "1"
$Gateway6 = $Network6 + "1"

$Nic = Get-NetAdapter -name Ethernet
$Nic | Set-NetIPInterface -DHCP Disabled
$Nic | New-NetIPAddress -AddressFamily IPv4 `
                    -IPAddress $IPv4 `
                    -PrefixLength 24 `
```

```
                              -type Unicast `
                              -DefaultGateway $Gateway4
Set-DnsClientServerAddress -InterfaceAlias $Nic.Name `
                              -ServerAddresses 192.168.10.2,2001:db8:0:10::2
$NIC |  New-NetIPAddress -AddressFamily IPv6 `
                              -IPAddress $IPv6 `
                              -PrefixLength 64 `
                              -type Unicast `
                              -DefaultGateway $Gateway6
ipconfig /all
```

Install the Active Directory role on the server

When you have the networking configured, the next step is to add the Active Directory role to the server. Use the Install-WindowsFeature cmdlet to add the AD-Domain-Services role to the server.

> **TIP** Use Get-WindowsFeature to get a list of the actual installable names of the roles and features of Windows Server. If you only know the display name, or a portion of it, use a command such as the following to find the correct name.
>
> ```
> Get-WindowsFeature `
>              | Where-Object {$_.DisplayName -match "Active" `
>                    -AND $_.InstallState -eq "Available" } `
>              | Format-Table -auto DisplayName,Name,InstallState
> ```

The command to install the Active Directory Domain Services role, including the management tools, is as follows.

```
Install-WindowsFeature -Name AD-Domain-Services -IncludeManagementTools
```

When you run this on your server, you should get something like the following.

```
Install-WindowsFeature -Name AD-Domain-Services -IncludeManagementTools


Success Restart Needed Exit Code       Feature Result
------- -------------- ---------       --------------
True    No             Success         {Active Directory Domain Services, Group P...

WARNING: Windows automatic updating is not enabled. To ensure that your newly-
installed role or feature is automatically updated, turn on Windows Update.
```

As you can tell from the output, no restart is required. In addition to installing the Active Directory Domain Services role, Install-WindowsFeature has installed the full set of Remote Server Administration Tools (RSAT) related to Active Directory Domain Services (AD DS) and the Group Policy Management Console.

There's one more task you'll want to do before you join the computer to the domain and promote it to a domain controller: update the Windows PowerShell Get-Help files. Even if you had already done this, now that you've added additional modules, you need to get the help files for those modules. The command to update help from a local network share is as follows.

```
Update-Help -SourcePath \\cpr-labhost-6\pshelp -force
```

You'll obviously want to substitute a SourcePath value appropriate to your environment, or leave off the SourcePath parameter entirely to go directly to Microsoft for the files.

Join the server to the domain

You can promote a server to domain controller in a domain that it isn't a member of, but I prefer to keep my operations separate, especially for a new server that hasn't had its name changed from whatever obscure name it was assigned at creation time. This does cause an additional restart before you promote the server to domain controller, but you'd have to restart after changing the name anyway, so it's the same total number of restarts.

The command to rename the server to trey-dc-04 and join it to the TreyResearch.net domain is the following.

```
$domCred = Get-Credential -UserName "TreyResearch\Charlie" `
                         -Message "Enter the Domain password for Charlie."
Add-Computer -DomainName "TreyResearch.net" `
            -Credential $domCred -NewName trey-dc-04 -restart
```

The Get-Credential command prompts me for domain credentials to join the server to the domain, and the Add-Computer command combines the domain join with a computer rename operation. When the server reboots, I can log on with my domain credentials and it will have its new name applied.

> **NOTE** If your need is only to rename the computer, use the Rename-Computer cmdlet. This allows you to rename a server, even after it has been promoted to domain controller in most cases. But it does require a restart after running the command.

Promote a server to domain controller

Promoting a server to domain controller uses only one command, Install-ADDSDomainController. There are a lot of options and parameters to the process, most of which you won't need except in specialized circumstances, but they're there for when you do. Some relate to creating a read-only domain controller (RODC), a subject we're leaving for Chapter 5, "Deploy read-only domain controllers (RODCs)." The parameters for Install-ADDSDomainController are shown in Table 4-1.

TABLE 4-1 Parameters for Install-ADDSDomainController

Parameter	Type	Description
DomainName	String	The FQDN where the new domain controller will be installed.
SiteName	String	Specifies the name of an existing site to which the new domain controller is added.
SkipPreChecks	Toggle	When specified, only basic validation is performed before the domain controller is promoted.
SafeModeAdministratorPassword	SecureString	The password for the Administrator account when the server is started in Safe Mode or Directory Services Restore Mode. If not specified, the cmdlet prompts for the password and a confirmation.
ADPrepCredential	PSCredential	The credentials of the account to use to run the adprep utility to prepare the directory prior to installation of the domain controller.
AllowDomainControllerReinstall	Switch	Allows the installation to continue if an existing domain controller account has the same name.
AllowPasswordReplicationAccountName	String[]	An array of user, group, and computer account names that are permitted to replicate to this RODC. By default, only those accounts in the Allowed RODC Password Replication Group are permitted.
ApplicationPartitionsToReplicate	String[]	An array of application partitions to replicate during promotion.
CreateDnsDelegation	Switch	Specifies whether to create a DNS delegation to this new domain controller. If not specified, the value is calculated based on the environment.
Credential	PSCredential	The credentials of the account performing the domain controller promotion.
CriticalReplicationOnly	Switch	When $True, only critical replication occurs before the initial reboot, the rest completing after. When $False, both critical and non-critical replication completes before the domain controller reboots. Default is $False.
DatabasePath	String	Specifies the path to the domain database. This path *must* be on a local fixed disk. UNC paths or removable disks are not supported. Default value is %systemroot%\NTDS.
DnsDelegationCredential	PSCredential	The credential object for the account to use to create the DNS delegation. Ignored if the DNS delegation is computed or specified to be $False.

Parameter	Type	Description
NoDnsOnNetwork	Switch	Specifies that no DNS server exists on the network and the new domain controller should be configured for name resolution. If not specified, the DNS settings of the network card are used to contact an authoritative DNS server.
NoGlobalCatalog	Switch	When $True, the new domain controller is not configured as a Global Catalog server.
InstallationMediaPath	String	The path to installation media used to install a new domain controller.
InstallDns	Switch	If specified as $True, Active Directory–integrated DNS is installed. If specified as $False, it is not. Default is calculated as $True if Active Directory–integrated DNS is discovered on the network, and $False if it is not.
LogPath	String	Specifies the path to the domain log files. This path *must* be on a local fixed disk. UNC paths or removable disks are not supported. Default value is %systemroot%\NTDS.
MoveInfrastructureOperationMasterRoleIfNecessary	Switch	When specified, the infrastructure operation master FSMO role is transferred to the new domain controller if necessary.
NoRebootOnCompletion	Switch	When specified, the post-installation reboot is suppressed. This leaves the new domain controller in an indeterminate state.
ReadOnlyReplica	Switch	When specified, the new domain controller is installed as an RODC.
ReplicationSourceDC	String	Specifies the domain controller to use as the initial replication source.
SkipAutoConfigureDns	Switch	When specified, automatic configuration of an existing DNS Server service on the target server is suppressed.
SystemKey	SecureString	The system key for the data replication source media. Default is none.
SysvolPath	String	Specifies the path to the system volume. This path *must* be on a local fixed disk. UNC paths or removable disks are not supported. Default value is %systemroot%\SYSVOL.
UseExistingAccount	Switch	Attaches a new server to an existing RODC account.

Before you deploy a new domain controller, it's a good practice to test the deployment to ensure that it will work. This allows you to pre-test your environment during working hours and then perform the actual deployment during off-hours when the extra replication traffic is less likely to affect overall network speeds. To test the deployment, you'll use the same command parameters you expect to use during the actual deployment. Then, if the deployment is reasonably close in time to your test, you can skip the pre-check stage (-SkipPreChecks) during the actual deployment, because that just repeats the prerequisite checks that the Test cmdlet uses.

```
Test-ADDSDomainControllerInstallation `
      -NoGlobalCatalog:$false `
      -CreateDnsDelegation:$false `
      -CriticalReplicationOnly:$false `
      -DatabasePath "C:\Windows\NTDS" `
      -DomainName "TreyResearch.net" `
      -LogPath "C:\Windows\NTDS" `
      -NoRebootOnCompletion:$false `
      -SiteName "Default-First-Site-Name" `
      -SysvolPath "C:\Windows\SYSVOL" `
      -InstallDns:$true `
      -Force
```

Running this on trey-dc-04 in my lab environment produces the result shown in Figure 4-1.

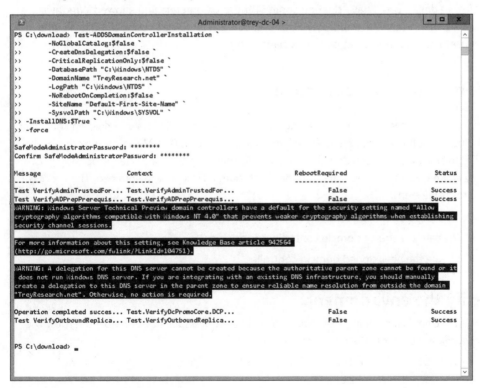

FIGURE 4-1 Using Test-ADDSDomainControllerInstallation

As shown in the figure, there are two warnings, both of which we can safely ignore. The critical column is the fourth column, Status, in which all four rows show Success. Now, if you don't get any ugly messages back from running the Test cmdlet, you're ready to deploy a new domain controller to your existing TreyResearch.net domain. We're still in our original site; therefore, you can use the following command.

```
Install-ADDSDomainController `
    -SkipPreChecks `
    -NoGlobalCatalog:$false `
    -CreateDnsDelegation:$false `
    -CriticalReplicationOnly:$false `
    -DatabasePath "C:\Windows\NTDS" `
    -DomainName "TreyResearch.net" `
    -InstallDns:$true `
    -LogPath "C:\Windows\NTDS" `
    -NoRebootOnCompletion:$false `
    -SiteName "Default-First-Site-Name" `
    -SysvolPath "C:\Windows\SYSVOL" `
    -Force:$true
```

Now I admit, I could have skipped some of those parameters and allowed Windows PowerShell to compute the appropriate values, but I prefer to be specific when I can, and it's a useful way to show what is actually happening.

Clone a domain controller

Windows Server doesn't support copying the .vhd or .vhdx (VHD) files of a domain controller to clone the domain controller. However, in Windows Server 2012, Microsoft introduced the ability to clone a virtualized domain controller. By following the supported process, you can safely clone the domain controller with data and domain integrity maintained. The process requires three steps:

1. Verify that the environment meets cloning requirements.
2. Prepare the source domain controller for cloning.
3. Create the new, cloned domain controller.

Verify the environment

The requirements for cloning a domain controller are quite specific but hardly onerous. The environment must meet the following requirements:

- The PDC emulator FSMO role must be hosted on a domain controller running Windows Server 2012 or later.
- The PDC emulator must be available during the entire cloning process.
- The source and target domain controllers must be running Windows Server 2012 or later.

- The virtualization host platform must support VM-Generation ID (VMGID).
- The following Microsoft virtualization platforms are supported:
  - Windows Server 2012 with Hyper-V
  - Windows Server 2012 R2 with Hyper-V
  - Windows Server Technical Preview with Hyper-V
  - Microsoft Hyper-V Server 2012
  - Microsoft Hyper-V Server 2012 R2
  - Microsoft Hyper-V Server Technical Preview
  - Windows 8 with Hyper-V client
  - Windows 8.1 with Hyper-V client
  - Windows 10 Technical Preview with Hyper-V client

Prepare the source domain controller

If the requirements for cloning have been met, you can prepare the source domain controller. The steps are:

- Add the source domain controller to the Cloneable Domain Controllers security group.
- Identify any applications that will prevent cloning, and add any safe applications that aren't identified to the CustomDCCloneAllowList.xml.
- Remove any stand-alone managed service accounts (MSAs) from the source domain controller. Group MSAs (gMSAs) are supported.
- Create the DCCloneConfig.xml file.
- Shut down the source domain controller.

Add the source to the Cloneable Domain Controllers security group

Before you can clone a domain controller, you must first add it to the Cloneable Domain Controllers security group in Active Directory. This is a special group that should only contain members during the actual process of cloning. After the cloning is complete, remove the source domain controller from the group. To add trey-dc-04 to the group, use the following command.

```
Add-ADGroupMember -Identity "Cloneable Domain Controllers" `
            -Members (Get-ADComputer -Identity trey-dc-04).SAMAccountName `
            -PassThru
```

> **TIP** You can't use Add-ADGroupMember to add a member by specifying its name, or by passing an object through the pipeline. If you remember that the SAMAccountName property for a computer object is usually Name$, you can do it that way, but this way is sure.

The results of the preceding command yield the following output.

```
DistinguishedName : CN=Cloneable Domain Controllers,CN=Users,DC=TreyResearch,DC=net
GroupCategory     : Security
GroupScope        : Global
Name              : Cloneable Domain Controllers
ObjectClass       : group
ObjectGUID        : b12b23c1-499b-4dbe-8206-846a17cd2df2
SamAccountName    : Cloneable Domain Controllers
SID               : S-1-5-21-910751839-3601328731-670513855-522
```

To remove the source domain controller from the Cloneable Domain Controllers group, replace the Add verb in the previous command with the Remove verb, yielding the following command.

```
Remove-ADGroupMember -Identity "Cloneable Domain Controllers" `
                     -Members (Get-ADComputer -Identity trey-dc-04).SAMAccountName `
                     -PassThru
```

Identify problem applications

Some programs and services can prevent a successful cloning and will block the process. Use the Get-ADDCCloningExcludedApplicationList cmdlet to get a list of potential problem applications. Any application that is listed by the cmdlet must either be excluded from consideration or removed from the source domain controller. One service that should never be excluded is the Dynamic Host Configuration Protocol (DHCP) service. If you have DHCP installed on the source domain controller, you should either choose a different domain controller to clone or remove the service and add it back only after the cloning is complete. To get the list of applications on our source domain controller, trey-dc-04, run the command locally. In my lab, I got the following.

```
Get-ADDCCloningExcludedApplicationList
```

Name	Type
----	----
HyperSnap 8	Program
Vim 7.4 (self-installing)	Program
ClipSVC	Service
CoreUIRegistrar	Service
DiagTrack	Service
NgcCtnrSvc	Service
NgcSvc	Service
SlbMux	Service
WdNisSvc	Service
WinDefend	Service

The two programs listed are my screen capture program, HyperSnap, and my editor, Vim. Both are always added to any computer I have as essential productivity tools. Neither is likely to be an issue with cloning, so both can be safely excluded. The Windows services need to be examined a bit more closely. The one that looks likely to be an issue is Windows Defender (WinDefend service)—antivirus applications are always tricky. To uninstall Windows Defender, use the following command.

```
Uninstall-WindowsFeature -Name Windows-Defender
```

```
Success Restart Needed Exit Code      Feature Result
------- -------------- ---------      --------------
True    Yes            SuccessRest... {Windows Defender}
WARNING: You must restart this server to finish the removal process.
```

Removing Windows Defender requires a reboot, which is not surprising. To reboot, use the following.

```
Restart-Computer -Wait 0
```

Now we'll log back on and re-run the Get-ADDCCloningExcludedApplicationList command, but this time we'll generate an exclusion list with the command.

```
Get-ADDCCloningExcludedApplicationList -GenerateXML
```

```
The inclusion list was written to 'C:\Windows\NTDS\CustomDCCloneAllowList.xml'.
```

Good. The next step is to check whether we have any MSAs.

Remove managed service accounts

Windows stand-alone MSAs are not supported for domain controller cloning operations. If you have any on the source controller, you need to remove them prior to cloning, and then add them back after. To check whether you have any on trey-dc-04, use this command.

```
Get-ADComputer -Identity trey-dc-04 | Get-ADComputerServiceAccount
```

If there are no MSAs, you'll get nothing back from the command, but if any are found, you'll get a listing of each of them. Use Uninstall-ADServiceAccount to remove them, and then Install-ADServiceAccount to add the account back after cloning has completed.

> **NOTE** Group MSAs (gMSAs) are supported for cloning and can be left in place. Only stand-alone MSAs need to be removed.

Create DCCloneConfig.xml

Now that you've identified and either excluded or removed programs and services that were reported by Get-ADDCCloningExcludedApplicationList, you're ready to create the DCCloneConfig.xml file that controls the cloning process. Use the New-ADDCCloneConfigFile cmdlet to create the DCCloneConfig.xml file. New-ADDCCloneConfigFile accepts the parameters shown in Table 4-2.

TABLE 4-2 Parameters for New-ADDCCloneConfigFile

Parameter	Type	Description
None		Creates a blank DCCloneConfig.xml file.
CloneComputerName	String	Specifies the target cloned domain controller name.
Path	String	Path to the DCCloneConfig.xml file. If not specified, the default value is $env:windir\ntds. When the command is run in offline mode, this parameter is required.
SiteName	String	The Active Directory site name for the target domain controller. If not specified, the site of the source domain controller is used.
IPv4Address	String	The static IPv4 address of the source domain controller.
IPv4SubnetMask	String	The static IPv4 subnet mask of the source domain controller.
IPv4DefaultGateway	String	The static IPv4 default gateway address of the source domain controller.
IPv4DNSResolver	String[]	An array of static IPv4 DNS entries of the source domain controller. This is an array data type of up to four entries in a comma-separated list.
IPv6DNSResolver	String	The static IPv6 DNS entries of the cloned computer. This is an array data type in a comma-separated list.
PreferredWINSServer	String	The static IPv4 address of the primary WINS server.
AlternateWINSServer	String	The static IPv4 address of the secondary WINS server.
Offline	Switch	Specifies that the command is being run against an offline image. Any existing DCCloneConfig.xml file is overwritten. No validation tests are performed.
Static	Switch	Required if you specify static IP address arguments.

To create a new, cloned domain controller called trey-dc-10 at a static IP address of 192.168.10.10, use the following command.

```
New-ADDCCloneConfigFile -Static `
                -CloneComputerName trey-dc-10 `
                -IPv4Address 192.168.10.10 `
                -IPv4SubnetMask 255.255.255.0 `
                -IPv4DefaultGateway 192.168.10.1 `
                -IPv4DNSResolver 192.168.10.2
```

The results of running New-ADDCCloneConfigFile on trey-dc-04 as the source controller are shown in Figure 4-2.

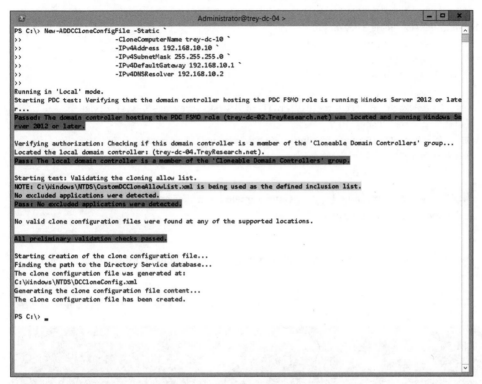

```
Administrator@trey-dc-04 >

PS C:\> New-ADDCCloneConfigFile -Static `
>>                      -CloneComputerName trey-dc-10 `
>>                      -IPv4Address 192.168.10.10 `
>>                      -IPv4SubnetMask 255.255.255.0 `
>>                      -IPv4DefaultGateway 192.168.10.1 `
>>                      -IPv4DNSResolver 192.168.10.2
>>
Running in 'Local' mode.
Starting PDC test: Verifying that the domain controller hosting the PDC FSMO role is running Windows Server 2012 or late
r...
Passed: The domain controller hosting the PDC FSMO role (trey-dc-02.TreyResearch.net) was located and running Windows Se
rver 2012 or later.

Verifying authorization: Checking if this domain controller is a member of the 'Cloneable Domain Controllers' group...
Located the local domain controller: (trey-dc-04.TreyResearch.net).
Pass: The local domain controller is a member of the 'Cloneable Domain Controllers' group.

Starting test: Validating the cloning allow list.
NOTE: C:\Windows\NTDS\CustomDCCloneAllowList.xml is being used as the defined inclusion list.
No excluded applications were detected.
Pass: No excluded applications were detected.

No valid clone configuration files were found at any of the supported locations.

All preliminary validation checks passed.

Starting creation of the clone configuration file...
Finding the path to the Directory Service database...
The clone configuration file was generated at:
C:\Windows\NTDS\DCCloneConfig.xml
Generating the clone configuration file content...
The clone configuration file has been created.

PS C:\> _
```

FIGURE 4-2 The results of running New-ADDCCloneConfigFile on trey-dc-04

When New-ADDCCloneConfigFile has been successfully run against the source domain controller, shut down the source domain controller before proceeding. Remove any snapshots of the source domain controller, and merge any differencing disks.

Create the cloned domain controller

After the source domain controller has been shut down, all snapshots have been removed, and any differencing disks merged, you can then choose a method to use to create a new VM from a copy of the source domain controller VHDs. If you're copying a single-NIC (network interface card), single-VHD source domain controller, you can just create a new VM from the copied VHD.

I used the following, interactively.

```
Copy-Item "D:\VMs\trey-dc-04\Virtual Hard Disks\trey-dc-04-system.vhdx" `
        "V:\trey-dc-10\Virtual Hard Disks\trey-dc-10-system.vhdx"
$ClonedDC=New-VM -Name trey-dc-10 `
        -MemoryStartupBytes 1024MB `
        -Generation 2 `
        -BootDevice VHD `
        -Path "V:\" `
        -VHDPath "V:\trey-dc-10\Virtual Hard Disks\trey-dc-10-system.vhdx" `
        -Switch "Local-10"
Set-VM -VM $ClonedDC -ProcessorCount 2 -DynamicMemory -PassThru
Start-VM $ClonedDC
```

> **NOTE** The virtual machine for your clone domain controller must be the same generation as the source domain controller.

The result of running these commands is a new, cloned domain controller, as shown in Figure 4-3.

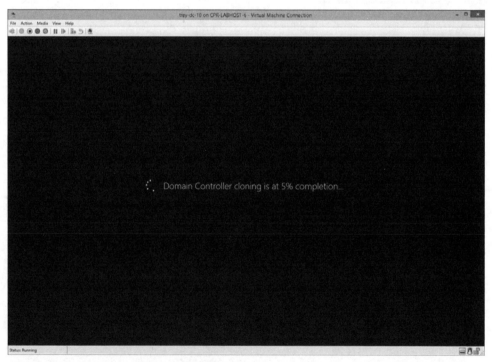

FIGURE 4-3 The domain controller cloning in process

After the files from the source domain controller have been copied, you can restart that domain controller.

> **NOTE** Don't forget to remove the source and target domain controllers from the Clone-able Domain Controllers security group. This group should only be populated during the actual cloning process.

Manage FSMO roles

There are five flexible single master operations (FSMO) roles in Windows domains. Each role plays an important part in the ongoing maintenance of the domain, and each resides on only a single domain controller. When a new forest and domain are created, all the FSMO roles reside on a single domain controller, the first domain controller in the forest. The five roles are:

- **Schema master** The schema master is the forest-wide role responsible for all updates to the AD DS schema. The schema master is the only domain controller that can write to the directory schema. By default, only members of the Schema Admins group have the right to transfer or seize the schema master role.

- **Domain naming master** The domain naming master is the forest-wide role responsible for both the addition and removal of domains and directory partitions. By default, only members of the Enterprise Admins group have the right to transfer or seize the domain naming master role.

- **RID master** The RID master is the domain-wide role responsible for allocating blocks of relative identifiers (RIDs) to each domain controller in the domain. When a domain controller creates a new security principal, such as a group, user, or computer object, the object is assigned a new, *globally unique* security identifier (SID). This SID is a combination of the domain SID plus an RID assigned to the object by the RID Master. By default, only members of the Domain Admins group have the right to transfer or seize the RID master role.

- **PDC emulator** The PDC emulator is the definitive source of password information, and the PDC emulator in the forest-root domain is the Windows Time Service source for the entire forest. The PDC emulator role is a domain-wide role. By default, only members of the Domain Admins group have the right to transfer or seize the PDC emulator role.

- **Infrastructure master** The infrastructure master is the domain-wide role responsible for updating references to objects in other domains, and for replicating those changed references to other domain controllers in the domain.

Transfer FSMO roles

When a new forest is created, all five FSMO roles reside on the first domain controller. In a small domain, that's perfectly acceptable, but it is not appropriate for a large enterprise. Distributing the FSMO roles across multiple domain controllers provides a more balanced allocation of resources. Typically, the PDC emulator and the RID master roles for each domain reside on a single domain controller, and the two forest-wide roles, schema master and domain naming master, reside on a single domain controller.

You can transfer the FSMO roles from one domain controller to another by using the Move-ADDirectoryServerOperationMasterRole cmdlet. One big advantage to using Windows PowerShell for this operation is that you can move more than one role at a time. So, for example, if you wanted to move the three domain-wide roles from their current location to trey-dc-04, you might start by looking to find out where they currently reside. For that, use Get-ADDomain, which also gives you quite a bit of other information about the domain.

```
Get-ADDomain -Identity treyresearch.net
```

```
AllowedDNSSuffixes              : {}
ChildDomains                    : {}
ComputersContainer              : CN=Computers,DC=TreyResearch,DC=net
DeletedObjectsContainer         : CN=Deleted Objects,DC=TreyResearch,DC=net
DistinguishedName               : DC=TreyResearch,DC=net
DNSRoot                         : TreyResearch.net
DomainControllersContainer      : OU=Domain Controllers,DC=TreyResearch,DC=net
DomainMode                      : Windows2012R2Domain
DomainSID                       : S-1-5-21-910751839-3601328731-670513855
ForeignSecurityPrincipalsContainer :
CN=ForeignSecurityPrincipals,DC=TreyResearch,DC=net
Forest                          : TreyResearch.net
InfrastructureMaster            : trey-dc-02.TreyResearch.net
LastLogonReplicationInterval    :
LinkedGroupPolicyObjects        : {CN={31B2F340-016D-11D2-945F-00C04FB984F9},
CN=Policies,CN=System,DC=TreyResearch,DC=net}
LostAndFoundContainer           : CN=LostAndFound,DC=TreyResearch,DC=net
ManagedBy                       :
Name                            : TreyResearch
NetBIOSName                     : TREYRESEARCH
ObjectClass                     : domainDNS
ObjectGUID                      : 43bdaeeb-4bac-431e-9e82-176c2dc7d8b9
```

```
ParentDomain                    :
PDCEmulator                     : trey-dc-02.TreyResearch.net
QuotasContainer                 : CN=NTDS Quotas,DC=TreyResearch,DC=net
ReadOnlyReplicaDirectoryServers : {}
ReplicaDirectoryServers         : {trey-dc-02.TreyResearch.net, trey-dc-
09.TreyResearch.net,

                                  trey-dc-04.TreyResearch.net}
RIDMaster                       : trey-dc-02.TreyResearch.net
SubordinateReferences           : {DC=ForestDnsZones,DC=TreyResearch,DC=net,
                                  DC=DomainDnsZones,DC=TreyResearch,DC=net,
                                  CN=Configuration,DC=TreyResearch,DC=net}
SystemsContainer                : CN=System,DC=TreyResearch,DC=net
UsersContainer                  : CN=Users,DC=TreyResearch,DC=net
```

To move the three domain-wide roles, use the following command.

```
Move-ADDirectoryServerOperationMasterRole `
              -OperationMaster PDCEmulator,RIDMaster,InfrastructureMaster `
              -Identity trey-dc-04
```

And, after a prompt to confirm that we really want move the roles, it's done. Use Get-ADDomainController to view the result, as shown in Figure 4-4.

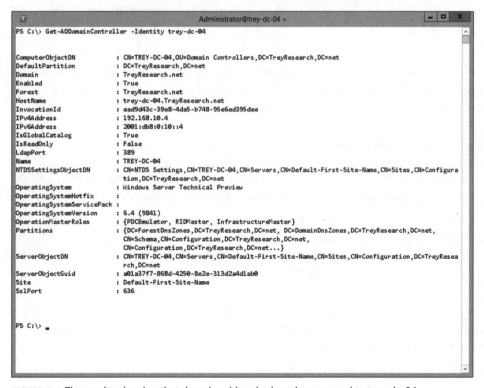

FIGURE 4-4 The results, showing that domain-wide roles have been moved to trey-dc-04

To find out where the forest-wide roles are, use the Get-ADForest cmdlet. This shows that both the schema master and domain naming master roles currently reside on trey-dc-02. To move them to trey-dc-09, use the following.

```
Move-ADDirectoryServerOperationMasterRole `
                    -Identity 'trey-dc-09' `
                    -OperationMasterRole SchemaMaster,DomainNamingMaster
```

Again, to make sure that the roles have transferred successfully, use either Get-ADForest or Get-ADDomainController.

Seize FSMO roles

The preferred method to move roles between domain controllers is to politely transfer them, as described in the previous section. But sometimes that's simply not possible. The cause could be something planned, like a domain migration, or something unplanned, like a major disaster recovery scenario. As long as there is still one domain controller in the domain, you can seize the roles to that domain controller. You should not do this if there is *any* chance that the original domain controller hosting the role you are seizing might ever come back online.

> **IMPORTANT**   Let me repeat that, just to be crystal clear. After a FSMO role has been seized from a domain controller, that domain controller should not ever be allowed to connect to the domain. Ever. Bad and unpredictable things can and will happen. You've been warned.

So, if your FSMO role holder isn't currently available but you expect it to be restored and available soon, what should you do? Wait for it, or seize the roles and decommission the server? Decommissioning is easy if it's a virtual machine. It's a bit more of a nuisance if it's a physical server.

Seizing the operations master roles uses the same command as transferring the roles, except that seizing uses the Force parameter. Even when you use the Force parameter, however, AD DS attempts to transfer the role if it can reach the current holder of the role. Only if that fails will AD DS allow you to seize the role. To seize the three domain-wide roles back to trey-dc-02, use the following command.

```
Move-ADDirectoryServerOperationMasterRole `
                    -OperationMaster PDCEmulator,RIDMaster,InfrastructureMaster `
                    -Identity trey-dc-02 `
                    -Force
```

Again, you're prompted to confirm each seizure, and then the roles are seized. The process takes somewhat longer, because an attempt is made to contact the current role holder to attempt a transfer operation first.

Now, because I've seized roles from trey-dc-04, a bit of cleanup is required.

```
Remove-VM -Name trey-dc-04 ; rm -r D:\VMs\trey-dc-04
```

Gone, never to return.

Summary

In this chapter, you learned how to deploy additional domain controllers in your domain. You learned how to create a new domain controller from an existing server by configuring the networking, installing the Active Directory role, and then promoting the server to domain controller. You also learned how to clone an existing virtualized domain controller to create a new virtualized domain controller, saving many steps over the standard deployment. Finally, you learned how to manage the five flexible single master operations roles and how to move them or seize them.

In the next chapter, you'll learn how to create and deploy read-only domain controllers, and you'll learn some tricks that can be used to deploy a domain controller even when it is in a remote location with slow or unreliable connectivity.

CHAPTER 5

Deploy read-only domain controllers (RODCs)

Microsoft introduced the read-only domain controller (RODC) with the release of Windows Server 2008. Those of you with long memories can be forgiven if you think you've seen this before; however, back then they were called backup domain controllers (BDCs). BDCs existed starting with the original release of Windows NT, right up until Windows 2000, when Active Directory was introduced and all domain controllers became multimaster domain controllers—which was great, but there are actually some really useful scenarios for having a read-only domain controller available at a remote location to facilitate logons, name resolution, and Group Policy deployment.

Remote sites, such as branch offices, frequently have less reliable and slower network bandwidth, and they are also likely to have less rigorous security. By using an RODC, these sites can protect the integrity of Active Directory Domain Services (AD DS). By using a staged deployment, it's possible to deploy a domain controller from media, greatly speeding up deployment to poorly connected sites.

Active Directory Windows PowerShell nouns used in this chapter:

- ADDSReadOnlyDomainControllerAccount
- ADDSDomainController

Other Windows PowerShell commands used in this chapter:

- Install-WindowsFeature
- Update-Help
- Get-NetAdapter
- New-NetIPAddress
- Set-DnsClientServerAddress
- Get-Credential

Prepare the forest and domain

Before you can add an RODC to a domain, you need to prepare the domain. If it is an existing forest and domain, with domain controllers that are running Windows Server 2008, Windows Server 2008 R2, or Windows Server 2012, you can prepare the forest and the domain for the inclusion of a Windows Server 2012 R2 or Windows Server Technical Preview domain controller by using the adprep.exe tool.

You should always use the version of adprep.exe that is located on the installation media of the latest version of Windows Server that you want to add to the domain or forest as a domain controller. However, starting with Windows Server 2012 R2, the Install-ADDSDomain-Controller cmdlet runs adprep automatically for most scenarios. So, for example, if you have a forest and domain with only Windows Server 2008 R2 domain controllers but want to introduce a Windows Server 2012 R2 domain controller, the promotion of that domain controller with the Install-ADDSDomainController also runs the adprep command to automatically prepare the domain and the forest if necessary. When you create a new domain by using Install-ADDSDomain, the command runs any necessary adprep commands. However, if you are installing an RODC into a domain that hasn't had one before, you need to run adprep to prepare the domain to accept an RODC.

If you're installing a Windows Server 2012 R2 RODC, you need to run the adprep.exe tool that resides in the \support\adprep folder on the Windows Server 2012 R2 installation media. If you're installing a Windows Server Technical Preview RODC, you need to run the adprep utility from the \support\adprep folder of the Windows Server Technical Preview installation media.

For each existing domain that hasn't had a Windows Server 2012 or later domain controller added, you need to prepare the Group Policy by using the following command.

```
adprep /domainprep /gpprep
```

This command requires Domain Admins privileges and should only be done once per domain. This command must be run when the infrastructure master operations master (also known as flexible single master operations or FSMO) role holder is reachable and online.

Finally, for any domain where you are deploying an RODC, you need to prepare the domain for that RODC by using the following command.

```
adprep /rodcprep
```

This command requires Enterprise Admins privileges and needs to be run only once per *forest*. Rodcprep needs to be able to contact both the domain naming master FSMO role holder for the forest and the infrastructure master FSMO role holder for the domains where RODCs are to be deployed. This command can be run again if an infrastructure master role holder was offline at the time of the initial rodcprep.

Staged deployment of an RODC

The simplest way to deploy RODCs is to pre-stage them. When you pre-stage an RODC, the staging of the account requires you to be a member of the Domain Admins group, but the actual deployment of the RODC can be delegated to a non-administrative account, making it easy to deploy to remote sites that might not have an administrator. Staging an RODC also gives you the ability to install the RODC from media that contains a copy of the Active Directory database, speeding up replication and reducing the load on network resources.

A staged deployment creates the RODC account before the computer is deployed. Then you join the new RODC to the domain and promote it to an RODC in one step. Whether you use the install from media (IFM) option or allow the AD DS database replication to occur across the network, the preparation steps are identical:

- Prepare the RODC account.
- Prepare the target RODC server.
- Deploy the target RODC server.

Prepare the RODC account

Read-only domain controllers are members of a special security group in AD DS, the read-only domain controllers security group. When you do a staged RODC deployment, you pre-populate the group with the target RODC account, and you can also pre-populate the two security groups that control which user, group, and computer accounts are replicated to the new RODC server and which ones are prevented from replicating. By default, if no accounts are specified, the Allowed RODC Password Replication Group is empty. By default, Administrators, Server Operators, Backup Operators, Account Operators, and the members of the Denied RODC Password Replication Group do not have their passwords replicated to RODCs in the domain. The Denied RODC Password Replication Group includes, by default:

- Cert Publishers
- Domain Admins
- Enterprise Admins

- Schema Admins
- Group Policy Creator Owners
- krbtgt (Key Distribution Center Service Account)
- Domain Controllers
- Read-only Domain Controllers

To prepare an RODC account for trey-rodc-200, use the following command.

```
Add-ADDSReadOnlyDomainControllerAccount `
        -DomainControllerAccountName "trey-rodc-200" `
        -DomainName "TreyResearch.net" `
        -SiteName "Default-First-Site-Name" `
        -DelegatedAdministratorAccountName "TREYRESEARCH\Stanley" `
        -InstallDNS `
        -AllowPasswordReplicationAccountName "Dave","Alfie","Stanley"
```

As shown in Figure 5-1, this creates the account and doesn't require a reboot. The required parameters for Add-ADDSReadOnlyDomainControllerAccount are the first three in the previous command: DomainControllerAccountName, DomainName, and SiteName. If you plan to have the RODC deployed by a non-administrator, be sure to include the DelegatedAdministratorAccountName parameter.

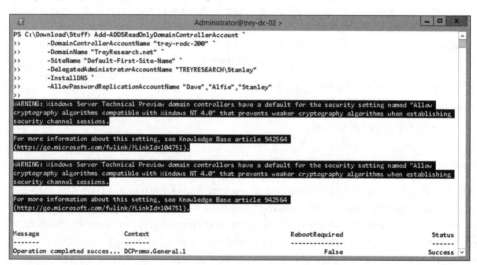

FIGURE 5-1 Adding a staged RODC account

You can test the creation of an RODC account before actually running the Add-ADDS-ReadOnlyDomainControllerAccount cmdlet, by using the Test-ADDSReadOnlyDomain-ControllerAccount cmdlet, which runs all the prerequisite checks for creating the RODC account without actually creating it.

Prepare the RODC target server

Before deploying the new read-only domain controller, you should configure the networking of the RODC target server to support its use as an RODC. This means configuring fixed IP addresses for both IPv4 and IPv6. This is especially important if the RODC is also acting as a DNS server.

To configure the network adapters in the RODC, use the Set-NetIPInterface and New-NetIPAddress cmdlets. Use the Set-DnsClientServerAddress cmdlet to set the DNS server address.

Use Get-NetAdapter to discover the names and Interface Index values of your network adapters.

```
Get-NetAdapter
```

Name	InterfaceDescription	ifIndex	Status	MacAddress	LinkSpeed
Ethernet	Microsoft Hyper-V Netw...	3	Up	00-10-5D-33-10-C8	10 Gbps

We only have a single network adapter, "Ethernet," so that makes things simple. First, assign the adapter to a variable.

```
$Nic = Get-NetAdapter -Name Ethernet
```

Now we need to reconfigure $Nic to disable the DHCP.

```
$Nic | Set-NetIPInterface -DHCP Disabled
```

Next configure an IPv4 address.

```
$Nic | New-NetIPAddress -AddressFamily IPv4 `
                        -IPAddress 192.168.10.200 `
                        -PrefixLength 24 `
                        -type Unicast `
                        -DefaultGateway 192.168.10.1
```

Now configure the DNS setting for $Nic.

```
Set-DnsClientServerAddress -InterfaceAlias $Nic.Name `
                        -ServerAddresses 192.168.10.2,2001:db8:0:10::2 `
                        -PassThru
```

InterfaceAlias	Interface Index	Address Family	ServerAddresses
Ethernet	3	IPv6	{2001:db8:0:10::2}
Ethernet	3	IPv4	{192.168.10.2}

And finally, configure the IPv6 settings for $Nic.

```
$Nic |  New-NetIPAddress -AddressFamily IPv6 `
                         -IPAddress 2001:db8:0:10::c8 `
                         -PrefixLength 64 `
                         -type Unicast `
                         -DefaultGateway 2001:db8:0:10::1
```

And, to confirm that everything is as we expect, here are the results from ipconfig.

```
ipconfig
```

```
Windows IP Configuration


Ethernet adapter Ethernet:

   Connection-specific DNS Suffix  . :
   IPv6 Address. . . . . . . . . . : 2001:db8:0:10::c8
   Link-local IPv6 Address . . . . : fe80::2c84:9c6d:8f86:8fa0%3
   IPv4 Address. . . . . . . . . . : 192.168.10.200
   Subnet Mask . . . . . . . . . . : 255.255.255.0
   Default Gateway . . . . . . . . : 2001:db8:0:10::1
                                     192.168.10.1

Tunnel adapter isatap.{71508A35-E9FB-4CD9-8022-E56B057C67BE}:

   Media State . . . . . . . . . . : Media disconnected
   Connection-specific DNS Suffix  . :
```

Of course, if you grabbed my quick-and-dirty Set-myIP.ps1 script from Chapter 4, "Deploy additional domain controllers," you can use that (assuming you've adjusted it for your environment).

```
Set-myIP -IP4 200 -IP6 C8
```

Either way, the result is that the RODC server is configured to fixed IP addresses, and those addresses are configured to get their DNS information from the writeable domain controller, trey-dc-02.

Finally, you need to change the name of the server to the name you used to stage the RODC account. Use the Rename-Computer cmdlet to rename the server.

```
Rename-Computer -NewName trey-rodc-200 -Restart -Force
```

Deploy the RODC target server

After you've set the networking, you can install AD DS by using the following command.

```
Install-WindowsFeature `
    -Name AD-Domain-Services `
    -IncludeAllSubFeature `
    -IncludeManagementTools
```

You can ignore the warning about automatic updating not being enabled. I don't allow automatic updating of any domain controller, even an RODC, and I doubt that very many other system administrators do either. However, if this RODC is exposed (such as an RODC in a perimeter network), you might want to consider enabling automatic updating and running the RODC as a core installation.

In addition to installing the Active Directory Domain Services role, Install-WindowsFeature has installed the full set of Remote Server Administration Tools (RSAT) related to AD DS and the Group Policy Management Console. And because that installation has also included new Windows PowerShell modules, now's a good time to update the Get-Help files.

```
Update-Help -SourcePath \\trey-dc-02\pshelp -force
```

Network deployment

When you are able to deploy an RODC over a fast and reliable network connection, it makes sense to do a straightforward network deployment. You don't need to create the IFS media, just join the RODC to the domain and promote it in one step. To join the RODC to the domain and promote it to a read-only domain controller, use the following commands.

```
$domCred = Get-Credential -UserName "TREYRESEARCH\Stanley" `
                          -Message "Enter your domain credentials"
Install-ADDSDomainController -DomainName "TreyResearch.net" `
                             -Credential $domCred `
                             -Force `
                             -UseExistingAccount:$True
```

Because the account is a staged account, this will join the computer to the domain and automatically promote it to RODC status. Also, because this account was pre-staged, I was able to join the RODC to the domain and promote it to a domain controller from a standard user account.

Because I didn't include the SafeModeAdministratorPassword parameter, this prompts for the safe mode password and a confirmation of the password. If you are automating deployment to a lab environment, where password security might not be as rigorously enforced as in a production environment, you can use the ConvertTo-SecureString cmdlet with the SafeModeAdministratorPassword parameter to eliminate the need for any prompting.

Media deployment

You can speed up the process of initial replication to a new domain controller by installing the AD DS database from a disk file. By using this process, *install from media (IFM)*, combined with staging, you can deploy a remote RODC even over a slow link and without any specialized knowledge or privileges at the remote site.

CREATE THE IFM MEDIA

Use the Ntdsutil.exe ifm command to create the media. You can also create the installation media by restoring a critical-volume backup of a domain controller in the same domain. Unfortunately, there isn't a simple Windows PowerShell cmdlet for this. The requirements for IFM are detailed but not surprising:

- You can't use IFM to create the first domain controller in a domain; there must be an existing Windows Server 2008 or later domain controller.
- The IFM media must be taken from the same domain as the new domain controller.
- If you're creating a global catalog server, the IFM must be from a domain controller that is also a global catalog.
- To install a domain controller that is also a DNS server, the IFM must be from a domain controller that is also a DNS server.
- To create installation media for a writable domain controller, you must create the IFM on a writeable domain controller that is running Windows Server 2008 or later.
- To create installation media for an RODC, you can create the IFM on either a writeable domain controller or an RODC.
- To create installation media that includes SYSVOL, you must create the IFM on a domain controller running Windows Server 2008 Service Pack 2 or later.

To create the IFM media, you need to use an account with Domain Admins privileges. Open a Windows PowerShell window, *as administrator*, while logged on to an account that is a member of the Domain Admins security group. In the shell, enter the following commands to create RODC media that includes SYSVOL, and save it to the C:\IFM folder.

```
ntdsutil
activate instance ntds
ifm
create sysvol RODC "C:\IFM"
quit
quit
```

```
ntdsutil "activate instance ntds" ifm "create sysvol RODC C:\IFM" q q
```

The IFM media can now be copied to a network share or a removable drive for use during the RODC promotion process.

INSTALL FROM MEDIA

To pre-stage the RODC account, use the Add-ADDSReadOnlyDomainControllerAccount cmdlet. For this media installation version, we'll use a non-administrative account, just as we did during the network installation. Again, the account creation must be run by an account with domain-level administrator privileges.

```
Add-ADDSReadOnlyDomainControllerAccount `
      -DomainControllerAccountName "trey-rodc-201" `
      -DomainName "TreyResearch.net" `
      -SiteName "Default-First-Site-Name" `
      -DelegatedAdministratorAccountName "TREYRESEARCH\Wally" `
      -InstallDNS `
      -AllowPasswordReplicationAccountName "Dave","Alfie","Wally"
```

Prepare the target RODC server exactly as you did for the network installation, giving it fixed IP addresses and making sure to rename it to match the name you've used in the Add-ADDSReadOnlyDomainControllerAccount command. Don't forget to use Install-Windows-Feature to install AD DS and all the management tools. For my lab, I'm using the following commands to create trey-rodc-201 and prepare it for promotion to an RODC.

```
Install-WindowsFeature       -Name AD-Domain-Services `
                             -IncludeAllSubFeature `
                             -IncludeManagementTools
$Nic = Get-NetAdapter        -Name Ethernet
$Nic | New-NetIPAddress      -AddressFamily IPv4 `
                             -IPAddress 192.168.10.201 `
                             -PrefixLength 24 `
                             -type Unicast `
                             -DefaultGateway 192.168.10.1
Set-DnsClientServerAddress -InterfaceAlias $Nic.Name `
                             -ServerAddresses 192.168.10.2,2001:db8:0:10::2 `
                             -PassThru
```

```
$Nic | New-NetIPAddress    -AddressFamily IPv6 `
                           -IPAddress 2001:db8:0:10::c9 `
                           -PrefixLength 64 `
                           -type Unicast `
                           -DefaultGateway 2001:db8:0:10::1
Rename-Computer -NewName trey-rodc-201 -Restart -Force
```

After the target RODC server reboots, you can promote it to an RODC and join it to the TreyResearch.net domain by using the following command.

```
$domCred = Get-Credential    -UserName "TREYRESEARCH\Wally" `
                             -Message "Enter your domain credentials"
Install-ADDSDomainController -DomainName "TreyResearch.net" `
                             -Credential $domCred `
                             -InstallationMediaPath "C:\IFM" `
                             -UseExistingAccount:$True
```

This assumes that we've copied the IFM media to C:\IFM. Also, I want to include a caution about the InstallationMediaPath parameter: it's *fussy*. If you leave a trailing backslash, it will fail. If you include the Active Directory folder in the path ("C:\IFM\Active Directory"), it will fail.

Non-staged deployment of an RODC

The process for doing a non-staged deployment of an RODC is similar to doing a staged deployment, except that you don't first create the account in AD DS. You still need to prepare the RODC target server, and you still have a choice of network deployment or IFM deployment. However, the option to deploy with a non-administrative account is gone, and options that were a part of the pre-staging, such as whether to install DNS, now have to be part of the Install-ADDSDomainController command.

Prepare the RODC target server

Before deploying a read-only domain controller, you should configure the networking of the RODC target server to support its use as an RODC. This means configuring fixed IP addresses for both IPv4 and IPv6. This is especially important if the RODC is also acting as a DNS server.

To configure the network adapters in the RODC, use the Set-NetIPInterface and New-NetIPAddress cmdlets. Use the Set-DnsClientServerAddress cmdlet to set the DNS server address.

Use Get-NetAdapter to discover the names and Interface Index values of your network adapters.

```
Get-NetAdapter
```

Name	InterfaceDescription	ifIndex	Status	MacAddress	LinkSpeed
Ethernet	Microsoft Hyper-V Network...	3	Up	00-10-5D-33-10-CA	10 Gbps

We only have a single network adapter, "Ethernet," so that makes things simple. First, assign the adapter to a variable.

```
$Nic = Get-NetAdapter -Name Ethernet
```

Now we need to reconfigure $Nic to disable the DHCP.

```
$Nic | Set-NetIPInterface -DHCP Disabled
```

Next configure an IPv4 address.

```
$Nic | New-NetIPAddress -AddressFamily IPv4 `
                    -IPAddress 192.168.10.202 `
                    -PrefixLength 24 `
                    -type Unicast `
                    -DefaultGateway 192.168.10.1
```

Now configure the DNS setting for $Nic.

```
Set-DnsClientServerAddress -InterfaceAlias $Nic.Name `
                    -ServerAddresses 192.168.10.2,2001:db8:0:10::2 `
                    -PassThru
```

InterfaceAlias	Interface Index	Address Family	ServerAddresses
Ethernet	3	IPv6	{2001:db8:0:10::2}
Ethernet	3	IPv4	{192.168.10.2}

And finally, configure the IPv6 settings for $Nic.

```
$Nic | New-NetIPAddress -AddressFamily IPv6 `
                    -IPAddress 2001:db8:0:10::ca `
                    -PrefixLength 64 `
                    -type Unicast `
                    -DefaultGateway 2001:db8:0:10::1
```

And, to confirm that everything is as we expect, here are the results from ipconfig.

```
ipconfig
```

```
Windows IP Configuration

Ethernet adapter Ethernet:
   Connection-specific DNS Suffix  . : TreyResearch.net
      IPv6 Address. . . . . . . . . : 2001:db8:0:10::ca
      IPv6 Address. . . . . . . . . : 2001:db8:0:10:c450:46c9:e0bf:d17
      Link-local IPv6 Address . . . . : fe80::2862:1cbd:5203:a58f%3
      IPv4 Address. . . . . . . . . : 192.168.10.202
      Subnet Mask . . . . . . . . . : 255.255.255.0
      Default Gateway . . . . . . . : 2001:db8:0:10::1
                                      192.168.10.1


Tunnel adapter isatap.{2C852E90-0A1E-434F-9230-FDE6F5620D78}:

   Media State . . . . . . . . . : Media disconnected
   Connection-specific DNS Suffix  . : TreyResearch.net
```

Of course, if you grabbed my quick-and-dirty Set-myIP.ps1 script from Chapter 4, you can use that (assuming that you've adjusted it for your environment).

```
Set-myIP -IP4 202 -IP6 CA
```

Either way, the result is that the RODC server is configured to fixed IP addresses, and those addresses are configured to get their DNS information from the writeable domain controller, trey-dc-02.

Finally, you need to change the name of the server to the name you used to stage the RODC account. Use the Add-Computer cmdlet to join the domain and change the name in a single step.

```
$domCred = Get-Credential -UserName "TreyResearch\Charlie" `
                        -Message "Enter the Domain password for Charlie."

Add-Computer -DomainName TreyResearch.net `
            -NewName trey-rodc-202 `
            -Credential $domCred `
            -Restart `
            -Force
```

Deploy the non-staged RODC target server

Use the following command to install the AD-Domain-Services server role.

```
Install-WindowsFeature -Name AD-Domain-Services -IncludeManagementTools
```

In addition to installing the Active Directory Domain Services role, the IncludeManagementTools parameter has caused the full set of RSAT tools related to AD DS and the Group Policy Management Console to be installed. And because that installation has also included new Windows PowerShell modules, now's a good time to update the Get-Help files.

```
Update-Help -SourcePath \\trey-dc-02\pshelp -force
```

Network deployment

When you are able to deploy an RODC over a fast and reliable network connection, it makes sense to do a straightforward network deployment. You don't need to create the IFS media, just promote the domain controller. Because this isn't a staged deployment, you must either run the command in an elevated Windows PowerShell window from an account that is a member of the Domain Admins group, or you must provide credentials for such an account. Also, you should specify whether to install DNS, and you must specify the SiteName. But because we're running this without pre-staging the account, I like to test that the promotion will happen without issues, so we'll use the same command as we will use for the actual deployment, but change the verb from Install to Test and add an Install to the end of the noun, like this.

```
Test-ADDSDomainControllerInstallation `
                -DomainName "TreyResearch.net" `
                -InstallDNS `
                -SiteName "Default-First-Site-Name" `
                -Force `
                -AllowPasswordReplicationAccountName "Dave","Alfie" `
                -ReadOnlyReplica:$True
```

As you can tell from Figure 5-2, all three preliminary tests for RODC deployment were successful. We did get an obligatory warning about Windows NT 4.0 compatibility due to cryptography algorithms, but that was expected.

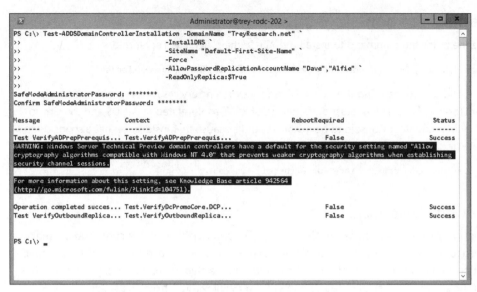

```
Administrator@trey-rodc-202 >

PS C:\> Test-ADDSDomainControllerInstallation -DomainName "TreyResearch.net" `
>>                          -InstallDNS `
>>                          -SiteName "Default-First-Site-Name" `
>>                          -Force `
>>                          -AllowPasswordReplicationAccountName "Dave","Alfie" `
>>                          -ReadOnlyReplica:$True
>>
SafeModeAdministratorPassword: ********
Confirm SafeModeAdministratorPassword: ********

Message                  Context                    RebootRequired          Status
-------                  -------                    --------------          ------
Test VerifyADPrepPrerequis... Test.VerifyADPrepPrerequis...                False          Success
WARNING: Windows Server Technical Preview domain controllers have a default for the security setting named "Allow
cryptography algorithms compatible with Windows NT 4.0" that prevents weaker cryptography algorithms when establishing
security channel sessions.

For more information about this setting, see Knowledge Base article 942564
(http://go.microsoft.com/fwlink/?LinkId=104751).

Operation completed succes... Test.VerifyDcPromoCore.DCP...                False          Success
Test VerifyOutboundReplica... Test.VerifyOutboundReplica...                False          Success


PS C:\>
```

FIGURE 5-2 Testing the RODC deployment

Because the test was successful, we're ready to do the actual deployment. You'll notice that the parameters are exactly the same as they were for the Test-ADDSDomainControllerInstallation cmdlet, except that I've added the SkipPreChecks parameter. We don't need the pre-checks, because we just ran them with the Test-ADDSDomainControllerInstallation command. Now, to promote trey-rodc-202 to an RODC, use the following command.

```
Install-ADDSDomainController -DomainName "TreyResearch.net" `
                            -SkipPreChecks `
                            -InstallDNS `
                            -SiteName "Default-First-Site-Name" `
                            -Force `
                            -AllowPasswordReplicationAccountName "Dave","Alfie" `
                            -ReadOnlyReplica:$True
```

You'll notice that this command is slightly different than the one used to deploy a staged RODC from the network. I've added the InstallDNS, AllowPasswordReplicationAccountName, and SiteName parameters, and changed the UseExistingAccount parameter to the ReadOnly-Replica parameter. These parameters were covered by the Add-ADDSReadOnlyDomain-ControllerAccount cmdlet when we staged the deployment. But the result will be exactly the same whether staged or not.

Media deployment

Prepare your RODC target server as described earlier in the "Prepare the RODC target server" section. For this media deployment, I'm creating trey-rodc-203, and I'm setting my networking with the following.

```
Set-myIP 203 CB
```

I'm joining the server to the domain and changing the name in a single Windows PowerShell command by calling Get-Credential directly into the Credential parameter.

```
Add-Computer -DomainName TreyResearch.net `
            -NewName trey-rodc-203 `
            -Credential (Get-Credential -Message "Enter Domain Admin Creds") `
            -Restart `
            -Force
```

Now, with the IFM copied to drive C on trey-rodc-203, I can deploy the RODC by using the following command.

```
Install-ADDSDomainController -DomainName "TreyResearch.net" `
                            -Credential $domCred `
                            -SiteName "Default-First-Site-Name" `
                            -InstallDNS `
                            -InstallationMediaPath "C:\IFM" `
                            -ReadOnlyReplica:$True
```

After I enter and re-enter the safe mode administrator password, and confirm that I really want to do this, my target server is rebooted and is an RODC.

Now, to confirm that everything in this chapter has worked, see Figure 5-3, which is a screen shot of Active Directory Users And Computers.

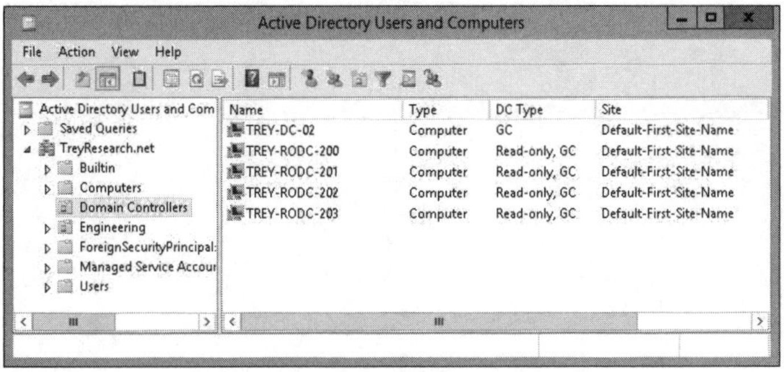

FIGURE 5-3 Four RODCs deployed in the TreyResearch.net domain

> **NOTE** The techniques and commands used in this section on deploying RODCs that are not pre-staged apply equally to writeable domain controllers, including the ability to install from media. Writeable domain controllers can't be staged, but they can be deployed from media.

Summary

In this chapter, you learned how to prepare a server to be a domain controller, how to pre-pare the forest and domain to accept a read-only domain controller, and how to pre-stage the RODC accounts to allow deployment to sites that might not have local resources that are domain administrators. In addition, you learned how to create IFM media so that domain controllers can be deployed from media, facilitating deployment to remote and poorly con-nected sites. Finally, you also learned how to deploy an RODC without pre-staging it first.

In the next chapter, you'll learn how to deploy additional domains in the forest, and how to create additional forests.

CHAPTER 6

Deploy additional domains and forests

In previous chapters, you learned how to deploy a forest and domain, set up networking, add users and groups, and add additional domain controllers, including read-only domain controllers, to that initial domain. In this chapter, you'll learn how to deploy additional domains and subdomains (also known as *child domains*) and how to configure cross-forest trusts.

We'll start with our existing TreyResearch.net domain and add a child domain to it, NorthAmerica.TreyResearch.net. Then we'll create another tree in our forest by adding WingtipToys.com to the forest. Finally, as a result of Trey Research acquiring Tailspin Toys, we'll add a cross-forest trust to the TailspinToys.com domain.

Active Directory Windows PowerShell nouns used in this chapter:

- ADDSDomainControllerInstallation
- ADDSDomainController
- ADDSDomainInstallation
- ADDSDomain
- ADGroupMember
- ADDSForestInstallation
- ADDSForest

Other Windows PowerShell commands used in this chapter:

- Rename-Computer
- Get-NetIPAddress
- Set-NetIPInterface
- New-NetIPAddress
- Get-Member
- Get-NetAdapter
- Set-DnsClientServerAddress
- Install-WindowsFeature
- Format-Table
- Update-Help

- Import-Module
- Get-Credential
- New-Object

Create a child domain

Although it's certainly possible (and often preferable) to have your entire organization in a single Active Directory domain, there are frequently good reasons to segregate portions of the organization into separate domains, whether these are child domains or tree domains.

> **NOTE** A child domain is a sub-domain in the same namespace as the parent domain—thus, NorthAmerica.TreyResearch.net is a child domain of TreyResearch.net. A tree domain has a separate namespace—thus, WingtipToys.com, which was created in the existing Trey-Research.net forest, is a tree domain. The parent of a child domain is the domain higher up the tree, whereas the parent of a tree domain is the forest.

A child domain needs to be a single-level domain (NorthAmerica) within the same DNS namespace (TreyResearch.net) as its parent.

Prepare the server

Before you can promote a server to be the domain controller for a child domain, you need to prepare the server and configure the networking to support the promotion. Because we're creating a new domain in this example, we do *not* want to join the domain first. If you try to promote a server while it's a member of the parent domain, it will fail and promptly unjoin you from the domain and reboot. This might seem drastic, but it does make the point. So, to prepare the server, we need to:

- Rename the server to a name that meets our naming conventions.
- Assign fixed IP addresses for all network adapters.
- Configure the DNS settings for the network adapters.

Rename the server

To rename the server, we use the Rename-Computer cmdlet. This cmdlet has a simple syntax.

```
syntax Rename-Computer
```

```
Syntax for Rename-Computer is:

Rename-Computer [-NewName] <string> [-ComputerName <string>] [-PassThru]
[-DomainCredential <pscredential>][-LocalCredential <pscredential>] [-Force] [-Restart]
[-WhatIf] [-Confirm] [<CommonParameters>]
```

Assuming that we are logged on as a local administrator, we can ignore the ComputerName and LocalCredential parameters, and because we're not in a domain, we can ignore the DomainCredential parameter. For the rest, we obviously want the NewName parameter, and for this specific situation, we can use -Restart:$False. We're going to configure the networking before we trigger the reboot.

The server name we're going to use in the lab for this domain controller is na-dc-05. So, to rename the server, use the following.

```
Rename-Computer -NewName na-dc-05 -Restart:$False
```

This gives us a warning that the changes will not take place until we restart the computer. We know that.

Assign fixed IP addresses

We need to change the Dynamic Host Configuration Protocol (DHCP) addresses on the server to fixed IP addresses. The lab server has two network adapters, one on 192.168.10.0/24, and the other on 192.168.11.0/24. Both adapters need to be set. First, let's find out which network adapter is connected to which network. We could use Get-NetIPAddress for that, but the output is pretty messy. Let's just get what we need in a format we can read.

```
Get-NetIPAddress -AddressFamily IPv4 `
            | Format-Table -Auto ifIndex,InterfaceAlias,IPAddress
```

```
ifIndex InterfaceAlias              IPAddress
------- --------------              ---------
      4 Ethernet 2                  192.168.11.22
      3 Ethernet                    192.168.10.21
      1 Loopback Pseudo-Interface 1 127.0.0.1
```

We're going to change the IP addresses for both IPv4 and IPv6, but it's easy enough to identify which adapter is which with just the IPv4 address, and it makes the output a lot less messy. Oh, and in case you were wondering, ifIndex is an alias for InterfaceIndex, as you can tell if you use the following.

```
Get-NetIPAddress | Get-Member
```

Now that we can identify which adapter is which, we can get the two adapters into variables we can work with.

```
$Nic10 = Get-NetAdapter -ifIndex 3
$Nic11 = Get-NetAdapter -ifIndex 4
```

Now we need to reconfigure the two adapters to disable the DHCP.

```
$Nic10 | Set-NetIPInterface -DHCP Disabled
$Nic11 | Set-NetIPInterface -DHCP Disabled
```

Then we configure the IPv4 addresses.

```
$Nic10 | New-NetIPAddress -AddressFamily IPv4 `
                          -IPAddress 192.168.10.5 `
                          -PrefixLength 24 `
                          -type Unicast `
                          -DefaultGateway 192.168.10.1
$Nic11 | New-NetIPAddress -AddressFamily IPv4 `
                          -IPAddress 192.168.11.5 `
                          -PrefixLength 24 `
                          -type Unicast
```

Now we configure the IPv6 addresses.

```
$Nic10 | New-NetIPAddress -AddressFamily IPv6 `
                          -IPAddress 2001:db8:0:10::5 `
                          -PrefixLength 64 `
                          -type Unicast `
                          -DefaultGateway 2001:db8:0:10::1
$Nic11 | New-NetIPAddress -AddressFamily IPv6 `
                          -IPAddress 2001:db8:0:11::5 `
                          -PrefixLength 64 `
                          -type Unicast
```

You'll notice that we set $Nic10 so that the default gateway is assigned to it, and $Nic11 doesn't have a setting for a DefaultGateway. That's because with Windows you should have only a single default gateway; the New-NetIPAddress cmdlet will fail if you try to assign a second default gateway.

Configure the DNS settings

Now, while we've still got those variables, let's configure the DNS setting for the adapters. We can't just pass the variables through the pipeline, so we use the Name property of each.

```
Set-DnsClientServerAddress -InterfaceAlias $Nic10.Name `
                           -ServerAddresses 192.168.10.2,2001:db8:0:10::2 `
                           -PassThru
Set-DnsClientServerAddress -InterfaceAlias $Nic11.Name `
                           -ServerAddresses 127.0.0.1,::1 `
                           -PassThru
```

You'll also notice that we've set $Nic11 to use itself for the DNS server by pointing to the loopback addresses for the DNS server, even though we don't yet have DNS installed on the server. But that's all going to change soon.

Install the Active Directory Domain Services role

Before we can promote the server to be a domain controller, we need to install the Active Directory Domain Services (AD DS) role on the server. The feature name is AD-Domain-Services.

```
Install-WindowsFeature -Name AD-Domain-Services -IncludeManagementTools
```

When you run this on your server, you should get something like the following output.

```
Success Restart Needed Exit Code      Feature Result
------- -------------- ---------      --------------
True    No             Success        {Active Directory Domain Services, Group P...

WARNING: Windows automatic updating is not enabled. To ensure that your newly-
installed role or feature is automatically updated, turn on Windows Update.
```

As shown in the output, no restart is required. In addition to installing the Active Directory Domain Services role, Install-WindowsFeature has installed the full set of Remote Server Administration Tools (RSAT) related to AD DS, and the Group Policy Management Console.

There's one more task we'll want to do before we promote the server to a domain controller—update the Windows PowerShell Get-Help files. Even if we had already done this, now that we've added additional modules, we need to get the Help files for those modules. The command to update Help from a local network share is as follows.

```
Update-Help -SourcePath \\cpr-labhost-6\pshelp -force
```

Create the new domain

Now that we've prepared the server and installed the Active Directory Domain Services role, we're prepared to create the child domain. We'll use the same Test-ADDSDomainController-Installation and Install-ADDSDomainController cmdlets we first used in Chapter 4, "Deploy additional domain controllers." There the parameters for Install-ADDSDomainController are listed in Table 4-1. We'll use a somewhat different set of parameters this time. We'll start by testing the promotion first, as shown in Figure 6-1. To test, we're running the following.

```
$myDomCreds = Get-Credential -UserName "TreyResearch\Charlie" `
                             -Message "Enter Domain Password"
Test-ADDSDomainInstallation `
     -NoGlobalCatalog:$false `
     -CreateDnsDelegation:$True `
     -Credential $myDomCreds `
     -DatabasePath "C:\Windows\NTDS" `
     -DomainMode "Win2012R2" `
     -DomainType "ChildDomain" `
     -InstallDns:$True `
     -LogPath "C:\Windows\NTDS" `
```

```
-NewDomainName "NorthAmerica" `
-NewDomainNetbiosName "NORTHAMERICA" `
-ParentDomainName "TreyResearch.net" `
-NoRebootOnCompletion:$False `
-SiteName "Default-First-Site-Name" `
-SysvolPath "C:\Windows\SYSVOL" `
-Force:$True
```

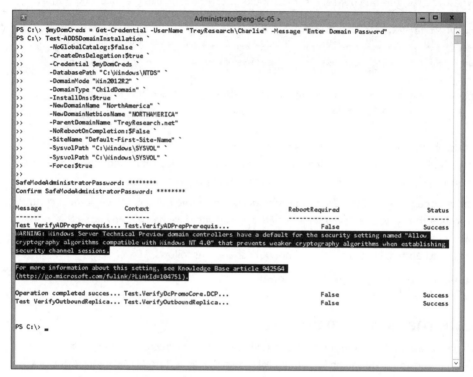

FIGURE 6-1 Testing the domain promotion before we execute it

The choice of parameters controls the child domain promotion. As you can tell in the figure, the new domain controller will host the global catalog (GC) and will attempt to create a DNS delegation from the parent. The parent domain is TreyResearch.net, and this is a child domain of domain type "Win2012R2". (We could also have specified the domain type as "6" with the same result, but that's a lot less friendly.) Also required is the SiteName parameter, even though we still only have a single site in our forest. The three path parameters aren't required, because they're just specifying the default paths, but in the real world you might want to tweak those in large Active Directory deployments. The result of the test was success (with the expected warnings), so we're ready to do the actual promotion.

If we are in the same session, we already have a $domCreds value, so we can change the cmdlet from Test to Install as follows.

```
Install-ADDSDomain -NoGlobalCatalog:$False `
                   -CreateDnsDelegation:$True `
                   -Credential $myDomCreds `
                   -DatabasePath "C:\Windows\NTDS" `
                   -DomainMode "Win2012R2" `
                   -DomainType "ChildDomain" `
                   -InstallDns:$True `
                   -LogPath "C:\Windows\NTDS" `
                   -NewDomainName "NorthAmerica" `
                   -NewDomainNetbiosName "NORTHAMERICA" `
                   -ParentDomainName "TreyResearch.net" `
                   -NoRebootOnCompletion:$False `
                   -SiteName "Default-First-Site-Name" `
                   -SysvolPath "C:\Windows\SYSVOL" `
                   -Force:$True
```

The process of creating a new child domain can take a while, and the larger your Active Directory is, the longer it will take. Also, if you're installing DNS on the new domain controller, the process will also include the time it takes to install and configure the DNS Server service, as shown in Figure 6-2.

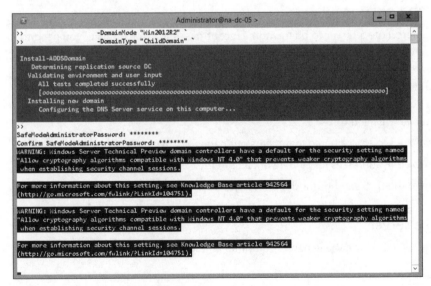

FIGURE 6-2 Creating the new child domain

The Builtin\Administrators group automatically adds any local administrators from before the server was promoted to a domain controller and converts the accounts to AD DS accounts in the NorthAmerica.TreyResearch.net domain. It also adds Enterprise Admins from the parent domain and Domain Admins from the child domain to the Builtin\Administrators group.

```
Get-ADGroupMember -Identity Administrators | ft -auto Name,DistinguishedName

Name              DistinguishedName
----              -----------------
Enterprise Admins CN=Enterprise Admins,CN=Users,DC=TreyResearch,DC=net
Domain Admins     CN=Domain Admins,CN=Users,DC=NorthAmerica,DC=TreyResearch,DC=net
Charlie           CN=Charlie,CN=Users,DC=NorthAmerica,DC=TreyResearch,DC=net
Administrator     CN=Administrator,CN=Users,DC=NorthAmerica,DC=TreyResearch,DC=net
```

Create a tree domain

Creating a tree domain creates a completely different DNS namespace, and the root of the tree must follow DNS naming conventions. Unlike a child domain, which is a single-level domain (northamerica), the tree domain must be a two-level domain (wingtiptoys.com).

Prepare the server

Before you can promote a server to be the domain controller for a tree domain, you need to prepare the server and configure the networking to support the promotion. Because we're creating a new domain in this example, we do *not* want to join another domain first. If you try to promote a server while it's a member of another domain, it will fail and promptly unjoin you from the domain and reboot. This might seem drastic, but it does make the point. So, to prepare the server, we need to:

- Rename the server to a name that meets our naming conventions.
- Assign fixed IP addresses for all network adapters.
- Configure the DNS settings for the network adapters.

Rename the server

To rename the server, we use the Rename-Computer cmdlet. This cmdlet has a simple syntax.

```
syntax Rename-Computer
```

```
Syntax for Rename-Computer is:

Rename-Computer [-NewName] <string> [-ComputerName <string>] [-PassThru]
[-DomainCredential <pscredential>] [-LocalCredential <pscredential>] [-Force]
[-Restart] [-WhatIf] [-Confirm] [<CommonParameters>]
```

Assuming that we are logged on as a local administrator, we can ignore the Computer-Name and LocalCredential parameters, and because we're not in a domain, we can ignore the DomainCredential parameter. For the rest, we obviously want the NewName parameter, and for this specific situation, we can use -Restart:$False. We're going to configure the networking before we trigger the reboot.

The server name we're going to use in the lab for this domain controller is wing-dc-06. So, to rename the server, use the following.

```
Rename-Computer -NewName wing-dc-06 -Restart:$False
```

This gives us a warning that the changes will not take place until we restart the computer. We know that.

Assign fixed IP addresses

We need to change the DHCP addresses on the server to fixed IP addresses. The target lab server has two network adapters, one on 192.168.10.0/24, and the other on 192.168.12.0/24. Both adapters need to be set. First, let's find out which network adapter is connected to which network. We could use Get-NetIPAddress for that, but the output is pretty messy. Let's just get what we need in a format we can read.

```
Get-NetIPAddress -AddressFamily IPv4 `
            | Format-Table -Auto ifIndex,InterfaceAlias,IPAddress
```

```
ifIndex InterfaceAlias             IPAddress
------- --------------             ---------
      6 Ethernet 2                 192.168.10.23
      3 Ethernet                   192.168.12.22
      1 Loopback Pseudo-Interface 1 127.0.0.1
```

We're going to change the IP addresses for both IPv4 and IPv6, but it's easy enough to identify which adapter is which with just the IPv4 address, and it makes the output a lot less messy.

Now that we can identify which adapter is which, we can get the two adapters into variables we can work with.

```
$Nic12 = Get-NetAdapter -ifIndex 3
$Nic10 = Get-NetAdapter -ifIndex 6
```

Now we need to reconfigure the two adapters to disable the DHCP.

```
$Nic10 | Set-NetIPInterface -DHCP Disabled
$Nic12 | Set-NetIPInterface -DHCP Disabled
```

Then we configure the IPv4 addresses.

```
$Nic12 | New-NetIPAddress -AddressFamily IPv4 `
                          -IPAddress 192.168.12.6 `
                          -PrefixLength 24 `
                          -type Unicast
$Nic10 | New-NetIPAddress -AddressFamily IPv4 `
                          -IPAddress 192.168.10.6 `
                          -PrefixLength 24 `
                          -type Unicast `
                          -DefaultGateway 192.168.10.1
```

Now we configure the IPv6 addresses.

```
$Nic12 | New-NetIPAddress -AddressFamily IPv6 `
                          -IPAddress 2001:db8:0:12::6 `
                          -PrefixLength 64 `
                          -type Unicast
$Nic10 | New-NetIPAddress -AddressFamily IPv6 `
                          -IPAddress 2001:db8:0:10::6 `
                          -PrefixLength 64 `
                          -type Unicast `
                          -DefaultGateway 2001:db8:0:10::1
```

You'll notice that we set $Nic10 so that the default gateway is assigned to it, and $Nic12 doesn't have a setting for a DefaultGateway. That's because with Windows you should have only a single default gateway; the New-NetIPAddress cmdlet will fail if you try to assign a second default gateway.

Configure the DNS settings

Now, while we've still got those variables, let's configure the DNS setting for the adapters. We can't just pass the variables through the pipeline, so we use the Name property of each.

```
Set-DnsClientServerAddress -InterfaceAlias $Nic10.Name `
                           -ServerAddresses 192.168.10.2,2001:db8:0:10::2 `
                           -PassThru
```

Because we used the PassThru parameter, we get output from Set-DnsClientServerAddress.

```
InterfaceAlias          Interface Address ServerAddresses
                        Index     Family

--------------          --------- ------- ---------------
Ethernet 2                      6 IPv4    {192.168.10.2}
Ethernet 2                      6 IPv6    {2001:db8:0:10::2}
```

Now we set $Nic12.

```
Set-DnsClientServerAddress -InterfaceAlias $Nic12.Name `
                           -ServerAddresses 127.0.0.1,::1 `
                           -PassThru
```

InterfaceAlias	Interface Index	Address Family	ServerAddresses
Ethernet	3	IPv4	{127.0.0.1}
Ethernet	3	IPv6	{::1}

We've set $Nic12 to use itself for the DNS server by pointing to the loopback addresses for the DNS server, even though we don't yet have DNS installed on the server. That's OK because the promotion to domain controller will include the installation of DNS.

Install the Active Directory Domain Services role

Before we can promote the server to be a domain controller, we need to install the AD DS role on the server. The feature name is AD-Domain-Services.

```
Install-WindowsFeature -Name AD-Domain-Services -IncludeManagementTools
```

When you run this on your server, you should get something like the following output.

Success	Restart Needed	Exit Code	Feature Result
True	No	Success	{Active Directory Domain Services, Group P...

```
WARNING: Windows automatic updating is not enabled. To ensure that your newly-
installed role or feature is automatically updated, turn on Windows Update.
```

As shown in the output, no restart is required. In addition to installing the Active Directory Domain Services role, Install-WindowsFeature has installed the full set of RSAT related to AD DS, and the Group Policy Management Console.

There's one more task we'll want to do before we promote the server to a domain controller—update the Windows PowerShell Get-Help files. Even if we had already done this, now that we've added additional modules, we need to get the Help files for those modules. The command to update Help from a local network share is as follows.

```
Update-Help -SourcePath \\cpr-labhost-6\pshelp -force
```

Create the new domain

Now that we've prepared the server and installed the Active Directory Domain Services role, we're prepared to create the tree domain. We'll use the same Test-ADDSDomainController-Installation and Install-ADDSDomainController cmdlets we first used in Chapter 4. There the parameters for Install-ADDSDomainController are listed in Table 4-1. We'll use a somewhat different set of parameters this time. We'll start by testing the promotion first, by using the following.

```
$myDomCreds = Get-Credential -UserName "TreyResearch\Administrator" `
                             -Message "Enter Domain Password"
Test-ADDSDomainInstallation   -NoGlobalCatalog:$false `
                              -Credential $myDomCreds `
                              -DatabasePath "C:\Windows\NTDS" `
                              -DomainMode "Win2012R2" `
                              -DomainType "TreeDomain" `
                              -InstallDns:$True `
                              -LogPath "C:\Windows\NTDS" `
                              -NewDomainName "WingtipToys.com" `
                              -NewDomainNetbiosName "WINGTIP" `
                              -ParentDomain "TreyResearch.net" `
                              -NoRebootOnCompletion:$True `
                              -SiteName "Default-First-Site-Name" `
                              -SysvolPath "C:\Windows\SYSVOL" `
                              -Force:$True
```

The choice of parameters controls the tree domain promotion. As shown in the code, the new domain controller will host the GC and will have DNS installed. I deliberately didn't specify DNS delegation, wanting Windows to compute that according to the environment. The parent domain is TreyResearch.net, and this is a tree domain of domain type "Win2012R2".

> **NOTE** If this is a tree domain, you might ask, why do we have to specify a parent domain? And what domain does one specify for a parent? These are good questions! If we don't have a parent, we're in a new forest entirely, which requires different cmdlets and creates a completely different environment. For a tree domain, specify the root domain of the forest (the first domain created in the forest) as the parent.

If we are in the same session, we already have a $domCreds value, so we can change the cmdlet from Test to Install and the NoRebootOnCompletion to $False to get the following.

```
Install-ADDSDomain -NoGlobalCatalog:$false `
                   -Credential $myDomCreds `
                   -DatabasePath "C:\Windows\NTDS" `
                   -DomainMode "Win2012R2" `
                   -DomainType "TreeDomain" `
```

```
-InstallDns:$True `
-LogPath "C:\Windows\NTDS" `
-NewDomainName "WingtipToys.com" `
-NewDomainNetbiosName "WINGTIP" `
-ParentDomain "TreyResearch.net" `
-NoRebootOnCompletion:$False `
-SiteName "Default-First-Site-Name" `
-SysvolPath "C:\Windows\SYSVOL" `
-Force:$True
```

Even though we specified -Force:$True, there's still a confirmation prompt if we're running the command interactively. And, of course, we need to specify the safe mode password for domain recovery. But, after those are done, the process continues automatically and reboots the new domain controller when it's finished. The process of creating a new tree domain can take a while, and the larger your Active Directory is, the longer it will take. Also, if you're installing DNS on the new domain controller, the process will also include the time it takes to install and configure the DNS Server service.

The promotion process automatically converts any local accounts from before the server was promoted to a domain controller to AD DS accounts and adds the AD DS accounts to the corresponding Builtin groups in the WingtipToys.com domain. It also adds the Enterprise Admins group from the parent domain and the Domain Admins group from the tree domain to the Builtin\Administrators group. The Administrator's group now has the following.

```
Get-ADGroupMember -Identity Administrators | ft -auto Name,DistinguishedName
```

Name	DistinguishedName
Enterprise Admins	CN=Enterprise Admins,CN=Users,DC=TreyResearch,DC=net
Domain Admins	CN=Domain Admins,CN=Users,DC=WingtipToys,DC=com
Charlie	CN=Charlie,CN=Users,DC=WingtipToys,DC=com
Administrator	CN=Administrator,CN=Users,DC=WingtipToys,DC=com

SECURITY Even though the Charlie account is converted to a domain account and added to the Builtin\Administrators group, Charlie's account is not added to the Domain Admins group. If you search for Domain Admins, you will not find his account listed. This has the potential to be a somewhat hidden back door if you're not aware of it, because most administrators monitor Domain Admins and Enterprise Admins account members but could easily miss an account that is in the Builtin\Administrators group.

The pre-promotion Users group members are automatically converted to domain accounts and are also added directly to the Builtin\Users group and the Domain Users group.

Create a new forest

Creating a new forest, TailspinToys.com, is the same as creating our original TreyResearch.net forest. But then creating a trust relationship between that original TreyResearch.net forest and the new TailspinToys.com forest gets a bit more complicated if we restrict ourselves to Windows PowerShell. I'd still create the new forest entirely by using Windows PowerShell—it's definitely the best tool for the job. But even though I'll give you a script to create a one-way forest trust, this is actually a job I'd do with the graphical interface by using the Active Directory Domains and Trusts snap-in (domains.msc). But first, let's create the forest. To do that, we start by configuring the networking.

Configure networking

We need to prepare the server that will be the root of the TailspinToys.com forest. We configure the networking to be on the 192.168.10.0/24 subnet and the 2001:db8:0:10::/64 prefix. Then we assign an IPv4 address of 192.168.10.210 and an IPv6 address of 2001:db8:0:10::d2.

```
$Nic = Get-NetAdapter -Name Ethernet
$Nic | Set-NetIPInterface -DHCP Disabled
$Nic | New-NetIPAddress -AddressFamily IPv4 `
                     -IPAddress 192.168.10.210 `
                     -PrefixLength 24 `
                     -Type Unicast `
                     -DefaultGateway 192.168.10.1
Set-DnsClientServerAddress -InterfaceAlias $Nic.Name `
                     -ServerAddresses 192.168.10.2,2001:db8:0:10::2
$Nic | New-NetIPAddress -AddressFamily IPv6 `
                     -IPAddress 2001:db8:0:10::d2 `
                     -PrefixLength 64 `
                     -Type Unicast `
                     -DefaultGateway 2001:db8:0:10:1
```

Now we rename the server to tail-dc-210 by using Rename-Computer.

```
Rename-Computer -NewName tail-dc-210 -Force -Restart
```

This will cause the server to restart. Now we're ready to create the forest.

Test the promotion to domain controller

To verify that our deployment of TailspinToys will complete satisfactorily before we commit to the creation, we should test it first. To make that easy, I've included Test-TailspinForest, which installs the Active Directory Domain Services role, if it isn't already installed, and then runs the Test-ADForestInstallation cmdlet.

Test-TailspinForest.ps1

```
<#
.SYNOPSIS
Test the environment to verify that a new forest of TailspinToys.com can be created.

.DESCRIPTION
Test-TailspinForest tests if the AD-Domain-Services feature is installed, and
if not, installs it. It then tests the current environment to verify that
a new forest, TailspinToys.com can be successfully installed. This script
expects no parameters or inputs, and does not trigger a restart upon completion.

.EXAMPLE
Test-TailspinForest
Tests whether a Promotion of the current server to be the root domain controller of
TailspinToys.com will succeed.

.NOTES
     Author: Charlie Russel
  Copyright: 2015 by Charlie Russel
           : Permission to use is granted but attribution is appreciated
    Initial: 4/17/2015 (cpr)
    ModHist:
           :
#>
if ( (Get-WindowsFeature -Name AD-Domain-Services).InstallState -ne "Installed" ) {
  Install-WindowsFeature -Name AD-Domain-Services -IncludeManagementTools
}

Import-Module ADDSDeployment
Test-ADDSForestInstallation `
      -DomainName 'TailspinToys.com' `
      -DomainNetbiosName 'TAILSPINTOYS' `
      -DomainMode 6 `
      -ForestMode 6 `
      -InstallDNS `
      -Force
```

Test-TailspinForest completes successfully, as shown in Figure 6-3, which means that we're ready to run Install-TailspinForest to actually create the new forest.

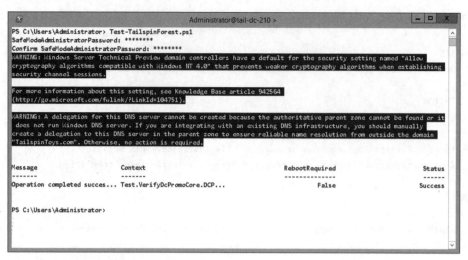

FIGURE 6-3 Testing whether TailspinToys.com can be created as a new forest

Deploy the new forest

Because we have confidence that the server and the environment are ready for the new forest and domain, we're ready to do the actual deployment. I've included a script to do the deployment, Install-TailspinForest.ps1.

Install-TailspinForest

```
<#
.SYNOPSIS
Deploy a new forest of TailspinToys.com on the target server.

.DESCRIPTION
Install-TailspinForest tests if the AD-Domain-Services feature is installed, and
if not, installs it. It then deploys the new forest, TailSpinToys.com on the server
and installs DNS. This script expects no parameters or inputs, and triggers a restart
upon completion.

.EXAMPLE
Install-TailSpinForest
Installs the TailSpinToys.com domain on the current server as the root domain controller
of the forest.

.NOTES
     Author: Charlie Russel
  Copyright: 2015 by Charlie Russel
           : Permission to use is granted but attribution is appreciated
    Initial: 4/17/2015 (cpr)
    ModHist:
```

```
        :
#>
if ( (Get-WindowsFeature -Name AD-Domain-Services).InstallState -ne "Installed" ) {
  Install-WindowsFeature -Name AD-Domain-Services -IncludeManagementTools
}

Import-Module ADDSDeployment
Install-ADDSForest `
      -DomainName 'TailspinToys.com' `
      -DomainNetbiosName 'TAILSPINTOYS' `
      -DomainMode 6 `
      -ForestMode 6 `
      -InstallDNS `
      -Force
```

And with that, we have a new forest after the installation completes and tail-dc-210 reboots.

Create a trust

Forest trusts are one-way, nontransitive trusts. This is the opposite of the way the default trust relationships work within a forest. Within a forest, trusts are automatically created and are two-way, transitive trusts, ensuring that every user in the forest can be authenticated anywhere in the forest and can receive the appropriate level of authentication and authorization. But sometimes you need a bit more than the standard trusts in a forest, so let's start by looking at two-way, *shortcut* trusts between two leaves of a tree or between adjacent trees in the forest. First, however, there is a useful Windows PowerShell command you can use to find the current trust relationships: Get-ADTrust.

```
Get-ADTrust -Filter *
```

```
Direction                  : BiDirectional
DisallowTransivity         : False
DistinguishedName          : CN=TreyResearch.net,CN=System,DC=WingtipToys,DC=com
ForestTransitive           : False
IntraForest                : True
IsTreeParent               : False
IsTreeRoot                 : False
Name                       : TreyResearch.net
ObjectClass                : trustedDomain
ObjectGUID                 : 571b8821-3339-4ec2-b306-fbeb0c6df59b
SelectiveAuthentication    : False
SIDFilteringForestAware    : False
SIDFilteringQuarantined    : False
Source                     : DC=WingtipToys,DC=com
```

```
Target                 : TreyResearch.net
TGTDelegation          : False
TrustAttributes        : 32
TrustedPolicy          :
TrustingPolicy         :
TrustType              : Uplevel
UplevelOnly            : False
UsesAESKeys            : False
UsesRC4Encryption      : False
```

Create a shortcut trust

The path that authentication has to take in a complicated forest structure can affect usability when two domains are widely separated. For example, look at Figure 6-4, which shows a forest diagram for our TreyResearch.net forest, with a couple of nodes added.

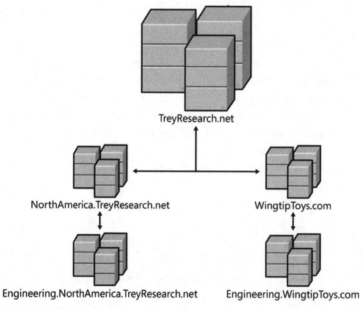

FIGURE 6-4 The TreyReseach.net forest diagram

If the two Engineering domains end up working on joint projects, the authentication traffic could pose a problem because the only trust path between the two domains is all the way up through the root TreyResearch.net domain and back down. This is not a problem for the occasional user, but it is not ideal if the two engineering domains work closely together and share resources. The solution is to create a shortcut trust between Engineering. NorthAmerica.TreyResearch.net and Engineering.WingtipToys.com. There isn't yet a simple Windows PowerShell cmdlet to create or manipulate trusts, but you can do it by using the old netdom command.

```
Netdom trust /d:engineering.northamerica.treyresearch.net engineering.wingtiptoys.com
/add /twoway /Ud:TREYRESEARCH\Charlie /Uo:WINGTIPTOYS\Administrator
```

You must have Domain Admin credentials for each domain, and you'll be prompted for the password for both accounts. But when you're done, you'll have the trust relationship shown in Figure 6-5.

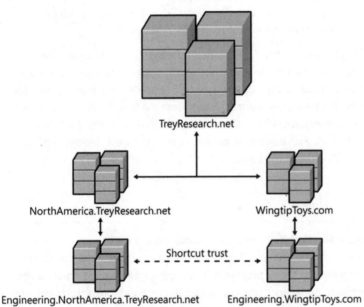

FIGURE 6-5 Using a shortcut trust to improve usability

Netdom still works in Windows Server 2012 R2 and in the Windows Server Technical Preview I'm using in this book, but its time is short, and I can only hope that we get some new Windows PowerShell AD DS nouns soon.

Create a forest trust

Unfortunately, netdom doesn't work to create a forest trust, so to create a forest trust you must use some more advanced Windows PowerShell commands. To create a forest trust between TailspinToys.com and TreyResearch.net, use the following to create the two-way trust. You'll need to run with Enterprise Admins privileges from the TreyResearch.net domain.

```
$remCred = Get-Credential `
          -Name "TailspinToys\Charlie" `
          -Message "Enter Remote Creds"
$remForest = New-Object `
          System.DirectoryServices.ActiveDirectory.DirectoryContext(`
          'Forest',`
          'TailspinToys.com',`
          $remCred.UserName,`
          $remCred.GetNetworkCredential().Password)
$locForest=[System.DirectoryServices.ActiveDirectory.Forest]::GetCurrentForest()
$locForest.CreateTrustRelationship($remForestObject,'Bidirectional')
```

These commands take advantage of the Forest class of the System.DirectoryServices. ActiveDirectory .NET namespace. We first get credentials to the remote root domain, then create a forest object by setting our context to the remote forest. We get a forest object for the current forest by calling the GetCurrentForest() method on the System.DirectoryServices. ActiveDirectory Forest class. Finally, we call the CreateTrustRelationship method on that current forest object ($locForest), with our target being the remote forest ($remForestObj), specifying that we want a bidirectional trust.

Summary

In this chapter you learned how to create both a child domain and a tree domain, also learning the network configuration that is required. You also learned how to test the domain creation before you actually commit to the deployment. You then learned how to create a new forest and how to create trusts, both shortcut trusts within a forest and forest trusts between forests.

In the next chapter, you'll learn how to configure account policies and how to create and manage service accounts.

CHAPTER 7

Configure service authentication and account policies

In this chapter, we'll extend what we did in Chapter 3, "Create and manage users and groups," by looking at a special kind of user account—the service account—and how the different kinds of service accounts can be used for service authentication. We'll also cover how to create and apply fine-grained user policies to user accounts, so that you can have different password policies for different sets of users.

Active Directory Windows PowerShell nouns used in this chapter:

- ADUser
- ADServiceAccount
- ADComputerServiceAccount
- ADGroup
- ADGroupMember
- ADDefaultDomainPasswordPolicy
- ADFineGrainedPasswordPolicy
- ADFineGrainedPasswordPolicySubject
- ADUserResultantPasswordPolicy
- ADOrganizationalUnit
- ADObject

Other Windows PowerShell commands used in this chapter:

- [ADSI]"WinNT://*computername*"
- Import-Module
- Read-Host
- Get-WMIObject
- Install-WindowsFeature
- Get-WindowsFeature
- Add-KDSRootKey

- Get-Date
- New-ScheduledTaskAction
- New-ScheduledTaskTrigger
- New-ScheduledTaskPrincipal
- Register-ScheduledTask

Manage service authentication

Services that run on computers running Windows Server need to run under an account. Windows Server 2003 introduced *service accounts*, which provide the authentication and authorization necessary for services and applications that run on servers running Windows Server. Initially, service accounts were local accounts only, managed manually at each server that required an account or accounts. This was not a problem in small business environments, but it was a nightmare in large and diverse enterprises. The next step was the use of domain accounts as service accounts, which facilitated central management in Active Directory Domain Services (AD DS). But this was still less than a winning solution, and the flexibility and manageability of service accounts have continued to improve. Managed service accounts (MSAs) and virtual accounts were introduced in Windows Server 2008 R2, and group MSAs (gMSAs) were introduced in Windows Server 2012.

Create service accounts

The Windows PowerShell ActiveDirectory module can be used to create domain user service accounts in exactly the same manner as any other user account in AD DS. But that approach won't work for machine local accounts, which are supported by the ActiveDirectory module. Instead, you need to use direct Active Directory Services Interface (ADSI) calls.

Create a local service account

Local service accounts are specific to the server on which they are created and are limited to that server. If you have multiple servers that provide the same service, you still need separate accounts on each server, and you need to manage those accounts individually. This is not at all a good situation, but there might be some older environments where you don't have any choice. You can use Windows PowerShell, however, to make the management a bit easier. First, you can use Windows PowerShell to create the local service account, and you can also use Windows PowerShell to manage passwords for your service accounts. We'll start by creating a local service account on the trey-dhcp-03 server. Because there isn't a built-in module that supports local account management, the process is a bit more complicated than a simple one-line command. There is, however, a module you can download from the Microsoft TechNet Script Center that encapsulates the steps I'll detail here. The process to create a local user, ServiceUsr, on the trey-dhcp-03 server is shown in Figure 7-1.

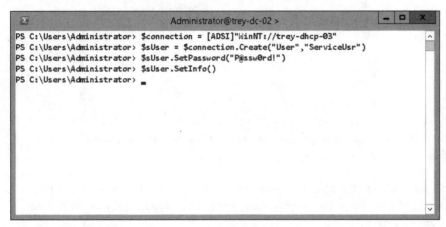

FIGURE 7-1 Creating a service account by using type [ADSI]

Here are the steps:

- Connect to the local computer user account database by using ADSI.
- Use the Create method, specifying that you're creating a user.
- Use the SetPassword method to assign a password.
- Use the SetInfo method to actually create the user object.

```
#The WinNT in the following IS CASE SENSITIVE
$connection = [ADSI]"WinNT://trey-dhcp-03"
$sUser = $connection.Create("User","ServiceUsr")
$sUser.SetPassword("P@ssw0rd!")  # No Spaces!
$sUser.SetInfo()
```

The good thing about this process is that it can be run on a local computer against a remote computer, enabling you to script the process across your domain. Figure 7-2 shows lusrmgr.msc running on trey-dhcp-03, showing that the local account is created, even though we ran the script from trey-dc-02.

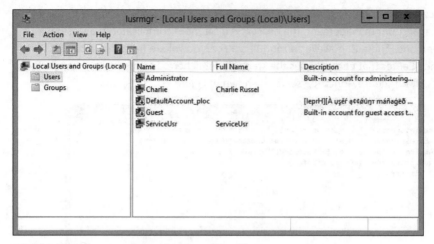

FIGURE 7-2 Local users and groups on trey-dhcp-03

To add a description to the account we just created, we'll use the following command. (This assumes that we're still in the same session and Windows PowerShell window that we used to create the account.)

```
$sUser.description = "Service Account User"
$sUser.SetInfo()
```

You can use the [ADSI] adapter to create, modify, or remove local users and groups without additional modules, but sometimes it's just easier to add a module in which someone has already done all the work for you. That's certainly the case here, with Ed Wilson of Microsoft having created a useful and well-written module, complete with built-in Get-Help support. You can download the module from the TechNet Script Center at *gallery.technet.microsoft.com /scriptcenter/f75801e7-169a-4737-952c-1341abea5823*. To use the module, follow these steps:

1. Copy the entire text of the script from the Script Center page. Be sure to get *all* of it.
2. Open your favorite text editor. I use gVim, but you can use Notepad, or the Windows PowerShell ISE, or any other script editor that you want, as long as it creates pure text-only files.
3. Paste the copied text into the editor.
4. Create a new directory called **Local_User** in your modules directory.
5. Save the Local_User.psm1 file in the directory you just created.

> **NOTE** Your personal modules directory is the first element of $ENV:PSModulePath. Also note that the directory name and the name of the .psm1 file must match.

6. You can begin using the module immediately. You can use Import-Module Local_User to import the module explicitly or allow Windows PowerShell to automatically load it. Because the module is in your PSModulePath, it is automatically loaded when needed.

Using the module makes it simpler to do what we just did.

```
New-LocalUser -UserName ServiceUsr `
              -Password "P@ssw0rd!" `
              -ComputerName trey-dhcp-03 `
              -Description "Service Account User"
```

The module also includes a Set-LocalUserPassword command, making it easy to change the passwords for remote accounts.

Create a domain service account

Creating a domain service account gets around the problem of having to create separate accounts for every server and service—instead, you create a domain service account and use regular AD DS tools and scripts to manage it. To create a domain service account in our TreyResearch.net domain, we'll use the following command.

```
$svcPW = Read-Host -Prompt "Enter a Pwd to use: " -AsSecureString
New-ADUser -Name ServiceUser `
           -SamAccountName ServiceUser `
           -Enabled $True `
           -ChangePasswordAtLogon $False `
           -Description "Domain-wide Service Account" `
           -AccountPassword $svcPW `
           -PassThru
```

And, because we specified the -PassThru parameter, we get the following.

```
DistinguishedName : CN=ServiceUser,CN=Users,DC=TreyResearch,DC=net
Enabled           : True
GivenName         :
Name              : ServiceUser
ObjectClass       : user
ObjectGUID        : ee53b73d-57e8-48b1-82a1-0132e4b3c624
SamAccountName    : ServiceUser
SID               : S-1-5-21-955785887-403849375-625509144-1117
Surname           :
UserPrincipalName :
```

Configure managed service accounts (MSAs)

Managed service accounts (MSAs) were introduced in Windows Server 2008 R2. An MSA is an AD DS account that is assigned to a specific computer. The passwords for MSAs are long and complex and are automatically maintained. MSA passwords are changed on the same schedule, using the same mechanism as computer accounts.

Usually, an MSA is created with a generated password that is set automatically, and that password is automatically changed every 30 days. You can set an MSA password to an explicit value, but the password can be reset to a new generated value on demand.

MSA accounts do not have permission to log on interactively, and they can't be locked out. They are created in the Managed Service Accounts container of Active Directory and require a minimum AD DS domain functional level of Windows Server 2008 R2 for automatic service principal name (SPN) and automatic password management to work. If your domain functional level is less than Windows Server 2008 R2, you can still use the automatic password management features of MSAs by updating the schema of your AD DS. However, automatic SPN management would still not be supported.

Create and install an MSA

Creating an MSA is the first step of the process, but then you need to install the MSA on the computer it is assigned to. This requires the Windows PowerShell ActiveDirectory module to be installed on the target server, along with the Microsoft .NET Framework 3.5 core. Installing the Remote Server Administration Tools Active Directory module for Windows PowerShell (RSAT-AD-PowerShell) is easy, but installing the .NET Framework requires access to the Internet or to the installation media for Windows Server. If you use Get-WindowsFeature on a server running Windows Server 2012 R2 or Windows Server Technical Preview to find out whether the .NET Framework is available, you'll discover that it has an Install State of Removed.

```
Get-WindowsFeature -name NET-Framework-Core
```

Display Name	Name	Install State
[ ] .NET Framework 3.5 (includes...	NET-Framework-Core	Removed

This means that it's not available on the computer on which Windows Server is installed. Therefore, you need to provide access to the original installation media or Windows Update to install it. This is a total nuisance for which I have *never* heard a reasonable explanation from anyone at Microsoft, especially given that so many things still require it. If your server is not connected to the Internet, or if you're using Windows Server Update Services (WSUS) and the binaries for the .NET Framework aren't available, you need to use the Source parameter to tell Install-WindowsFeature where to find the necessary files. This can be a locally mounted copy of the Windows Server installation media, a locally available copy of the WIM file for Windows

Server, or a network share of the SxS folder from the Windows Server installation media. To install the two required features, use the following.

```
Install-WindowsFeature -ComputerName trey-dhcp-03 `
                    -Name RSAT-AD-PowerShell,NET-Framework-Core `
                    -Source \\cpr-labhost-6\SxS
```

This will install the required prerequisites on the remote server. Now we can create an MSA by using the following command.

```
New-ADServiceAccount -Name TestMSA `
                    -RestrictToSingleComputer `
                    -Enabled $True `
                    -PassThru
```

```
DistinguishedName : CN=TestMSA,CN=Managed Service Accounts,DC=TreyResearch,DC=net
Enabled           : True
Name              : TestMSA
ObjectClass       : msDS-ManagedServiceAccount
ObjectGUID        : cfbf2deb-62bf-49aa-abb0-6cc247a72d08
SamAccountName    : TestMSA$
SID               : S-1-5-21-955785887-403849375-625509144-1122
UserPrincipalName :
```

We then associate the MSA with trey-dhcp-03 by using the following command.

```
Add-ADComputerServiceAccount -Identity trey-dhcp-03 `
                    -ServiceAccount TestMSA `
                    -PassThru
```

```
DistinguishedName : CN=TREY-DHCP-03,CN=Computers,DC=TreyResearch,DC=net
DNSHostName       : trey-dhcp-03.TreyResearch.net
Enabled           : True
Name              : TREY-DHCP-03
ObjectClass       : computer
ObjectGUID        : d0ea8644-9025-4298-8f0c-d87fac24e52b
SamAccountName    : TREY-DHCP-03$
SID               : S-1-5-21-955785887-403849375-625509144-1111
UserPrincipalName :
```

Finally, we need to log on to trey-dhcp-03 to install the MSA. First, we'll check to make sure our prerequisites are installed, and then we'll do the actual installation of the MSA to the server.

```
Get-WindowsFeature -Name NET-Framework-Core,RSAT-AD-PowerShell
Install-ADServiceAccount -Identity TestMSA
```

There's no PassThru parameter for Install-ADServiceAccount, and no indication that the account was installed on the server. But if it isn't, we'll get an error message.

Even though MSAs don't require explicit setting of a password, there can be some good reasons for using a well-known password during the initial setup. By choosing a well-known password, you can pre-create the MSA in AD DS and then install the MSA on a server that has no writeable domain controllers, only read-only domain controllers (RODCs), such as a server in a perimeter network. In that scenario, you can install the MSA by using the AccountPassword parameter or the PromptForPassword parameter to provide the well-known password that was assigned when the account was created.

Associate an MSA with a service

When you assign an MSA to a computer, it doesn't actually do anything until you associate the MSA with a service. This assigns a Log On value to the service of *<domain>\<MSA$>* where *<domain>* is the Active Directory domain name and *<MSA$>* is the SAMAccountName of the managed service account. Therefore, to associate the MSA just created to the TestSvc service, we use Windows Management Instrumentation (WMI).

```
$MSA = 'TREYRESEARCH\TestMSA$'
$SvcName = 'TestSvc'
$Password = $Null
$Svc = Get-WMIObject Win32_Service -filter "Name=""$SvcName"" "
$InParams = $Svc.psbase.getMethodParameters("Change")
$InParams["StartName"] = $MSA
$InParams["StartPassword"] = $Password
$Svc.invokeMethod("Change",$InParams,$null)
```

Remove an MSA

You can uninstall an MSA from a computer by using the Uninstall-ADServiceAccount cmdlet. This leaves it still assigned to the computer, but not installed.

```
Uninstall-ADServiceAccount -Identity TestMSA
```

If you're uninstalling an MSA that is isolated from a writeable domain controller, you can add the ForceRemovalLocal parameter to allow the MSA to be uninstalled.

To remove the computer assignment but leave the MSA account still present in AD DS for later reuse, use the Remove-ADComputerServiceAccount cmdlet.

```
Remove-ADComputerServiceAccount -Identity trey-dhcp-03 `
                                -ServiceAccount TestMSA `
                                -PassThru
```

The ServiceAccount parameter accepts an array (comma-separated list) of MSAs that can be identified by SAMAccountName, distinguished name, GUID, or security identifier (SID).

Finally, to remove the MSA entirely from AD DS, use Remove-ADServiceAccount.

```
Remove-ADServiceAccount -Identity TestMSA
```

> **TIP** None of these commands support a -Force parameter; therefore, if you're scripting the removal of an MSA, add the -Confirm:$False parameter to the Uninstall-ADServer-Account, Remove-ADComputerServiceAccount, and Remove-ADServiceAccount commands. This will bypass the requirement to confirm that you really want to uninstall and remove the accounts.

Configure group managed service accounts (gMSAs)

Microsoft introduced group managed service account (gMSAs) with the release of Windows Server 2012. gMSAs extend the functionality of the stand-alone MSAs introduced in Windows Server 2008 R2 across multiple servers, allowing gMSAs to be used for services that span multiple hosts. In addition, gMSAs can be used for scheduled tasks, Internet Information Services (IIS) application pools, and Microsoft Exchange Server.

The automatic password management that was introduced with MSAs is extended to work across multiple computers by using Key Distribution Services (KDS). KDS needs to be running on a Windows Server 2012 or later domain controller to distribute the keys. Group MSAs can only be created by using Windows PowerShell; there isn't a GUI way to do it yet.

Prepare the domain

Before you can create the first gMSA in a domain, you need to create the KDS root key. This is a step that is required only once per domain. Use the Add-KDSRootKey command to create the KDS root key.

```
Add-KDSRootKey -EffectiveImmediately
```

```
Guid
----
caa08165-7fce-3a43-a12a-2389ee544487
```

Unfortunately, although EffectiveImmediately is the name of the parameter, the reality is that the new KDS root key is not effective for 10 hours. This delay is to ensure that the key is fully deployed to all domain controllers within the domain.

> **NOTE** You can bypass the 10-hour wait time, but you should only do so in a lab environment. To bypass the waiting time, use the following command.
>
> ```
> Add-KdsRootKey -EffectiveTime ((Get-Date).AddHours(-10))
> ```

Create a security group

While you're waiting, you can create a new security group for the computers that use the gMSA. This makes it easier to keep track of which computers have the gMSA assigned to them, and makes management simpler. Of course, there is a downside—the group membership won't become effective until the target computers are rebooted.

```
New-ADGroup  -Name TestMSA `
            -GroupScope DomainLocal `
            -Description "Group for servers using TestMSA" `
            -DisplayName "Test gMSA Group" `
            -GroupCategory Security `
            -SAMAccountName TestMSA `
            -PassThru
Add-ADGroupMember  -Identity TestMSA `
            -Members "trey-rodc-200$","trey-rodc-201$" `
            -PassThru
```

```
DistinguishedName : CN=TestMSA,CN=Users,DC=TreyResearch,DC=net
GroupCategory     : Security
GroupScope        : DomainLocal
Name              : TestMSA
ObjectClass       : group
ObjectGUID        : e03c13ad-df06-45d4-86d7-b56ee0f7d148
SamAccountName    : TestMSA
SID               : S-1-5-21-955785887-403849375-625509144-1123
```

> **TIP** The SamAccountName of a computer account is the computer's name with a trailing $ appended. When listing the computers to add to a security group, use the SamAccountName, not the computer name.

Create the account

To create the gMSA, we use the same New-ADServiceAccount cmdlet that we used for the stand-alone MSA. However, this time we won't use the RestrictToSingleComputer parameter, and we need to give the gMSA a DNS host name. Thus the command to create a gMSA with a name of SvcAcnt1 is as follows.

```
New-ADServiceAccount  -Name SvcAcnt1 `
            -DNSHostName SvcAcnt1.treyresearch.net `
            -PassThru
```

This would work equally well without the PassThru parameter, but we would get absolutely no indication of success. With the PassThru parameter, we get the following output.

```
DistinguishedName : CN=SvcAcnt1,CN=Managed Service Accounts,DC=TreyResearch,DC=net
Enabled           : True
Name              : SvcAcnt1
ObjectClass       : msDS-GroupManagedServiceAccount
ObjectGUID        : b0d55ffc-677a-450d-932d-62cda908a5be
SamAccountName    : SvcAcnt1$
SID               : S-1-5-21-955785887-403849375-625509144-1127
UserPrincipalName :
```

There are many available options for MSA and gMSA accounts. Table 7-1 lists the relevant parameters supported by New-ADServiceAccount.

TABLE 7-1 New-ADServiceAccount parameters

Parameter	Type
Name	String
DNSHostName	String
AccountExpirationDate	Datetime
AccountNotDelegated	Boolean
AccountPassword	SecureString
AuthenticationPolicy	ADAuthenticationPolicy
AuthenticationPolicySilo	ADAuthenticationPolicySilo
AuthType	ADAuthType
Certificates	String[]
CompoundIdentitySupported	Boolean
Credential	PSCredential
Description	String
DisplayName	String
Enabled	Boolean
HomePage	String
Instance	ADServiceAccount
KerberosEncryptionType	ADKerberosEncryptionType
ManagedPasswordIntervalInDays	Int
OtherAttributes	Hashtable
PassThru	Switch

Parameter	Type
Path	String
PrincipalsAllowedToDelegateToAccount	ADPrincipal[]
PrincipalsAllowedToRetrieveManagedPassword	ADPrincipal[]
RestrictToOutboundAuthenticationOnly	Switch
RestrictToSingleComputer	Switch
SamAccountName	String
Server	String
ServicePrincipalNames	String[]
TrustedForDelegation	Boolean

Install the gMSA

The gMSA is installed on a host by using the Install-ADServiceAccount cmdlet, but before we do that, we need to designate which computers can manage the password for the account. (We could also have done this as part of the New-ADServiceAccount creation.) It's a good idea to use a security group as the principal that can retrieve the managed password. This allows you to automatically add and remove computers from the gMSA by adding or removing them from the security group. We created the TestMSA security group earlier, and it has two RODCs in it. We'll use that group for our gMSA with the following command.

```
Set-ADServiceAccount -Identity SvcAcnt1 `
                -PrincipalsAllowedToRetrieveManagedPassword TestMSA `
                -PrincipalsAllowedToDelegateToAccount TestMSA `
                -PassThru
```

This yields no particular new information from the PassThru parameter, but at least it confirms that all is still well.

```
DistinguishedName : CN=SvcAcnt1,CN=Managed Service Accounts,DC=TreyResearch,DC=net
Enabled           : True
Name              : SvcAcnt1
ObjectClass       : msDS-GroupManagedServiceAccount
ObjectGUID        : b0d55ffc-677a-450d-932d-62cda908a5be
SamAccountName    : SvcAcnt1$
SID               : S-1-5-21-955785887-403849375-625509144-1127
UserPrincipalName :
```

Now, to install the account, we'll log on to one of the members of the TestMSA group and then use the following command.

```
Install-ADServiceAccount -Identity SvcAcnt1
```

There's no PassThru parameter and no information echoed to the command line unless there's a failure, but we can test the gMSA with the following.

```
Test-ADServiceAccount -Identity SvcAcnt1
```

```
True
```

Not exactly verbose output, but it tells us what we needed to know. The gMSA is working.

> **NOTE** A gentle reminder—computer account membership in security groups doesn't take effect until the computer is restarted.

Use the gMSA for a service

There isn't yet a way to configure a Windows service to use a gMSA by using Windows PowerShell. But you can still use the Services.msc console to configure a service to use a gMSA. Use the following steps to configure the Test Service to use the gMSA SvcAcnt1:

1. Open the Services console (services.msc).

2. Right-click the Test Service, and click Properties to open the properties dialog box for the Test Service.

3. Click the Log On tab.

4. Select This Account, and click Browse to open the Select User Or Service Account dialog box shown in Figure 7-3.

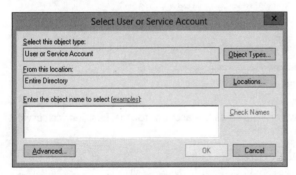

FIGURE 7-3 The Select User Or Service Account dialog box

5. Enter **SvcAcnt1**, and click Check Names. Click OK to return to the properties dialog box.

   The This Account field should have TREYRESEARCH\SvcAcnt1$ in it, as shown in Figure 7-4.

FIGURE 7-4 The Log On tab of the Test Service Properties (Local Computer) dialog box

6. Clear the Password and Confirm Password fields, and click OK.

The message shown in Figure 7-5 appears, informing you that the account has been granted Log On As A Service right.

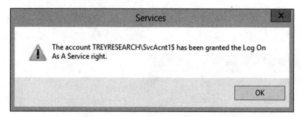

FIGURE 7-5 A Services message

7. Click OK. The gMSA is now configured as the account for the Test Service service.

Use the gMSA for a scheduled task

A significant improvement of gMSAs over stand-alone MSAs is that they can be used for scheduled tasks. To configure a scheduled task, Start-myBackup.ps1, to run at 8:00 every night, with the SvcAcnt1 account as the account running the task, use the following.

```
$myBackup = New-ScheduledTaskAction -Execute "C:\Tools\Start-myBackup.ps1"
$myTrig = New-ScheduledTaskTrigger -AT 20:00 -Daily
$myPrincipal = New-ScheduledTaskPrincipal `
                -UserID TREYRESEARCH\SvcAcnt1$ Password
```

Notice the UserID parameter that was used. We use the actual SAM account name, complete with the trailing $ character, and add Password as the argument. This tells Windows to retrieve the password associated with the gMSA. That privilege was granted to the TestMSA security group when we used the Set-ADServiceAccount command. Now that we've built the details of the task, we can register it with Register-ScheduledTask.

```
Register-ScheduledTask myBackupTask `
                    -Action $myBackup `
                    -Trigger $myTrig `
                    -Principal $myPrincipal
```

This yields confirmation that the task was actually scheduled.

```
TaskPath        TaskName       State
--------        --------       -----
\               myBackupTask   Ready
```

> **IMPORTANT** For a task to run as a scheduled job, you might need to add the gMSA account to a group that has the right to log on as a batch, or explicitly give that right to the account. Depending on the task, you might also need to add the account to a security group that gives it additional privileges that are necessary to perform the task, such as Backup Operators.

Configure virtual accounts

Virtual accounts are another way to have a service account that doesn't require you to manage passwords. Virtual accounts should be used for local resources only—use gMSAs for services that require network resources.

To use a virtual account for a service, enter **NT SERVICE\<servicename>** for the account name, and leave the password blank. There's no Windows PowerShell cmdlet for this. You can also use this command for IIS. The user name to use for IIS is IIS AppPool\<apppoolname>.

Configure account policies

Windows domains give you great flexibility and power to set policy for the users in your domain. And although some things are still more easily managed in the Group Policy Management Console (GPMC), many others are easily handled with two Windows PowerShell modules, the ActiveDirectory module and the GroupPolicy module.

Configure domain user password policy

The default domain user password policy forms the basis for all other password policies in the domain. Any user who isn't subject to a specific password settings object (PSO) is subject to the default domain user password policy.

We can get the default domain password policy for TreyResearch.net by using the Get-ADDefaultDomainPasswordPolicy cmdlet.

```
Get-ADDefaultDomainPasswordPolicy
```

```
ComplexityEnabled           : True
DistinguishedName           : DC=TreyResearch,DC=net
LockoutDuration             : 00:30:00
LockoutObservationWindow    : 00:30:00
LockoutThreshold            : 0
MaxPasswordAge              : 42.00:00:00
MinPasswordAge              : 1.00:00:00
MinPasswordLength           : 7
objectClass                 : {domainDNS}
objectGuid                  : e344a4a5-f533-4415-b7e1-085151b94a7d
PasswordHistoryCount        : 24
ReversibleEncryptionEnabled : False
```

That seems like both a rather weak and a rather annoying policy. Changing passwords every 42 days is just annoying to users, and with only a seven-character password requirement, it's really quite easy to crack. Let's change this to something a bit more reasonable. We'll increase the duration to 100 days, or just a bit more than three months. But, at the same time, we'll change the minimum password length to 10 characters and set the lockout threshold and duration.

```
Get-ADDefaultDomainPasswordPolicy -Identity TreyResearch.net `
    | Set-ADDefaultDomainPasswordPolicy -LockoutThreshold 10 `
                                        -LockoutDuration 00:10:00 `
                                        -LockoutObservationWindow 00:10:00 `
                                        -MinPasswordLength 10 `
                                        -MaxPasswordAge 100.00:00:00 `
                                        -PassThru
```

Notice that we had to change the LockoutObservationWindow at the same time we changed the LockoutDuration value. The LockoutDuration value must be greater than or equal to the value of the LockoutObservationWindow. This is a cmdlet that doesn't produce any output unless you specify the PassThru parameter. Doing so gives us the following output.

```
ComplexityEnabled           : True
DistinguishedName           : DC=TreyResearch,DC=net
LockoutDuration             : 00:10:00
LockoutObservationWindow    : 00:10:00
LockoutThreshold            : 10
MaxPasswordAge              : 100.00:00:00
MinPasswordAge              : 1.00:00:00
MinPasswordLength           : 10
objectClass                 : {domainDNS}
objectGuid                  : e344a4a5-f533-4415-b7e1-085151b94a7d
PasswordHistoryCount        : 24
ReversibleEncryptionEnabled : False
```

Configure password settings objects (PSOs)

Password settings objects (PSOs) are used to implement fine-grained account policies. Beginning with Windows Server 2008, it became possible to configure password policies in far greater detail than the basic default domain password policy that we configured earlier, in the "Configure domain user password policy" section.

Users might be subject to multiple PSOs. A PSO could be applied to all Finance users, for example, and a different PSO could be applied to all Executive users. Windows uses the precedence value of all relevant PSOs to determine which PSO is applied. The lower the precedence number, the higher the priority.

You can perform the entire process of creating, assigning, and managing fine-grained password policies by using the ADFineGrainedPasswordPolicy, ADFineGrainedPassword-PolicySubject, and ADUserResultantPasswordPolicy groups of cmdlets to configure PSOs and manage fine-grained password policies, but you can also use the Active Directory Administrative Center (ADAC), dsac.exe, to do the initial configuration. The ADAC is an extremely useful tool, one of the best Microsoft has given us in years. One of its more useful features is that it generates Windows PowerShell code for all of its actions, and you can save that code. So, for example, let's open up ADAC and create a new organizational unit (OU) called Executives. Use the following steps:

1. Open ADAC from Server Manager or by entering **dsac** at the command line and pressing Enter.

2. Expand the Windows PowerShell History pane by clicking the caret symbol (⌃) to show the Windows PowerShell commands that ADAC uses.

3. Click TreyResearch (local) in the list pane to set the focus to the TreyResearch.net domain, as shown in Figure 7-6.

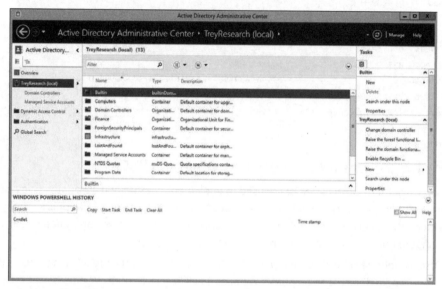

FIGURE 7-6 The Active Directory Administrative Center

4. Click New in the TreyResearch (local) area of the Tasks pane and select Organizational Unit on the menu to open the Create Organizational Unit dialog box, shown in Figure 7-7.

5. Enter **Executives** in the Name field, and enter **OU for Executives** in the Description field.

6. Click OK. The Executives OU is created.

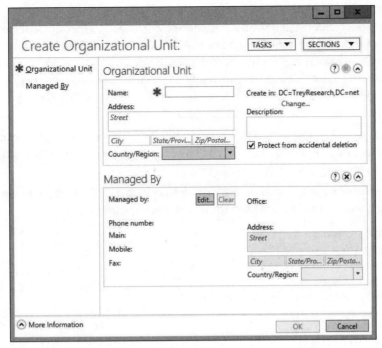

FIGURE 7-7 The Create Organizational Unit dialog box

Great—we created an OU. But now take a look at the Windows PowerShell history pane of ADAC. It shows the Windows PowerShell code used to create the OU. Two commands were issued, New-ADOrganizationalUnit and Set-ADObject. Click the plus sign (+) next to each to view the detail for each command.

```
New-ADOrganizationalUnit `
       -Description:"OU for Executives" `
       -Name:"Executives" `
       -Path:"DC=TreyResearch,DC=net" `
       -ProtectedFromAccidentalDeletion:$true `
       -Server:"trey-dc-02.TreyResearch.net"


Set-ADObject `
       -Identity:"OU=Executives,DC=TreyResearch,DC=net" `
       -ProtectedFromAccidentalDeletion:$true `
       -Server:"trey-dc-02.TreyResearch.net"
```

ADAC is nothing if not verbose, using more parameters than absolutely required—ProtectedFromAccidentalDeletion is the default, and you don't need to specify the server unless you're connecting from a different domain. ADAC also leaves out the PassThru parameter that we've been using to view more detail on the command line, and I'm not at all sure why it issues a Set-ADObject—there's nothing changing there from what the New-ADOrganizationalUnit did. But all those quibbles are just that, quibbles. You can use ADAC and build up your Windows PowerShell knowledge at the same time.

But now that we have an OU for Executives, let's create a security group called Executive Users in the OU and move a couple of users into that group. We'll then create a PSO and assign the PSO to the Executive Users security group.

First, let's create the security group. Notice that we have to specify the Path parameter, because we don't want this to just end up in the default Users container.

```
New-ADGroup -Name "Executive Users" `
            -GroupScope Universal `
            -Description "Executives of Trey Research" `
            -GroupCategory "Security" `
            -Path "OU=Executives,DC=TreyResearch,DC=net" `
            -SAMAccountName "Executive Users" `
            -PassThru
```

Because of the PassThru parameter, this yields the following output.

```
DistinguishedName : CN=Executive Users,OU=Executives,DC=TreyResearch,DC=net
GroupCategory     : Security
GroupScope        : Universal
Name              : Executive Users
ObjectClass       : group
ObjectGUID        : ffd3f830-5cf8-4826-9c83-ec397e8c3268
SamAccountName    : Executive Users
SID               : S-1-5-21-955785887-403849375-625509144-1129
```

And, because Trey Research has a new CFO, Sharon Crawford, we'll give her an account and add it to the new Executive Users group.

```
New-ADUser -Name "Sharon Crawford" `
           -GivenName "Sharon" `
           -SurName "Crawford" `
           -Department "Finance" `
           -Description "Chief Financial Officer" `
           -ChangePasswordAtLogon $True `
           -EmailAddress "Sharon@TreyResearch.net" `
```

```
      -Enabled $True `
      -PasswordNeverExpires $False `
      -SAMAccountName "Sharon" `
      -AccountPassword (ConvertTo-SecureString "Starting P@ssw0rd!" `
                                              -AsPlainText `
                                              -Force) `
      -Title "Chief Financial Officer" `
      -PassThru
```

This yields the following.

```
DistinguishedName : CN=Sharon Crawford,CN=Users,DC=TreyResearch,DC=net
Enabled           : True
GivenName         : Sharon
Name              : Sharon Crawford
ObjectClass       : user
ObjectGUID        : f6412fb7-3510-4bbb-a722-36a2638ee20d
SamAccountName    : Sharon
SID               : S-1-5-21-955785887-403849375-625509144-1132
Surname           : Crawford
UserPrincipalName :
```

Now we can make her a member of the Executive Users and Finance Users groups. We could do that by using two separate Add-ADGroupMember commands, one for each group, but instead, we'll use the following.

```
Add-ADPrincipalGroupMembership -Identity Sharon `
                               -MemberOf "Executive Users","Finance Users" `
                               -PassThru
```

The company policy at Trey Research is that users who have access to sensitive personnel data are subject to more stringent password policies than ordinary users. We can assign a PSO to Executive Users to enforce that, but first we need to create the PSO with the following.

```
New-ADFineGrainedPasswordPolicy `
    -description:"Set minimum 12 character passwords for all Executives." `
    -LockoutDuration 00:10:00 `
    -LockoutObservationWindow 00:10:00 `
    -LockoutThreshold 5 `
    -MaxPasswordAge 65.00:00:00 `
    -MinPasswordLength 12 `
    -Name:"Executive Users Pwd Policy" `
    -Precedence 10 `
    -PassThru
```

This new, fine-grained password policy only specifies the policy attributes that are different from the default domain password policy. Any attribute that we don't specify will be inherited from the default policy into this PSO.

Now we can assign this password policy to the Executive Users security group, and it will be applied to Sharon Crawford and any other users we add to that group later, unless that user is subject to a different PSO with a lower precedence.

```
Get-ADGroup -Identity "Executive Users" `
      | Add-ADFineGrainedPasswordPolicySubject `
      -Identity "Executive Users Pwd Policy"
```

We used a PSO here to tighten the password policy that applies to a specific set of users, but we could just as easily have used a PSO to apply a less-restrictive policy to a set of low-privilege users where the less-restrictive policy wouldn't create an undue risk to the organization.

You can view which users and groups are subject to a PSO in ADAC, or by using the Get-ADFineGrainedPasswordPolicySubject cmdlet. For example, to get the list of users and groups subject to our Executive Users Pwd Policy, use the following.

```
Get-ADFineGrainedPasswordPolicySubject -Identity "Executive Users Pwd Policy"
```

Summary

In this chapter, you learned how to create and manage service authentication, using the full range of service accounts from a simple local account on a single computer to the group managed service accounts introduced in Windows Server 2012. You also learned how to create a password settings object and apply that object to implement fine-grained password policies.

In the next chapter, you'll learn how to back up and restore Active Directory. You'll use Windows Server Backup to create a backup and enable Active Directory snapshots and create offline media. Then you'll do both authoritative and non-authoritative restores. Finally, you'll enable and use the Active Directory Recycle Bin.

CHAPTER 8

Back up and restore AD DS

Active Directory Domain Services (AD DS) is the heart of your organization and, by its very nature, holds important information in its database that is irreplaceable. If you had to rebuild your organization's computing environment from scratch as a result of a catastrophic event, it would be difficult, if not impossible, to do so without a restorable backup of AD DS. And yet many organizations, large and small, never explicitly back up their AD DS. And even of those that do, many have never tested a restore from backup. This is a scary thought if you've ever tried to recover from a major catastrophe that crippled all your domain controllers. But the process to back up AD DS is straightforward, and the recovery isn't much harder.

In this chapter, we'll back up our Active Directory by using Windows Server Backup, offline media, and Active Directory snapshots. Then we'll restore Active Directory and Active Directory objects by using our backups. You'll also discover how to enable and use the Active Directory Recycle Bin.

Active Directory Windows PowerShell nouns used in this chapter:

- ADDSDomainController
- ADSnapshot (functions)
- ADOptionalFeature
- ADObject
- ADUser

Other Windows PowerShell commands used in this chapter:

- Install-WindowsFeature
- Update-Help
- Get-Command
- Sort-Object
- Format-Table
- Get-WBPolicy
- New-WBPolicy
- Get-WBVolume
- Add-WBVolume
- Get-WBDisk

- New-WBFileSpec
- Add-WBFileSpec
- New-WBTarget
- Add-WBTarget
- Add-WBBareMetalRecovery
- Add-WBSystemState
- Set-WBSchedule
- Set-WBPolicy
- Ntdsutil
- Get-WBBackupSet
- Get-WBBackup
- Start-WBSystemStateRecovery
- Bcdedit
- Restart-computer

Back up Active Directory

There are three ways to back up Active Directory—by using the Windows Server Backup tool, by creating offline media, or by taking a snapshot. For normal operations, using Windows Server Backup is the preferred and supported way to back up Active Directory and the SYSVOL folder. However, using offline media to do an install from media (IFM) installation of AD DS can be a useful way to quickly recover a working domain controller in the event of a catastrophic failure, though it can't be used to create a domain from bare metal. Finally, for recovery of corrupted or inappropriately changed objects in AD DS, use Active Directory snapshots. The cautious and prudent administrator uses all three forms of backup and hopes never to need any of them—but knows that that hope is thin.

Windows Server Backup

The Windows Server Backup command-line tools can create backups that can restore Active Directory and the SYSVOL folder. Windows Server Backup supports system state, critical-volumes, and full-server backups from the WindowsServerBackup module of Windows PowerShell. These three key backup types are described here:

- **System state backup**   A system state backup can be used to recover the registry and directory service configuration and data, along with the SYSVOL.
- **Critical-volumes backup**   A critical-volumes backup or bare-metal backup can be used to recover in a fail-to-boot scenario and to recover Active Directory and the SYSVOL.
- **Full server backup**   A full server backup can be used to fully restore a failed server to new hardware. It can also be used to restore Active Directory and SYSVOL.

Install Windows Server Backup

The Windows Server Backup feature is not installed by default; it must be added after the server is built. The WindowsServerBackup module is included as part of the Windows Server Backup feature and can be used to initiate and automate backups. To install Windows Server Backup, use the following commands.

```
Install-WindowsFeature -Name Windows-Server-Backup
Update-Help -Module WindowsServerBackup -Force
```

If you use a local distribution source for Windows PowerShell Help files, include the SourcePath parameter in the Update-Help command.

To view the commands that were added with the WindowsServerBackup module, use the Get-Command cmdlet.

```
gcm -mod WindowsServerBackup
```

This gives you a list of commands, but they are not in the most useful format, so let's improve on that a bit.

```
gcm -Module WindowsServerBackup | Sort Noun,Verb | ft -auto Verb,Noun
```

Now that's a bit more useful. The list is reproduced here as Table 8-1.

TABLE 8-1 The cmdlets in the WindowsServerBackup module

Verb	Noun
Start	WBApplicationRecovery
Resume	WBBackup
Start	WBBackup
Get	WBBackupSet
Remove	WBBackupSet
Add	WBBackupTarget
Get	WBBackupTarget
New	WBBackupTarget
Remove	WBBackupTarget
Get	WBBackupVolumeBrowsePath
Add	WBBareMetalRecovery
Get	WBBareMetalRecovery
Remove	WBBareMetalRecovery
Remove	WBCatalog
Restore	WBCatalog
Get	WBDisk

Verb	Noun
Start	WBFileRecovery
Add	WBFileSpec
Get	WBFileSpec
New	WBFileSpec
Remove	WBFileSpec
Start	WBHyperVRecovery
Get	WBJob
Stop	WBJob
Get	WBPerformanceConfiguration
Set	WBPerformanceConfiguration
Get	WBPolicy
New	WBPolicy
Remove	WBPolicy
Set	WBPolicy
Get	WBSchedule
Set	WBSchedule
Get	WBSummary
Add	WBSystemState
Get	WBSystemState
Remove	WBSystemState
Start	WBSystemStateRecovery
Add	WBVirtualMachine
Get	WBVirtualMachine
Remove	WBVirtualMachine
Add	WBVolume
Get	WBVolume
Remove	WBVolume
Resume	WBVolumeRecovery
Start	WBVolumeRecovery
Get	WBVssBackupOption
Set	WBVssBackupOption

Configure a backup

The way Windows Server Backup works with Windows PowerShell can take a while to understand. We need to build a WBPolicy object. The WBPolicy object includes WBFileSpec objects to define what items should be backed up, a WBVolume object to define what volumes should be backed up, a WBDisk object that includes the list of internal and external disks that are available, a WBBackupTarget object that defines where the backups are stored, and finally, a WBSchedule object that defines when the backup runs. And before we can add each of those WB* objects to the WBPolicy object, we need to define the objects themselves.

Create the WBPolicy object   You can start with the existing WBPolicy object and edit it, or you can create a new WBPolicy from scratch and replace the current WBPolicy with the new one. To edit the existing policy, use the following command.

```
$wbPol = Get-WBPolicy -Editable
```

This retrieves an editable version of the current Windows Server Backup policy and stores it in the variable $wbPol. Of course, if you just installed Windows Server Backup and haven't yet scheduled a backup, there won't be a policy to get. Either way, let's create an entirely new policy with the following.

```
$newWbPol = New-WBPolicy
```

That was easy. We now have an empty policy object that we can build.

NOTE   There can only be one active Windows Server Backup policy at a time. When you finish defining a new WBPolicy, you use Set-WBPolicy to replace any existing policy with the new one.

Add a WBVolume object   You add a volume to back up by using the Add-WBVolume cmdlet. We need to specify a WBVolume object so that we can use Add-WBVolume, but with this cmdlet we can specify it in several ways. We'll add drive C by using the following.

```
$wbVol = Get-WBVolume -VolumePath C:
Add-WBVolume -Policy $newWBPol -Volume $wbVol
```

This produces output to confirm that drive C was added to the backup policy.

```
VolumeLabel : SystemVHD
MountPath   : C:
MountPoint  : \\?\Volume{50fe0d60-ead0-4bb1-90e4-cc548a7fb502}
FileSystem  : NTFS
Property    : Critical, ValidSource, IsOnDiskWithCriticalVolume
FreeSpace   : 125904564224
TotalSpace  : 135810514944
```

You can specify multiple volumes in a WBVolume object. Use Get-WBVolume with the AllVolumes parameter to identify which volumes are available. Unfortunately, you can't pipe Get-WBVolume directly to Add-WBVolume; you need to use a variable to hold the WBVolume object.

Add a WBFileSpec object   Before you can add a WBFileSpec object to a WBPolicy, you first need to create the file specification object and store it in a variable. You can add more than one file specification for inclusion, and you can add multiple file specifications for exclusion. File exclusions that aren't part of the file inclusions are ignored. We start by creating a WBFileSpec object by using New-WBFileSpec.

```
$incFSpec = New-WBFileSpec -FileSpec "D:\","C:\Temp"
$excFSpec = New-WBFileSpec -FileSpec "D:\PSHelp" -Exclude
```

Now we can add those two WBFileSpec objects to our WBPolicy by using the following commands.

```
Add-WBFileSpec -Policy $newWBPol -FileSpec $incFSpec
Add-WBFileSpec -Policy $newWBPol -FileSpec $excFSpec
```

And because that doesn't give us any output to tell us how we're doing, we can just check that with the following.

```
$newWBPol
```

```
Schedule               :
BackupTargets          :
VolumesToBackup        : {SystemVHD (C:)}
FilesSpecsToBackup     : {D:\*, C:\Temp\*}
FilesSpecsToExclude    : {D:\PSHelp\*}
ComponentsToBackup     :
BMR                    : False
SystemState            : False
OverwriteOldFormatVhd  : False
VssBackupOptions       : VssCopyBackup
```

Looking at our current policy, $newWBPol, we can tell that we still need at least a schedule and a backup target. We'll also want to do something about saving the system state, at least. Bare metal recovery (BMR) is less critical. Well, actually, for AD DS recovery, we really don't need drive D at all, and we don't need most of drive C.

Add a WBBackupTarget object   To create a backup target, we need to first identify the disks that are available by using Get-WBDisk. From this, we can identify the backup target disk and add a WBBackupTarget object to our WBPolicy object, $newWBPol. To get an array of connected internal and external disks, use Get-WBDisk.

```
$wbDisks = Get-WBDisk
$wbDisks
```

```
DiskName      : Microsoft Virtual Disk
DiskNumber    : 0
DiskId        : 19560519-351f-44e9-b0eb-604d19e85cb7
TotalSpace    : 136365211648
FreeSpace     : 125895063040
Volumes       : {EFI System Partition, SystemVHD (C:)}
ContainsBackup : False
BackupVolumeId : 00000000-0000-0000-0000-000000000000
Properties    : ContainsOemPartition, ContainsCriticalVolume

DiskName      : Microsoft Virtual Disk
DiskNumber    : 1
DiskId        : c151455e-d59b-45b5-b93a-080143ca0cd8
TotalSpace    : 536870912000
FreeSpace     : 524029472256
Volumes       : {trey-dc 2015_04_28 16:58 DISK_01}
ContainsBackup : True
BackupVolumeId : a52a0891-9484-41db-9b7d-76cf68230690
Properties    : ValidTarget

DiskName      : Microsoft Virtual Disk
DiskNumber    : 2
DiskId        : f4a48e9e-0484-4247-972e-b72fb7b078e9
TotalSpace    : 136365211648
FreeSpace     : 136107359744
Volumes       : {Data (D:)}
ContainsBackup : False
BackupVolumeId : 00000000-0000-0000-0000-000000000000
Properties    : ValidTarget
```

Both $wbDisks[1] and $wbDisks[2] are listed as valid targets, but $wbDisk[2] has the Data volume (D:) on it, so that's clearly not the one we want. Therefore, to add a WBBackupTarget to our WBPolicy, we first create a backup target object and then add it to the policy with the following.

```
$wbTarget = New-WBBackupTarget -Disk $wbDisks[1]
Add-WBBackupTarget -Policy $newWBPol -Target $wbTarget
```

Add a WBBareMetalRecovery object   You can add the files and partitions needed to perform a bare metal recovery (BMR) of your server to the WBPolicy object by using a single Add-WBBareMetalRecovery command. You don't need to first create an object before you can add it; the command does it in a single pass.

To add a BMR to our backup, we'll use the following.

```
Add-WBBareMetalRecovery -Policy $newWBPol
```

If we look at what our policy contains at this point, we get the following.

```
$newWBPol
```

```
Schedule              :
BackupTargets         : {Microsoft Virtual Disk}
VolumesToBackup       : {SystemVHD (C:)}
FilesSpecsToBackup    : {D:\*, C:\Temp\*}
FilesSpecsToExclude   : {D:\PSHelp\*}
ComponentsToBackup    :
BMR                   : True
SystemState           : True
OverwriteOldFormatVhd : False
VssBackupOptions      : VssCopyBackup
```

As you can tell, we've now got a BMR in the $newWBPol policy. If you want to add only the system state to your backup and don't need or want a full BMR, use the Add-WBSystemState cmdlet.

Add a WBSystemState object   You can directly add the system state to the backup policy object by using Add-WBSystemState; it isn't necessary to first create a system state object before you can add it. We can add the system state with the following.

```
Add-WBSystemState -Policy $newWBPol
```

Set the WBSchedule   The last thing we need to do to build a Windows Backup Policy object is to set the schedule for the policy. We'll use the Set-WBSchedule cmdlet to set the backup schedule for the policy. Set-WBSchedule accepts an array of times of the day to run the backup. So, for example, to set our $newWBPol object to run at noon and 8:00 in the evening, we'll use the following command.

```
Set-WBSchedule -Policy $newWBPol -Schedule 12:00,20:00
```

This leaves us with the following policy in $newWBPol.

```
$newWBPol
```

```
Schedule              : {4/30/2015 12:00:00 PM, 4/30/2015 8:00:00 PM}
BackupTargets         : {Microsoft Virtual Disk}
VolumesToBackup       : {SystemVHD (C:)}
FilesSpecsToBackup    : {D:\*, C:\Temp\*}
FilesSpecsToExclude   : {D:\PSHelp\*}
ComponentsToBackup    :
```

```
BMR                  : True
SystemState          : True
OverwriteOldFormatVhd : False
VssBackupOptions     : VssCopyBackup
```

It looks like we've covered what we need to for anything related to Active Directory; therefore, all we need to do is deploy the backup policy.

Deploy a backup

Because Windows Server Backup only supports one backup policy active at a time, we need to replace the current WBPolicy with the new one. To do that, we use Set-WBPolicy, but before we do that, I recommend that we capture the current policy, if there is one, into a variable, just in case something doesn't look right after we move the new one into place. That variable holding the current policy object is only viable as long as the current Windows PowerShell session is active, but it costs us only a single line of code.

```
$curPol = Get-WBPolicy
```

Having done that, we're ready to put our new Windows Server Backup policy in action with the following.

```
Set-WBPolicy -Policy $newWBPol -AllowDeleteOldBackups:$False -Force
```

This retains our existing backups while putting the new policy in place. However, because it doesn't give us any feedback at all, we should quickly double-check by using Get-WBPolicy.

```
Get-WBPolicy
```

```
Schedule             : {4/30/2015 12:00:00 PM, 4/30/2015 8:00:00 PM}
BackupTargets        : {trey 4/30/2015 7:39:20 PM Disk01}
VolumesToBackup      : {EFI System Partition, SystemVHD (C:)}
FilesSpecsToBackup   : {D:\*}
FilesSpecsToExclude  : {D:\PSHelp\*}
ComponentsToBackup   : {}
BMR                  : True
SystemState          : True
OverwriteOldFormatVhd : False
VssBackupOptions     : VssCopyBackup
```

To do an immediate backup with the new WBPolicy, use the following command.

```
Start-WBBackup -Policy $newWBPol
```

Create offline media

An alternative way to back up Active Directory is by creating offline media. This was covered in Chapter 5, "Deploy read-only domain controllers (RODCs)," but it is equally valid for writable domain controllers, including domain controllers that are DNS servers. This approach can't be used to re-create a domain from bare metal in the event of a disaster, but it can be used to quickly recover additional servers after the domain is back up and running. Unfortunately, you can't create the media from Windows PowerShell; you need to use a more arcane Microsoft tool, ntdsutil.

The requirements for an install from media (IFM) installation are detailed but not surprising:

- You can't use IFM to create the first domain controller in a domain; there must be an existing Windows Server 2008 or later domain controller.

- Create the IFM media from the same domain as the new domain controller.

- Create the IFM media from a domain controller that is also a global catalog server if the new domain controller is a global catalog server.

- Create the IFM media from a domain controller that is also a DNS server if the new domain controller is a DNS server.

- Create the IFM media on a writable domain controller that is running Windows Server 2008 or later to create installation media for a writable domain controller.

- Create the IFM media on either a writable domain controller or an RODC if the new domain controller is an RODC.

- Create the IFM media on a domain controller running Windows Server 2008 Service Pack 2 or later to create installation media that includes SYSVOL.

To create the IFM media, you need to use an account with Domain Admins privileges. Open a Windows PowerShell window, *as administrator*, while logged on to an account that is a member of the Domain Admins security group. In the shell, enter the following commands to create full domain controller media that includes SYSVOL and save it to the C:\IFM folder.

```
ntdsutil
activate instance ntds
ifm
create sysvol full "C:\IFM"
quit
quit
```

The IFM media can now be copied to a network share or a removable drive for use during the domain controller promotion process. Because the IFM media includes SYSVOL, use robocopy to copy the IFM folder.

To create the new domain controller from the IFM media, use the InstallationMediaPath parameter with the Install-ADDSDomainController cmdlet.

> **MORE INFO**   See Chapter 5 for more information about creating and using IFM media.

Configure Active Directory snapshots

Introduced in Windows Server 2008, Active Directory snapshots are point-in-time views of AD DS created by the Volume Shadow Copy Service (VSS). When combined with the Active Directory Recycle Bin, snapshots provide a way to recover from AD DS database corruption of an object or objects without doing a full-scale authoritative restore. Before creating any snapshots, you should enable the Active Directory Recycle Bin by using the following command.

```
Enable-ADOptionalFeature `
    -Identity "Recycle Bin Feature" `
    -Scope  ForestOrConfigurationSet `
    -Target "TreyResearch.net" `
    -Confirm:$False
```

> **IMPORTANT** The Enable-ADOptionalFeature command must be run on the domain controller that holds the domain naming master role for the forest.

Unfortunately, creating and working with snapshots means using ntdsutil again. To create a snapshot and list all of the currently available snapshots, run the following from an elevated Windows PowerShell prompt.

```
ntdsutil snapshot "activate instance ntds" create "list all" quit quit
```

There's a better way, however. Ashely McGlone, a Premier Field Service Engineer at Microsoft, has released a set of functions that wrap the ntdsutil commands in Windows PowerShell functions. They can be downloaded from *https://gallery.technet.microsoft.com /Active-Directory-Attribute-0f815689* and make working with snapshots much easier. These functions are not provided in the form of a module; they're just a group of functions, but they come complete with Help and parameters. After you have downloaded the functions, unzip the file and copy the contents to a directory where you can easily find them. I put them in my $home\psbin directory. You can add them to your current session by dot-sourcing the script, or by sourcing them in your $profile. To dot-source the AD_Snapshot_Functions, use the following.

```
. $home\psbin\AD_Snapshot_Functions
```

This loads the functions into your current session. You need to run them in an elevated Windows PowerShell session with an account that has Domain Admin permissions. The functions included are:

- **New-ADSnapshot**   Creates a snapshot.
- **Mount-ADDatabase**   Mounts a snapshot and advertises it. This function opens a separate window that runs dsamain.exe.
- **Show-ADSnapshot**   Lists the available AD DS snapshots on a domain controller.

- **Dismount-ADDatabase**   Dismounts the AD DS database snapshot and closes the open dsamain.exe window.
- **Remove-ADSnapshot**   Removes AD DS snapshots.
- **Repair-ADAttribute**   Recovers AD DS object attribute values from the mounted snapshot.
- **Repair-ADUserGroup**   Recovers group memberships for user accounts. (This can also be done with Repair-ADAttribute.)

To create a snapshot, use New-ADSnapshot. You'll get a report of the snapshot creation echoed back to the command line.

New-ADSnapshot

```
C:\Windows\system32\ntdsutil.exe: Activate Instance NTDS
Active instance set to "NTDS".
C:\Windows\system32\ntdsutil.exe: snapshot
snapshot: create
Creating snapshot...
Snapshot set {88b4d1b6-300f-4316-afc4-9dcbdb240974} generated successfully.
snapshot: quit
C:\Windows\system32\ntdsutil.exe: quit
```

To view a list of available snapshots, use Show-ADSnapshot.

Show-ADSnapshot

```
C:\Windows\system32\ntdsutil.exe: snapshot
snapshot: list all
 1: 2015/04/30:20:05 {19f8e0fa-cbec-4dda-87de-7bdb827b4ef7}
 2:     {990ac0b6-09fd-4eef-99b6-bedb22147bb1}

 3: 2015/05/01:12:03 {08fc9f6e-15b0-44b6-84f6-6a298981fd3f}
 4:     {4c8284fa-2027-495a-9d69-10ce8d246731}

 5: 2015/05/01:16:12 {88b4d1b6-300f-4316-afc4-9dcbdb240974}
 6:   C: {007982a4-2c1c-44d8-8513-09295f288776}

snapshot: quit
C:\Windows\system32\ntdsutil.exe: quit
```

Restore Active Directory

AD DS supports two kinds of full restores—an authoritative restore, which completely replaces any existing AD DS database with the version that is being restored; and a non-authoritative restore, which restores the database to the point at which it was backed up and then applies updates in the existing AD DS database to bring the restored domain controller into alignment with the rest of the domain.

You can also restore specific objects from an Active Directory snapshot. This goes beyond the basic undelete capability, enabling you to restore to a specific point-in-time snapshot.

Perform a non-authoritative restore

To perform a non-authoritative AD DS restore, you need to restart the domain controller in Directory Services Recovery Mode (DSRM). In DSRM, you can restore the AD DS database on a domain controller from the backup made by Windows Server Backup. To use a Windows Server Backup to restore the database, use the following from an elevated Windows PowerShell prompt.

```
bcdedit /set safeboot dsrepair
Restart-Computer
```

After the computer has restarted, you can log on with the DSRM password. From here, you can restore AD DS by using the Start-WBSystemStateRecovery command. First, to view a list of backups, use the following.

```
$Backups = Get-WBBackupSet
$Index = -2
$Backups | Format-Table -Auto `
          @{Label="Count"; `
            Expression={($Global:Index+=1)}},BackupTime
```

```
Index BackupTime
----- ----------
    0 5/2/2015 12:05:04 PM
    1 5/2/2015 8:00:07 PM
    2 5/3/2015 12:05:07 PM
    3 5/3/2015 8:00:08 PM
    4 5/4/2015 12:05:07 PM
    5 5/4/2015 8:00:06 PM
    6 5/5/2015 12:05:07 PM
    7 5/5/2015 8:00:07 PM
    8 5/6/2015 12:05:08 PM
```

This shows nine backups, with the most recent being $backups[8]. This works well if there are only a few backups, but the list could get really long over time. However, if we know we want the most recent backup, it's easy to find it.

```
$Backups = Get-WBBackupSet
$Backups[($Backups.count-1)]
```

```
VersionId        : 05/06/2015-19:05
BackupTime       : 5/6/2015 12:05:08 PM
BackupTarget     : \\?\Volume{eeaa152b-d4dd-47d1-8f68-b8f484793e51}
RecoverableItems : Volumes, SystemState, Applications, Files, BareMetalRecovery
Volume           : {EFI System Partition, SystemVHD (C:)}
Application      : {FRS, AD, Registry}
VssBackupOption  : VssCopyBackup
SnapshotId       : 63e1b96b-a092-40fb-9aec-80b5eface2a8
BackupSetId      : 7b6e554d-9d75-4905-9cc9-f72b48e7a9fd
```

To do a non-authoritative restore of that most recent backup, use the following.

```
Start-WBSystemStateRecovery -BackupSet $Backups[($Backups.count-1)]
```

This will prompt you to confirm and will restore from the backup. You can add a Force parameter to bypass the prompt and a RestartComputer parameter to automatically restart after the restore has completed.

> **NOTE** You shouldn't delay the restart that is required whenever you restore Active Directory. Until the restart has completed, the domain controller is in an indeterminate state.

When the domain controller restarts, log back on with the same DSRM password. You'll get a confirmation that the recovery completed successfully, as shown in Figure 8-1.

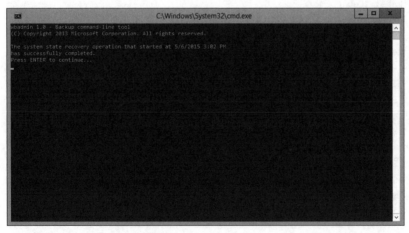

FIGURE 8-1 The recovery confirmation

Change the boot back to normal and reboot with the following.

```
bcdedit /deletevalue safeboot
Restart-Computer
```

During a non-authoritative Active Directory restore, any changes to the AD DS database that occurred after the restored system state backup are replicated from other domain controllers in the domain. The non-authoritative restore acts as a seed to reduce the total amount of replication traffic required.

Perform an authoritative restore

An authoritative restore is a last-resort restoration and shouldn't be undertaken lightly. You *will* lose data—any changes since the last backup will be overwritten on all domain controllers in the domain. However, when there's no choice, the option is there.

> **NOTE** For authoritative restoration of specific AD DS objects, see the "Restore an object by using the Active Directory Recycle Bin" and "Restore an object by using Active Directory snapshots" sections later in this chapter.

The steps to perform an authoritative restore are essentially similar to those for a non-authoritative restore. However, because of an apparent bug in Start-WBSystemStateRecovery, the cmdlet refuses to actually perform an authoritative restore. The command should be.

```
$Backups=Get-WBBackupSet
$backup = $Backups[($Backups.count-1)]
Start-WBSystemStateRecovery -BackupSet $Backup -AuthoritativeSysvolRecovery $True
```

However, this fails, reporting that it can't be recovered to an alternate location. Therefore, we need to use the graphical Windows Server Backup application to do this recovery. To do a full, authoritative restore of AD DS, use the following steps:

1. Start the domain controller in DSRM mode and log on with the DSRM password.
2. Start the Windows Server Backup application, and select Local Backup in the tree pane.
3. Select the backup you want to restore in the details pane, and click Recover in the actions pane.
4. Select This Server for the location where the backup is stored, and click Next. Select the backup by date and time on the Select Backup Date page of the Recovery Wizard.
5. Click Next to open the Select Recovery Type page of the Recovery Wizard, which is shown in Figure 8-2.

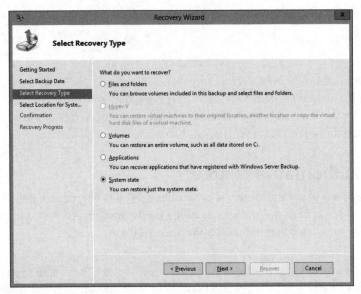

FIGURE 8-2 The Select Recovery Type page of the Recovery Wizard

6. Select System State, and click Next to open the Select Location For System State Recovery page of the Recovery Wizard, which is shown in Figure 8-3.

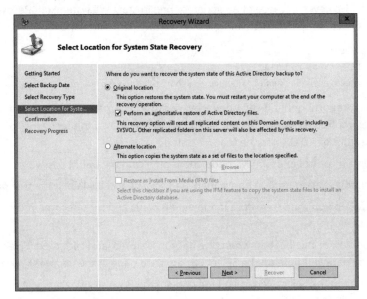

FIGURE 8-3 The Select Location For System State Recovery page of the Recovery Wizard

7. Select Original Location, and then select Perform An Authoritative Restore of Active Directory Files.

8. Click Next. You'll get a warning that there will be consequences, as shown in Figure 8-4.

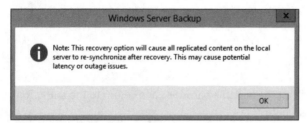

FIGURE 8-4 Windows Server Backup warning message

9. Click OK to open the Confirmation page of the Recovery Wizard.

10. Click Recover. You'll get one more confirmation dialog box, as shown in Figure 8-5.

FIGURE 8-5 Warning that system state recovery can't be paused or cancelled after it has started

11. Click Yes. The recovery will begin. When the recovery finishes, you'll be prompted to restart.

> **NOTE** When you recover an Active Directory database in DSRM mode, the database is mounted offline and doesn't go online until you return to normal mode. As long as we're in DSRM mode, the database remains offline even after a reboot.

12. After the restart, log back on to the domain controller with the DSRM account and password.

13. Press Enter to acknowledge the message shown earlier, in Figure 8-1.

14. Open a Windows PowerShell window, and enter **ntdsutil**.

15. In the ntdsutil shell, enter the following.

```
activate instance NTDS
Authoritative restore
list NC CRs
```

At this point, ntdsutil will list the writable partitions and return to the authoritative restore prompt, as shown here.

```
Opening DIT database... Done.

Listing locally instantiated writeable partitions and associated cross-refs:

1) Partition: DC=ForestDnsZones,DC=TreyResearch,DC=net
        cross-ref: CN=15852720-90d7-43f3-aaec-96ec31656a4a,
                   CN=Partitions,CN=Configuration,DC=TreyResearch,DC=net
2) Partition: DC=DomainDnsZones,DC=TreyResearch,DC=net
        cross-ref: CN=b1f2c892-7939-4b6f-b097-f216e9f5d75a,
                   CN=Partitions,CN=Configuration,DC=TreyResearch,DC=net
3) Partition: CN=Configuration,DC=TreyResearch,DC=net
        cross-ref: CN=Enterprise Configuration,CN=Partitions,
                   CN=Configuration,DC=TreyResearch,DC=net
4) Partition: CN=Schema,CN=Configuration,DC=TreyResearch,DC=net
        cross-ref: CN=Enterprise Schema,CN=Partitions,
                   CN=Configuration,DC=TreyResearch,DC=net
5) Partition: DC=TreyResearch,DC=net
        cross-ref: CN=TREYRESEARCH,CN=Partitions,
                   CN=Configuration,DC=TreyResearch,DC=net
Done.

authoritative restore:
```

16. The domain database that we want to authoritatively restore is the fifth one, so we enter the following.

```
restore subtree DC=TreyResearch,DC=net
```

Ntdsutil then restores the database, after a confirmation prompt, and increments the attribute version numbers by 100,000.

```
Opening DIT database... Done.

The current time is 05-06-15 19:01.17.
Most recent database update occured at 05-06-15 19:00.48.
Increasing attribute version numbers by 100000.

Counting records that need updating...
Records found: 0000000395
Done.


Found 395 records to update.

Updating records...
Records remaining: 0000000000
Done.


Successfully updated 395 records.

The following sub-NCs were not updated:
 (0) CN=Configuration,DC=TreyResearch,DC=net
 (1) DC=DomainDnsZones,DC=TreyResearch,DC=net
 (2) DC=ForestDnsZones,DC=TreyResearch,DC=net
 (3) DC=NorthAmerica,DC=TreyResearch,DC=net

The following text file with a list of authoritatively restored objects has
been created in the current working directory:
        ar_20150506-190118_objects.txt

One or more specified objects have back-links in this domain. The following LDIF
files with link restore operations have been created in the current
working directory:
        ar_20150506-190118_links_TreyResearch.net-Configuration.ldf
        ar_20150506-190118_links_TreyResearch.net.ldf

Authoritative Restore completed successfully.

authoritative restore:
```

17. Enter **quit**, press Enter, and enter **quit** again to return to the Windows PowerShell prompt.

18. Delete the safeboot attribute by using bcdedit, and restart the server.

```
bcdedit /deletevalue safeboot
Restart-Computer
```

I'm going to repeat my earlier warning here: An authoritative restore of all of AD DS is a last resort. You should always look for alternatives, including restoring just the corrupted objects.

Restore an object by using the Active Directory Recycle Bin

You can restore an Active Directory object that has been deleted if the Active Directory Recycle Bin is enabled. Enabling the Recycle Bin is a one-time, irreversible operation. You can enable the Recycle Bin for the entire forest, or only for the domain.

> **IMPORTANT** The Enable-ADOptionalFeature command must be run on the domain controller that holds the domain naming master role for the forest.

Use the following command to enable the Recycle Bin for the entire forest.

```
Enable-ADOptionalFeature `
    -Identity "Recycle Bin Feature" `
    -Scope  ForestOrConfigurationSet `
    -Target "TreyResearch.net" `
    -Confirm:$False
```

This command produces no output except a warning that it's irreversible. But we can verify that it has been successfully run by using the following command.

```
Get-ADOptionalFeature -Identity "Recycle Bin Feature"
```

```
DistinguishedName  : CN=Recycle Bin Feature,CN=Optional Features,
                     CN=Directory Service,CN=WindowsNT,CN=Services,
                     CN=Configuration,DC=TreyResearch,DC=net
EnabledScopes      : {CN=Partitions,CN=Configuration,DC=TreyResearch,
                     DC=net, CN=NTDS Settings,CN=TREY-DC-02,CN=Servers,
                     CN=Default-First-Site-Name,CN=Sites,
                     CN=Configuration,DC=TreyResearch,DC=net}
FeatureGUID        : 766ddcd8-acd0-445e-f3b9-a7f9b6744f2a
FeatureScope       : {ForestOrConfigurationSet}
IsDisableable      : False
Name               : Recycle Bin Feature
ObjectClass        : msDS-OptionalFeature
ObjectGUID         : 448afce4-93e9-4f0f-bc68-351d732e1ef4
RequiredDomainMode :
RequiredForestMode : Windows2008R2Forest
```

Now that we've enabled the Active Directory Recycle Bin, we can test deleting an object and restoring it. First, let's confirm that we have a user named Alfie, and then we'll delete him.

```
Get-ADUser -Identity Alfie
```

```
DistinguishedName : CN=Alfredo Fettuccine,CN=Users,DC=TreyResearch,DC=net
Enabled           : True
GivenName         : Alfredo
Name              : Alfredo Fettuccine
ObjectClass       : user
ObjectGUID        : dba98b99-421e-43f2-9c2c-2e671b25c874
SamAccountName    : Alfie
SID               : S-1-5-21-955785887-403849375-625509144-1105
Surname           : Fettuccine
UserPrincipalName : Alfie
```

Now, we'll remove him.

```
Get-ADUser -Identity Alfie | Remove-ADUser -Confirm:$False
Get-ADUser -Identity Alfie
```

```
get-aduser : Cannot find an object with identity: 'Alfie' under:
'DC=TreyResearch,DC=net'.
At line:1 char:1
+ get-aduser -Identity Alfie
+ ~~~~~~~~~~~~~~~~~~~~~~~~~~~
    + CategoryInfo          : ObjectNotFound: (Alfie:ADUser) [Get-ADUser],
ADIdentityNotFoundException
    + FullyQualifiedErrorId :ActiveDirectoryCmdlet:
Microsoft.ActiveDirectory.Management.ADIdentityNotFoundException,
Microsoft.ActiveDirectory.Management.Commands.GetADUser
```

No Alfie. But observe what happens if we change the Get-ADUser command to the following.

```
Get-ADObject -Filter {Name -like "Alfredo*"} -IncludeDeletedObjects
```

```
Deleted           : True
DistinguishedName : CN=Alfredo Fettuccine\0ADEL:dba98b99-421e-43f2-
                    9c2c-2e671b25c874,CN=Deleted Objects,DC=TreyResearch,DC=net
Name              : Alfredo Fettuccine
                    DEL:dba98b99-421e-43f2-9c2c-2e671b25c874
ObjectClass       : user
ObjectGUID        : dba98b99-421e-43f2-9c2c-2e671b25c874
```

There's Alfie. Notice that I had to use a -like operator on my filter and include a wildcard character. Alfie's name was changed to have DEL:dba98b99-421e-43f2-9c2c-2e671b25c874 added to it, which is the GUID used to identify the deleted object. We can restore him easily enough by using the following.

```
Get-ADObject -Filter {Name -like "Alfredo*"} `
          -IncludeDeletedObjects | Restore-ADObject
```

Now, if we search for Alfie again, we find that he is back.

```
Get-ADObject -Filter {Name -like "Alfredo*"}
```

DistinguishedName	Name	ObjectClass	ObjectGUID
CN=Alfredo Fettuccine,CN=U...	Alfredo Fettuccine	user	dba98b99-421e-43f2-...

Restore an object by using Active Directory snapshots

Sometimes the reason for restoring an object is not that it has been deleted, but that it has been corrupted. This is most commonly caused by the inadvertent and ill-considered actions of a system administrator—as I know only too well, having done it to myself. When this happens, restoring the object or objects from an Active Directory snapshot is the solution.

Usually, restoring an object from a snapshot is a fairly ugly process involving some arcane command-line tools. But, as you discovered earlier, in the "Configure Active Directory snapshots" section, there is a useful set of functions you can load to simplify things. As mentioned in that section, the Active Directory snapshot functions can be downloaded from *https://gallery.technet.microsoft.com/Active-Directory-Attribute-0f815689*. Unzip them and put them where you can find them—I've put mine in my $home/psbin directory. To dot-source the AD_Snapshot_Functions, use the following.

```
. $home\psbin\AD_Snapshot_Functions
```

Now we can start by finding out which snapshots are available.

```
Show-ADSnapshot
```

```
C:\Windows\system32\ntdsutil.exe: snapshot
snapshot: list all
 1: 2015/05/05:20:03 {f0d8b063-d243-4555-96bf-6dab379fa1df}
 2:     {5d80bf80-e8ce-4839-8247-8b630987bbf5}

 3: 2015/05/06:12:06 {4e7d2785-5a89-47b3-ba1e-cfbd07207feb}
 4:     {5cf6bc1b-f373-48b3-927c-068c19a0aa29}

 5: 2015/05/06:20:00 {ddcaa09a-38f9-4dd0-8d1c-ee04b3060fdf}
 6:   C: {d8adc9b4-9002-4e33-a9de-2768ac3f791b}
```

```
 7: 2015/05/06:20:05 {4fd1084e-a371-4b29-863d-ee06cf750411}
 8:    {1bcc26d0-c2d1-4016-b961-4aab6fe2b9fe}

 9: 2015/05/06:21:20 {58a5bf30-71c5-485a-b51f-4bffc0c03609}
10:    C: {ffb95ee3-4237-4bac-85cb-811b44e1d4c2}

snapshot: quit
C:\Windows\system32\ntdsutil.exe: quit
```

We have five snapshots available, all of which should have been created before someone inadvertently changed Alfie's DisplayName to Fettuccine. He's not happy about this, so we need to restore the Alfie user object from the snapshot we took earlier today. We'll start by mounting the most recent snapshot.

```
Mount-ADDatabase -LDAPPort 39990 -Last
```

This opens up a dsamain.exe window in the background that we need to leave alone until we're done. We'll start by comparing the Alfie user object in the two versions of the AD DS database. First, let's look at the snapshot database.

```
Get-ADUser -Identity Alfie -Property DisplayName -Server localhost:39990
```

```
DisplayName       : Alfie NoNose
DistinguishedName : CN=Alfredo Fettuccine,CN=Users,DC=TreyResearch,DC=net
Enabled           : True
GivenName         : Alfredo
Name              : Alfredo Fettuccine
ObjectClass       : user
ObjectGUID        : dba98b99-421e-43f2-9c2c-2e671b25c874
SamAccountName    : Alfie
SID               : S-1-5-21-955785887-403849375-625509144-1105
Surname           : Fettuccine
UserPrincipalName : Alfie
```

Now we'll look at the live database.

```
Get-ADUser -Identity Alfie -Property DisplayName -Server localhost
```

```
DisplayName       : Alfredo Fettuccine
DistinguishedName : CN=Alfredo Fettuccine,CN=Users,DC=TreyResearch,DC=net
Enabled           : True
GivenName         : Alfredo
Name              : Alfredo Fettuccine
ObjectClass       : user
ObjectGUID        : dba98b99-421e-43f2-9c2c-2e671b25c874
SamAccountName    : Alfie
```

```
SID              : S-1-5-21-955785887-403849375-625509144-1105
Surname          : Fettuccine
UserPrincipalName : Alfie
```

From this, we can tell that someone has tried to take away Alfie's preferred Display Name of Alfie NoNose. We can fix that with the following.

```
Get-ADUser -Identity Alfie -Server localhost `
        | Repair-ADAttribute -Property DisplayName -LDAPPort 39990

Action    : Replaced
NewObject : CN=Alfredo Fettuccine,CN=Users,DC=TreyResearch,DC=net
NewValue  : Alfredo Fettuccine
OldValue  : Alfie NoNose
Property  : DisplayName
Moved     : False
ObjGUID   : dba98b99-421e-43f2-9c2c-2e671b25c874
OldObject : CN=Alfredo Fettuccine,CN=Users,DC=TreyResearch,DC=net
```

And Alfie's back to his old self. You can close the dsmain window to finish, or use Dismount-ADDatabase.

> **NOTE** In case you are wondering, Alfie was a lovely blue-point Himalayan cat with the typical flat nose of the breed.

Summary

In this chapter, you learned three ways to back up an Active Directory database: using Windows Server Backup, offline media, and Active Directory snapshots. You then used four methods to recover Active Directory objects, including using the Active Directory Recycle Bin, which you enabled.

In the next chapter, you'll learn how to manage sites and replication, including Universal Group Membership Caching (UGMC).

CHAPTER 9

Manage sites and replication

Active Directory Domain Services (AD DS) uses *sites* to define boundaries between different business locations and different subnets. A site can include multiple subnets, but all subnets within a site should be connected by reliably available network connections. The connection between sites, however, can be over a slow or less reliable network connection. Active Directory replication uses two models—*intrasite replication* within a single site, and *intersite replication* between sites. In this chapter, you'll learn how to create a new subnet and a new site, create site links, and configure Universal Group Membership Caching (UGMC). You'll also configure a replication schedule and change a replication server.

Active Directory Windows PowerShell nouns used in this chapter:

- ADReplicationSite
- ADReplicationSubnet
- ADDomainController
- ADDSDomainController
- ADDirectoryServer
- ADGroupMember
- ADDCCloningExcludedApplicationList
- ADDCCloneConfigFile
- ADReplicationSiteLink
- ADReplicationSiteLinkBridge
- ADReplicationConnection

Other Windows PowerShell commands used in this chapter:

- Format-Table
- Get-NetFirewallRule
- Set-NetFirewallRule
- Enable-PSRemoting
- Copy-Item (cp)
- New-VM
- Set-VM
- Start-VM
- New-Object

Configure sites

Sites do not necessarily correlate to the AD DS namespace or domains, but they do correlate to the TCP/IP network topology. Although sites frequently correspond to business locations, this isn't a requirement. A site can contain multiple domains and their resources, in addition to multiple subnets. Furthermore, a single domain can reside in multiple sites. A single subnet, however, can't be spread across multiple sites; it can reside in only a single site.

The decision to use one or multiple sites is a decision that should be based on the physical realities of your network. You could, for example, choose to segment AD DS into sites based on physical buildings to manage the resource view of users in each building, even if the buildings are all adjacent to each other and connected by high-speed LAN links.

Create a new site

In this section, we will use New-ADReplicationSite to create a new site that will be associated with the 192.168.11.0/24 subnet and that will have trey-rodc-200 as the domain controller in the site. To create a new site named Redmond-11, use the following.

```
New-ADReplicationSite -Name Redmond-11 `
                      -Description "The .11 site/subnet on the Redmond Campus" `
                      -PassThru
```

Because we used the PassThru parameter, Windows PowerShell gives us the details on the created site, as shown here.

```
Description                        : The .11 site/subnet on the Redmond Campus
DistinguishedName                  : CN=Redmond-
1,CN=Sites,CN=Configuration,DC=TreyResearch,DC=net
InterSiteTopologyGenerator         :
ManagedBy                          :
Name                               : Redmond-11
ObjectClass                        : site
ObjectGUID                         : e272cfa0-047c-4fff-950d-cce00aae580f
ReplicationSchedule                :
UniversalGroupCachingRefreshSite   :
```

There are many more parameters available for New-ADReplicationSite, as shown in Table 9-1.

TABLE 9-1 Parameters for New-ADReplicationSite

Parameter	Type
Name	String
AuthType	ADAuthType
AutomaticInterSiteTopologyGenerationEnabled	Boolean
AutomaticTopologyGenerationEnabled	Boolean
Credential	PSCredential
Description	String
Instance	ADReplicationSite
InterSiteTopologyGenerator	ADDirectoryServer
ManagedBy	ADPrincipal
OtherAttributes	Hashtable
PassThru	Switch
ProtectedFromAccidentalDeletion	Boolean
RedundantServerTopologyEnabled	Boolean
ReplicationSchedule	ActiveDirectorySchedule
ScheduleHashingEnabled	Boolean
Server	String
TopologyCleanupEnabled	Boolean
TopologyDetectStaleEnabled	Boolean
TopologyMinimumHopsEnabled	Boolean
UniversalGroupCachingEnabled	Boolean
UniversalGroupCachingRefreshSite	ADReplicationSite
WindowsServer2000BridgeheadSelectionMethodEnabled	Boolean
WindowsServer2000KCCISTGSelectionBehaviorEnabled	Boolean
WindowsServer2003KCCBehaviorEnabled	Boolean
WindowsServer2003KCCIgnoreScheduleEnabled	Boolean
WindowsServer2003KCCSiteLinkBridgingEnabled	Boolean

Create a replication subnet

Now, to create an ADReplicationSubnet to associate with the site, use the New-ADReplication-
Subnet command.

```
New-ADReplicationSubnet -Name "192.168.11.0/24" `
                        -Site "Redmond-11" `
                        -Location "Redmond, WA" `
                        -PassThru
```

This creates the new subnet, as shown here.

```
DistinguishedName : CN=192.168.11.0/24,CN=Subnets,CN=Sites,CN=Configuration,
                    DC=TreyResearch,DC=net
Location          : Redmond, WA
Name              : 192.168.11.0/24
ObjectClass       : subnet
ObjectGUID        : f1dbe4fe-fda9-47ee-b2e8-3d94abeceef0
Site              : CN=Redmond-11,CN=Sites,CN=Configuration,DC=TreyResearch,DC=net
```

Also, because we never created a subnet for our main network, let's create one now. This subnet will be associated with the "Default-First-Site-Name" site, the site name that rarely gets changed, though we'll change it soon.

```
New-ADReplicationSubnet -Name "192.168.10.0/24" `
                        -Site "Default-First-Site-Name" `
                        -Location "Redmond, WA"
```

Now we can assign domain controllers to the appropriate sites. We'll start by discovering which domain controllers we have, whether they are read-only domain controllers or read-write domain controllers, and which sites they're in.

```
Get-ADDomainController -Filter * | Format-Table -auto @{Label="RODC"; `
                       Expression={$_.isReadOnly}; `
                       Width=6; `
                       Align="Right" `
                       }, Name, `
                       Site
```

```
RODC Name            Site
---- ----            ----
False TREY-DC-04     Default-First-Site-Name
False TREY-DC-02     Default-First-Site-Name
 True TREY-RODC-200  Default-First-Site-Name
```

As shown, we currently have three domain controllers, including the one RODC, trey-rodc-200, and all the domain controllers are in the Default-First-Site-Name site. To move the RODC to the site we created, Redmond-11, use the following command.

```
$site11 = Get-ADReplicationSite -Filter 'Name -eq "Redmond-11"'
Move-ADDirectoryServer -Identity trey-rodc-200 `
                       -site $site11.DistinguishedName
```

There's no feedback from this command, nor is there any confirmation, so to verify that it actually did what we intended, run the same Get-ADDomainController command we used earlier.

```
Get-ADDomainController -Filter * | Format-Table -auto @{Label="RODC"; `
                        Expression={$_.isReadOnly}; `
                        Width=6; `
                        Align="Right" `
                        }, Name, `
                        Site
```

Now the result is different, as shown here.

```
RODC  Name           Site
----  ----           ----
False TREY-DC-02     Default-First-Site-Name
False TREY-DC-04     Default-First-Site-Name
True  TREY-RODC-200  Redmond-11
```

Good. Now, to make life a bit more interesting in our two-site network, we'll add a new server, trey-dc-05, and promote it to domain controller in site Redmond-11. Use the steps detailed in Chapter 4, "Deploy additional domain controllers," to add an additional server, trey-dc-05, to the TreyResearch.net domain, and configure the server's networking to have a fixed IPv4 address of 192.168.11.5 and a fixed IPv6 address of 2001:db8:0:11::5.

To make it easier to connect to the server and manage it, configure the Windows Firewall to allow Remote Desktop Protocol (RDP), Windows Management Instrumentation (WMI), Windows Remote Management (WinRM), and file and printer sharing within the domain or private networks, by using the Set-myFirewall.ps1 script.

Set-myFirewall.ps1

```
.Synopsis
Enables Firewall rules for lab environment
.Description
Set-myFirewall gets a list of firewall rules related to Remote Desktop, File
and Print Sharing, and WMI, and enables them for both Domain and Private
Profiles. Finally, it enables PSRemoting. This script requires no parameters.
```

```
.Example
Set-myFirewall

Enables all RDP, WMI, and File & Printer Sharing firewall rules for Domain
and Private networks.
.Notes
     Author: Charlie Russel
  Copyright: 2015 by Charlie Russel
           : Permission to use is granted but attribution is appreciated
    Initial: 09 Apr, 2014
    ModHist: 10 May, 2015 - Set File&Print, WMI to enabled
           :
#>
[CmdletBinding()]

$RDPRules = Get-NetFirewallRule `
    | where {$_.DisplayName -match "Remote Desktop" }
$FPRules  = Get-NetFirewallRule `
    | Where {$_.DisplayName -match "File and Printer Sharing" }
$WMIRules = Get-NetFirewallRule `
    | Where {$_.DisplayName -match "Windows Management Instrumentation" }

ForEach ($rule in $RDPRules,$FPRules,$WMIRules ) {
   Set-NetFirewallRule -DisplayName $rule.DisplayName `
                       -Direction Inbound `
                       -Profile Domain,Private `
                       -Action Allow `
                       -Enabled True `
                       -PassThru
}
Enable-PSRemoting -Force
```

Finally, promote the server to domain controller by using the following command:

```
Install-ADDSDomainController `
            -NoGlobalCatalog:$false `
            -CreateDnsDelegation:$false `
            -CriticalReplicationOnly:$false `
            -DatabasePath "C:\Windows\NTDS" `
            -DomainName "TreyResearch.net" `
            -InstallDns:$true `
            -LogPath "C:\Windows\NTDS" `
            -NoRebootOnCompletion:$false `
            -SiteName "Redmond-11" `
            -SysvolPath "C:\Windows\SYSVOL" `
            -Force:$true
```

We now have two sites, each with a pair of domain controllers. That Default-First-Site-Name is annoying, however, and totally not descriptive, so we'll change it.

Rename a site

If you only have a single AD DS site, there's no particular need to rename it, nor is there any particular gain in renaming it. But if your network is more complicated than that single-site network, setting site names to consistently reflect their location or other property makes it easier for everyone who has to work on the network to understand it. And in Windows PowerShell, it's a lot easier to set the name as you want it when you first create the site than it is to change it later.

To rename the Default-First-Site-Name site to reflect its location (Vancouver, British Columbia) and subnet (192.168.10.0/24), we'll rename the site to Vancouver-10. This should be easy with Windows PowerShell, but it's actually easier to just use the GUI for this. Use the following steps to rename the Default-First-Site-Name site to Vancouver-10.

1. Log on to a domain controller with an account that is a member of the Enterprise Admins security group.

2. Open the Active Directory Sites And Services console (dssite.msc), shown in Figure 9-1.

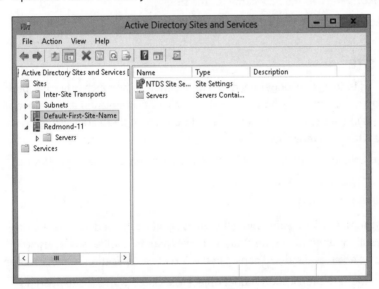

FIGURE 9-1 The Active Directory Sites And Services console

3. Navigate to Default-First-Site-Name in the tree pane, and right-click it.

4. Click Rename on the menu, as shown in Figure 9-2.

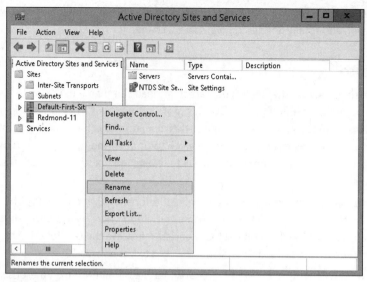

FIGURE 9-2 Renaming the Default-First-Site-Name site

5. Enter **Vancouver-10** as the new name for the site.
6. Exit the Active Directory Sites And Services console.

Remove a site

You can remove a site that is no longer needed—for example, if a branch office has been closed. Before you remove the site, however, you must first decommission and remove all domain controllers in the site or move them to a different site. If there are existing domain controllers in the site, the removal fails.

To remove the Calgary-12 site from the TreyResearch.net domain, use the following.

```
Get-ADReplicationSite -filter 'Name -eq "Calgary12"' `
    | Remove-ADReplicationSite
```

After you are prompted for confirmation, the site is silently removed. If there are domain controllers still assigned to the site, you can move them to another site by using Move-ADDirectoryServer, as discussed earlier, in the "Create a replication subnet" section.

You can also remove the replication subnet object associated with the site by using Remove-ADReplicationSubnet. To remove the 192.168.12.0/24 subnet associated with the Calgary-12 site, use the following command.

```
Remove-ADReplicationSubnet -Identity 192.168.12.0/24 -Confirm:$False
```

Because we specified the Confirm:$False parameter, the subnet is removed silently and without confirmation.

Configure Universal Group Membership Caching (UGMC)

Universal Group Membership Caching (UGMC) is a site-specific property that allows caching of the membership of universal security groups. This is particularly useful for sites where none of the domain controllers at the site are global catalog (GC) servers. You can designate a site as a UGMC-enabled site when you create the site, by using New-ADReplicationSite, or you can modify an existing site by using Set-ADReplicationSite.

To enable UGMC on a new site, Tokyo-13, and set the UGMC refresh site to our Redmond-11 site, we'll use the following command.

```
New-ADReplicationSite -Name Tokyo-13 `
                      -Description "Tokyo branch office on 13 subnet" `
                      -UniversalGroupCachingEnabled $True `
                      -UniversalGroupCachingRefreshSite Redmond-11 `
                      -PassThru
```

The result of this command shows that there isn't a replication schedule defined yet, nor is there an intersite topology generator designated. In addition, we haven't put a domain controller in that site yet.

```
Description                     : Tokyo branch office on 13 subnet
DistinguishedName               : CN=Tokyo-13,CN=Sites,CN=Configuration,
                                  DC=TreyResearch,DC=net
InterSiteTopologyGenerator      :
ManagedBy                       :
Name                            : Tokyo-13
ObjectClass                     : site
ObjectGUID                      : 8eed2f8c-b6f0-4e5b-bab3-c615c70c5e89
ReplicationSchedule             :
UniversalGroupCachingRefreshSite : CN=Redmond-11,CN=Sites,CN=Configuration,
                                  DC=TreyResearch,DC=net
```

Before we can create a site link, we need a domain controller in the Tokyo site. We'll quickly clone an existing RODC, trey-rodc-200, and put it in the office.

Run on trey-rodc-200

```
Add-ADGroupMember `
        -Identity "Cloneable Domain Controllers" `
        -Members (Get-ADComputer -Identity trey-rodc-200).SAMAccountName `
        -PassThru
Get-ADDCCloningExcludedApplicationList -GenerateXML
New-ADDCCloneConfigFile -Static `
                        -CloneComputerName trey-rodc-213 `
                        -Site Tokyo-13 `
                        -IPv4Address 192.168.13.213 `
                        -IPv4SubnetMask 255.255.255.0 `
                        -IPv4DefaultGateway 192.168.13.1 `
                        -IPv4DNSResolver 192.168.13.2
Stop-Computer
```

Run on Hyper-V host

```
mkdir "D:\vms\trey-rodc-213\Virtual Hard Disks"
cp "D:\vms\trey-rodc-200\Virtual Hard Disks\trey-rodc-200-System.vhdx" `
    "D:\vms\trey-rodc-213\Virtual Hard Disks\trey-rodc-213-System.vhdx"
$ClonedDC = New-VM -Name trey-rodc-213 `
                   -MemoryStartupBytes 1024MB `
                   -Generation 2 `
                   -BootDevice VHD `
                   -Path "D:\VMs\" `
                   -VHDPath "D:\VMs\trey-rodc-213\Virtual Hard Disks\trey-rodc-213-
system.vhdx" `
                   -Switch "Local-13"
Set-VM -VM $ClonedDC -ProcessorCount 2 -DynamicMemory -PassThru
Start-VM $ClonedDC
```

> **NOTE** The process of cloning a domain controller is covered in detail in Chapter 4.

OK, having cloned a domain controller, we can create a site link for the site.

Create a site link

Links and replication between domain controllers within a site are typically handled automatically by the Knowledge Consistency Checker (KCC) process, but with intersite replication, we'll create the link manually. We've just created the site, but it doesn't yet have a subnet associated with it. I inadvertently made the subnet first, but it isn't automatically associated with the site, as shown in Figure 9-3.

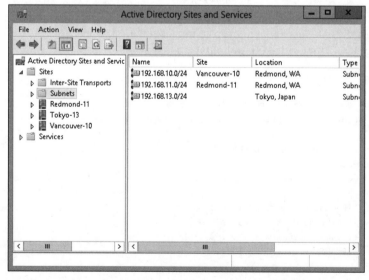

FIGURE 9-3 Subnets shown in the Active Directory Sites And Services console

To modify the 192.168.13.0/24 subnet to associate it with the Tokyo-13 site, use the following command.

```
Set-ADReplicationSubnet -Identity 192.168.13.0/24 -Site Tokyo-13 -PassThru
```

```
DistinguishedName : CN=192.168.13.0/24,CN=Subnets,CN=Sites,
                    CN=Configuration,DC=TreyResearch,DC=net
Location          : Tokyo, Japan
Name              : 192.168.13.0/24
ObjectClass       : subnet
ObjectGUID        : 366ad454-1532-45c1-b891-5b1f7e8cafd3
Site              : CN=Tokyo-13,CN=Sites,CN=Configuration,DC=TreyResearch,DC=net
```

Now we're going to create a site link between Tokyo-13 and Vancouver-10. There are many parameters you can specify for a site link, as shown in Table 9-2. Name is a required parameter, but all the others are optional and default to reasonable values. Setting the cost explicitly allows you to control the cost of each site link, with a lower cost being preferred for replication. The ReplicationFrequencyInMinutes defaults to 180 (three hours), but that might be too frequent for remote sites with limited bandwidth. By specifying the frequency and the schedule of replication, you can move the replication traffic to a time that won't interfere with normal work at the sites connected with this link.

TABLE 9-2 Parameters for New-ADReplicationSiteLink

Parameter	Type
Name	String
SitesIncluded	ADReplicationSite[]
Cost	Int32
Credential	PSCredential
Description	String
Instance	ADReplicationSiteLink
InterSiteTransportProtocol	{IP	SMTP}
OtherAttributes	Hashtable
PassThru	Switch
ReplicationFrequencyInMinutes	Int32
ReplicationSchedule	ActiveDirectorySchedule
Server	String

To set a new site link that connects our Vancouver-10 site to our Tokyo-13 site, with a cost of 500 and a frequency of every four hours, we use the following command.

```
New-ADReplicationSiteLink -Name 'CanadaWest-Japan' `
                          -SitesIncluded Vancouver-10,Tokyo-13 `
                          -Cost 500 `
                          -ReplicationFrequency 240 `
                          -InterSiteTransportProtocol IP `
                          -PassThru
```

```
Cost                        : 500
DistinguishedName           : CN=CanadaWest-Japan,CN=IP,CN=Inter-Site
                              Transports,CN=Sites,CN=Configuration,
                              DC=TreyResearch,DC=net
Name                        : CanadaWest-Japan
ObjectClass                 : siteLink
ObjectGUID                  : e1ca1043-4b10-42d6-bec2-d4f486c09774
ReplicationFrequencyInMinutes : 240
SitesIncluded               : {CN=Tokyo-13,CN=Sites,CN=Configuration,
                              DC=TreyResearch,DC=net,CN=Vancouver-10,
                              CN=Sites,CN=Configuration,DC=TreyResearch,DC=net}
```

For more complicated scenarios, you can use bridge connections that control the flow from site to site through a bridge site. In this scenario, for example, we could have a dedicated high-speed link between the headquarters at site A and a regional site B, and a moderate-speed link between site B and the branch office in the same region at site C, but only a slow, high-latency link possible between site A and site C. Rather than using that slower speed link, we could designate site B as a bridge site to site C. Use the ADReplicationSiteLinkBridge group of cmdlets to manage the site link bridge.

Manage replication

Replication between domain controllers occurs whether the domain controllers are in the same site or in different sites. Intrasite replication is used to replicate changes within a site, and intersite replication is used between different sites. Typically, intrasite replication is automatically configured by the KCC process, which runs every 15 minutes by default. The KCC creates replication connections between domain controllers in a single site automatically, and when site links are configured, the KCC can then create the intersite connections automatically.

For scenarios that are more complex, or where specialized network requirements or costs dictate manual control of site connections and replication, you can manually configure replication. For example, if a remote site has an expensive and limited connection to the rest of the network, you might want to limit replication frequency and control which domain controllers provide the link between the remote site and the main site by designating a site bridge between the remote site and a closer site with better connectivity, allowing the remote site to replicate to the bridge site.

Set the replication schedule

You can manually configure the replication schedule between domain controllers and between sites. The process for changing the replication between trey-dc-04 and trey-dc-05 is detailed in the following steps:

1. Create a new AD DS schedule object.

```
$schObj = New-Object -TypeName `
    System.DirectoryServices.ActiveDirectory.ActiveDirectorySchedule
```

2. Configure the schedule object to replace the current schedule with a new schedule that allows replication between midnight and 4:00, 8:00 to noon, and 16:00 to 20:00.

```
$schObj.ResetSchedule()
$schObj.SetDailySchedule(0,0,4,0)
$schObj.SetDailySchedule(8,0,12,0)
$schObj.SetDailySchedule(16,0,20,0)
```

3. Set the replication schedule for the replication between the two servers, trey-dc-04 and trey-dc-05.

```
$connection = Get-ADReplicationConnection `
    -filter {ReplicateToDirectoryServer -like "CN=trey-dc-05*"}
Set-ADReplicationConnection -Identity $connection `
                        -ReplicationSchedule $schObj `
                        -PassThru
```

This yields the result shown here.

```
AutoGenerated                      : False
DistinguishedName                  : CN=TREY-DC-04,CN=NTDS Settings,
                                     CN=TREY-DC-05,CN=Servers,CN=Redmond-11,
                                     CN=Sites,CN=Configuration,
                                     DC=TreyResearch, DC=net

InterSiteTransportProtocol         :
Name                               : TREY-DC-04
ObjectClass                        : nTDSConnection
ObjectGUID                         : 07c4e8c1-4335-4280-86c2-5a0919e11920
PartiallyReplicatedNamingContexts  : {}
ReplicatedNamingContexts           : {CN=Schema,CN=Configuration,
                                     DC=TreyResearch,DC=net,
                                     CN=Configuration,DC=TreyResearch,
                                     DC=net, DC=TreyResearch,DC=net}
```

```
ReplicateFromDirectoryServer        : CN=NTDS Settings,CN=TREY-DC-04,
                                      CN=Servers,CN=Vancouver-10,CN=Sites,
                                      CN=Configuration,DC=TreyResearch,DC=net
ReplicateToDirectoryServer          : CN=TREY-DC-05,CN=Servers,CN=Redmond-11,
                                      CN=Sites,CN=Configuration,
                                      DC=TreyResearch,DC=net
ReplicationSchedule                 :
System.DirectoryServices.ActiveDirectory.ActiveDirectorySchedule
```

This tells us that we set the schedule on the correct object, but it doesn't confirm what the schedule actually is. For that, we have to resort to the GUI.

4. Open Active Directory Sites And Services (dssite.msc).

5. Expand the Redmond-11 site in the tree pane, and select NTDS Settings for the TREY-DC-05 object, as shown in Figure 9-4.

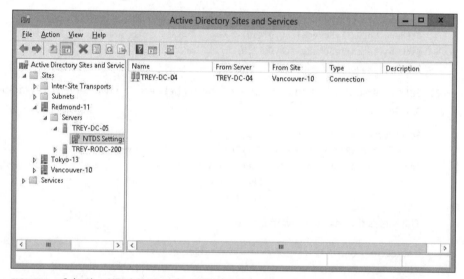

FIGURE 9-4 Selecting NTDS Settings for TREY-DC-05 in the Active Directory Sites And Services console

6. Right-click the connection in the details pane and click Properties on the menu to open the properties of the connection.

7. Click Change Schedule to show the Schedule For TREY-DC-04 dialog box shown in Figure 9-5, to confirm the hours for replication.

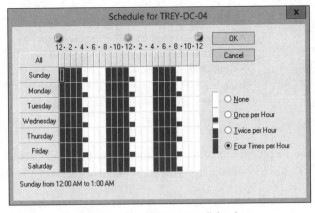

FIGURE 9-5 The Schedule For TREY-DC-04 dialog box

Change the replication server

When we created trey-rodc-200, AD DS automatically created a replication connection to trey-dc-02. That was an appropriate connection when trey-rodc-200 was the only server in the Redmond-11 site. But now that there's a second domain controller, trey-dc-05, and it's a writable domain controller, the RODC can easily replicate from it. Therefore, we can change the replication source server for trey-rodc-200 by using the Set-ADReplicationConnection command.

```
Set-ADReplicationConnection -Identity `
        (Get-ADReplicationConnection `
          -Filter {ReplicateToDirectoryServer -like "cn=trey-rodc-200*" }`
        ) -ReplicateFromDirectoryServer trey-dc-05 `
          -PassThru
```

Because we used the PassThru parameter, we get the details of the connection after the command completes, as shown here.

```
AutoGenerated                        : True
DistinguishedName                    : CN=RODC Connection (SYSVOL),CN=NTDS Settings,
                                       CN=TREY-RODC-200,CN=Servers,CN=Redmond-11,
                                       CN=Sites,CN=Configuration,
                                       DC=TreyResearch,DC=net

InterSiteTransportProtocol           :
Name                                 : RODC Connection (SYSVOL)
ObjectClass                          : nTDSConnection
ObjectGUID                           : f4bf5c14-8fbb-457f-bcdf-a06d00a9dbb1
PartiallyReplicatedNamingContexts    : {}
ReplicatedNamingContexts             : {CN=Schema,CN=Configuration,DC=TreyResearch,
                                       DC=net,CN=Configuration,DC=TreyResearch,
                                       DC=net,DC=TreyResearch,DC=net}
```

```
ReplicateFromDirectoryServer       : CN=NTDS Settings,CN=TREY-DC-05,CN=Servers,
                                     CN=Redmond-11,CN=Sites,CN=Configuration,
                                     DC=TreyResearch,DC=net
ReplicateToDirectoryServer         : CN=TREY-RODC-200,CN=Servers,
                                     CN=Redmond-11,CN=Sites,CN=Configuration,
                                     DC=TreyResearch,DC=net
ReplicationSchedule                :
```

There's no replication schedule set for this connection; therefore, it will replicate all day, every day. Because this is an intrasite connection, the replication frequency is every 15 minutes.

Summary

In this chapter you learned how to create, configure, and manage Active Directory sites and subnets; create and configure replication connections; create site links; and configure Universal Group Membership Caching.

In the next chapter, you'll learn how to connect your on-premises Active Directory to the cloud by using Microsoft Azure.

CHAPTER 10

Deploy Active Directory in the cloud

Enterprise environments are increasingly a mixture of on-premises and cloud services, mixed and intermingled to provide the geo-redundancy, flexibility, disaster recovery, and mobility that are expected in the modern world. This means that on-premises domain administrators are increasingly looking to the cloud, and specifically to Microsoft Azure, as a solution to meet the needs of the enterprise.

In this chapter, we'll connect our internal domain—msmvps.ca this time—to our Azure account, where we'll deploy a new virtual network (VNet), create a point-to-site virtual private network (VPN), and deploy a new virtual machine in Azure. We'll create a new Active Directory site and Active Directory subnet for msmvps.ca in Azure, and we'll deploy our new virtual machine as a full read-write domain controller in that site.

Active Directory Windows PowerShell nouns used in this chapter:

- ADReplicationSite
- ADReplicationSubnet
- ADDSDomainController

Other Windows PowerShell commands used in this chapter:

- Import-Module
- Get-Command
- Select-Object
- Where-Object
- Add-AzureAccount
- Get-AzureAccount
- Get-AzureSubscription
- New-SelfSignedCertificate
- Get-ChildItem
- ConvertTo-SecureString
- Export-PfxCertificate

- Import-PfxCertificate
- Get-AzureVNetConfig
- Set-AzureVNetConfig
- Remove-AzureVNetConfig
- Select-AzureSubscription
- Get-AzureLocation
- Format-Table
- New-AzureStorageAccount
- Get-AzureStorageAccount
- Set-AzureSubscription
- Get-AzureVMImage
- New-AzureVMConfig
- Get-Credential
- Add-AzureProvisioningConfig
- Set-AzureStaticVnetIP
- Set-AzureSubnet
- New-AzureQuickVM
- New-AzureVM
- Get-AzureVM
- Get-AzureRemoteDesktopFile
- Install-WindowsFeature
- Update-Help

> **NOTE** In this chapter, I assume you have an existing and functional Azure account. If you don't yet have one or want to create another one for working through the details in this chapter, you can get a free, 30-day trial account at *azure.microsoft.com/en-us/pricing /free-trial/*. There are also ways to get free accounts with much larger limits on them than this free trial, including Microsoft Developer Network (MSDN) accounts (up to $1,800 per year worth of free Azure), through school and academic programs, and through BizSpark (*azure.microsoft.com/en-us/pricing/member-offers/bizspark-startups/*).

Install the Windows PowerShell Azure model

Using Windows PowerShell with Azure requires the download and installation of the latest version of the Azure module. This module is updated frequently, with many new cmdlets being added all the time. When I wrote the Get-Help for the initial release of the Windows PowerShell Azure module three years ago, there were approximately 120 cmdlets. With release 0.9.1, there are 716 cmdlets, not including the resource cmdlets, which we won't be using for this chapter.

To get started, download the latest version of the Azure module at *https://github.com/Azure /azure-powershell/releases/latest*. Do this even if you already have the Windows PowerShell Azure module installed, because this module changes frequently. The version I used for this chapter is 0.9.1, and I chose to do a stand-alone Windows installation to ensure that I only installed the Windows PowerShell Azure module and not a bunch of other stuff that I didn't need.

Install the Windows PowerShell Azure module

To download and install the stand-alone Windows PowerShell Azure module, use the following steps:

1. Connect to the GitHub repository for Azure at *https://github.com/Azure/azure-power-shell/releases/latest*, as shown in Figure 10-1.

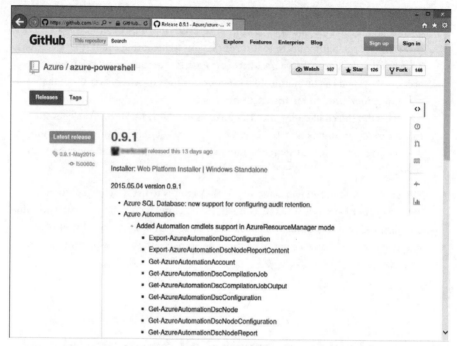

FIGURE 10-1 The GitHub repository for Azure PowerShell

2. Click Windows Standalone and save the downloaded file (azure-powershell.0.9.1.msi) to a location where you can find it.

3. Navigate to the location where you saved the installation file, and double-click it.

4. Accept the license agreement, as shown in Figure 10-2, and then click Install.

5. When the installation completes, click Finish to close the installation wizard.

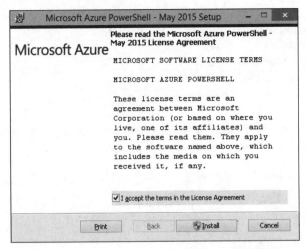

FIGURE 10-2 The Microsoft Azure PowerShell - May 2015 License Agreement dialog box

Load the Windows PowerShell Azure module

The Windows PowerShell Azure module is a 32-bit module that installs in a nonstandard location. The installer, however, adds that location to the $ENV:PSModulePath variable, allowing it to be found and automatically loaded by both the 32-bit and the 64-bit versions of Windows PowerShell. To explicitly load the Azure module, use the following command.

```
Import-Module Azure –PassThru
```

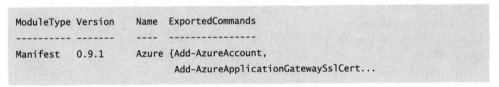

```
ModuleType Version    Name   ExportedCommands
---------- -------    ----   ----------------
Manifest   0.9.1      Azure  {Add-AzureAccount,
                               Add-AzureApplicationGatewaySslCert...
```

To get a count of the number of commands in the Azure module, use the following.

```
(Get-Command –Module Azure).count
```

```
716
```

The number of unique nouns in a module is a useful indicator of the scope of the module. To get a count of the unique nouns in the Azure module, use the following.

```
(Get-Command -Module Azure | Select Noun -Unique).count
```

```
297
```

Finally, let's actually find out what commands we have available, though we're certainly not going to use all of them in this chapter—that's a whole book in itself.

```
Get-Command -Module Azure | Select Noun -Unique
```

```
noun
----

AzureAccount
AzureApplicationGatewaySslCertificate
AzureCertificate
AzureDataDisk
AzureDisk
AzureDns
AzureEndpoint
AzureEnvironment
AzureHDInsightConfigValues
AzureHDInsightMetastore
AzureHDInsightScriptAction
AzureHDInsightStorage
AzureInternalLoadBalancer
AzureNetworkInterfaceConfig
AzureNodeWebRole
AzureNodeWorkerRole
AzurePHPWebRole
AzurePHPWorkerRole
AzureProvisioningConfig
AzureRemoteAppUser
AzureTrafficManagerEndpoint
AzureVhd
AzureVirtualIP
AzureVMImage
AzureWebRole
AzureWorkerRole
AzureProfile
AzureStorSimpleLegacyVolumeContainerStatus
AzureServiceProjectRemoteDesktop
AzureTrafficManagerProfile
```

```
AzureWebsiteApplicationDiagnostic
AzureWebsiteDebug
AzureRemoteAppSession
AzureVM
AzureAclConfig
AzureAffinityGroup
AzureApplicationGateway
AzureApplicationGatewayConfig
AzureAutomationAccount
AzureAutomationCertificate
AzureAutomationConnection
AzureAutomationCredential
AzureAutomationJob
AzureAutomationJobOutput
AzureAutomationModule
AzureAutomationRunbook
AzureAutomationRunbookDefinition
AzureAutomationSchedule
AzureAutomationScheduledRunbook
AzureAutomationVariable
AzureDeployment
AzureDeploymentEvent
AzureEffectiveRouteTable
AzureHDInsightCluster
AzureHDInsightJob
AzureHDInsightJobOutput
AzureHDInsightProperties
AzureIPForwarding
AzureLocation
AzureManagedCache
AzureManagedCacheAccessKey
AzureManagedCacheLocation
AzureManagedCacheNamedCache
AzureMediaServicesAccount
AzureNetworkSecurityGroup
AzureNetworkSecurityGroupAssociation
AzureNetworkSecurityGroupConfig
AzureNetworkSecurityGroupForSubnet
AzureOSDisk
AzureOSVersion
AzurePublicIP
AzurePublishSettingsFile
AzureRemoteAppCollection
AzureRemoteAppCollectionUsageDetails
AzureRemoteAppCollectionUsageSummary
```

```
AzureRemoteAppLocation
AzureRemoteAppOperationResult
AzureRemoteAppPlan
AzureRemoteAppProgram
AzureRemoteAppStartMenuProgram
AzureRemoteAppTemplateImage
AzureRemoteAppVNet
AzureRemoteAppVpnDevice
AzureRemoteAppVpnDeviceConfigScript
AzureRemoteAppWorkspace
AzureRemoteDesktopFile
AzureReservedIP
AzureRole
AzureRoleSize
AzureRouteTable
AzureSBAuthorizationRule
AzureSBLocation
AzureSBNamespace
AzureSchedulerJob
AzureSchedulerJobCollection
AzureSchedulerJobHistory
AzureSchedulerLocation
AzureService
AzureServiceADDomainExtension
AzureServiceAntimalwareConfig
AzureServiceAvailableExtension
AzureServiceDiagnosticsExtension
AzureServiceExtension
AzureServiceProjectRoleRuntime
AzureServiceRemoteDesktopExtension
AzureSiteRecoveryJob
AzureSiteRecoveryNetwork
AzureSiteRecoveryNetworkMapping
AzureSiteRecoveryProtectionContainer
AzureSiteRecoveryProtectionEntity
AzureSiteRecoveryRecoveryPlan
AzureSiteRecoveryRecoveryPlanFile
AzureSiteRecoveryServer
AzureSiteRecoverySite
AzureSiteRecoveryStorage
AzureSiteRecoveryStorageMapping
AzureSiteRecoveryVault
AzureSiteRecoveryVaultSettings
AzureSiteRecoveryVaultSettingsFile
AzureSiteRecoveryVM
```

```
AzureSqlDatabase
AzureSqlDatabaseCopy
AzureSqlDatabaseImportExportStatus
AzureSqlDatabaseOperation
AzureSqlDatabaseServer
AzureSqlDatabaseServerFirewallRule
AzureSqlDatabaseServerQuota
AzureSqlDatabaseServiceObjective
AzureSqlDatabaseUsages
AzureSqlRecoverableDatabase
AzureStaticVNetIP
AzureStorageAccount
AzureStorageBlob
AzureStorageBlobContent
AzureStorageBlobCopyState
AzureStorageContainer
AzureStorageContainerStoredAccessPolicy
AzureStorageFile
AzureStorageFileContent
AzureStorageKey
AzureStorageQueue
AzureStorageQueueStoredAccessPolicy
AzureStorageServiceLoggingProperty
AzureStorageServiceMetricsProperty
AzureStorageShare
AzureStorageTable
AzureStorageTableStoredAccessPolicy
AzureStoreAddOn
AzureStorSimpleAccessControlRecord
AzureStorSimpleDevice
AzureStorSimpleDeviceBackup
AzureStorSimpleDeviceBackupPolicy
AzureStorSimpleDeviceConnectedInitiator
AzureStorSimpleDeviceVolume
AzureStorSimpleDeviceVolumeContainer
AzureStorSimpleFailoverVolumeContainers
AzureStorSimpleJob
AzureStorSimpleLegacyVolumeContainerConfirmStatus
AzureStorSimpleLegacyVolumeContainerMigrationPlan
AzureStorSimpleResource
AzureStorSimpleResourceContext
AzureStorSimpleStorageAccountCredential
AzureStorSimpleTask
AzureSubnet
AzureSubnetRouteTable
```

```
AzureSubscription
AzureVMAccessExtension
AzureVMAvailableExtension
AzureVMBGInfoExtension
AzureVMChefExtension
AzureVMCustomScriptExtension
AzureVMDiagnosticsExtension
AzureVMDscExtension
AzureVMDscExtensionStatus
AzureVMExtension
AzureVMImageDiskConfigSet
AzureVMMicrosoftAntimalwareExtension
AzureVMPuppetExtension
AzureVMSqlServerExtension
AzureVNetConfig
AzureVNetConnection
AzureVNetGateway
AzureVNetGatewayDiagnostics
AzureVNetGatewayIPsecParameters
AzureVNetGatewayKey
AzureVNetSite
AzureWebHostingPlan
AzureWebHostingPlanMetric
AzureWebsite
AzureWebsiteDeployment
AzureWebsiteJob
AzureWebsiteJobHistory
AzureWebsiteLocation
AzureWebsiteLog
AzureWebsiteMetric
AzureWinRMUri
WAPackCloudService
WAPackLogicalNetwork
WAPackStaticIPAddressPool
WAPackVM
WAPackVMOSDisk
WAPackVMRole
WAPackVMSizeProfile
WAPackVMSubnet
WAPackVMTemplate
WAPackVNet
AzureHDInsightHttpServicesAccess
AzureHdinsightRdpAccess
AzureStorSimpleLegacyApplianceConfig
AzureStorSimpleLegacyVolumeContainer
```

```
AzureHDInsightHiveJob
AzureRemoteAppSessionLogoff
AzureCertificateSetting
AzureDataFactory
AzureHDInsightClusterConfig
AzureHDInsightHiveJobDefinition
AzureHDInsightMapReduceJobDefinition
AzureHDInsightPigJobDefinition
AzureHDInsightSqoopJobDefinition
AzureHDInsightStreamingMapReduceJobDefinition
AzureInternalLoadBalancerConfig
AzureMediaServicesKey
AzureQuickVM
AzureRoleTemplate
AzureSchedulerHttpJob
AzureSchedulerStorageQueueJob
AzureServiceADDomainExtensionConfig
AzureServiceDiagnosticsExtensionConfig
AzureServiceExtensionConfig
AzureServiceProject
AzureServiceRemoteDesktopExtensionConfig
AzureSiteRecoveryProtectionProfileObject
AzureSqlDatabaseServerContext
AzureSSHKey
AzureStorageBlobSASToken
AzureStorageContainerSASToken
AzureStorageContext
AzureStorageDirectory
AzureStorageQueueSASToken
AzureStorageTableSASToken
AzureStorSimpleDeviceBackupScheduleAddConfig
AzureStorSimpleDeviceBackupScheduleUpdateConfig
AzureStorSimpleInlineStorageAccountCredential
AzureStorSimpleNetworkConfig
AzureStorSimpleVirtualDevice
AzureVMConfig
AzureVMSqlServerAutoBackupConfig
AzureVMSqlServerAutoPatchingConfig
WAPackQuickVM
AzureVMDscConfiguration
AzureWebsiteProject
AzureAvailabilitySet
AzureNetworkSecurityGroupFromSubnet
AzureNetworkSecurityRule
AzureReservedIPAssociation
```

```
AzureRoute
AzureServiceAntimalwareExtension
AzureVMImageDataDiskConfig
AzureVMImageOSDiskConfig
AzureVNetGatewayDefaultSite
AzureRemoteAppVpnSharedKey
AzureRoleInstance
AzureServiceProjectPackage
AzureRemoteAppSessionMessage
AzureAutomationConnectionFieldValue
AzureHDInsightClusterSize
AzureHDInsightDefaultStorage
AzureLoadBalancedEndpoint
AzureNetworkSecurityGroupToSubnet
AzureServiceProjectRole
AzureStorageContainerAcl
AzureVMSize
AzureWalkUpgradeDomain
AzurePortal
AzureEmulator
AzureSiteRecoveryCommitFailoverJob
AzureSiteRecoveryPlannedFailoverJob
AzureSiteRecoveryProtectionProfileAssociationJob
AzureSiteRecoveryProtectionProfileDissociationJob
AzureSiteRecoveryTestFailoverJob
AzureSiteRecoveryUnplannedFailoverJob
AzureSqlDatabaseExport
AzureSqlDatabaseImport
AzureSqlDatabaseRecovery
AzureSqlDatabaseRestore
AzureStorageBlobCopy
AzureStorSimpleBackupCloneJob
AzureStorSimpleDeviceBackupJob
AzureStorSimpleDeviceBackupRestoreJob
AzureStorSimpleDeviceFailoverJob
AzureMode
AzureWebsiteSlot
AzureName
AzureTrafficManagerDomainName
AzureSiteRecoveryProtectionDirection
AzureWebsiteRepository
```

That's an impressive breadth of coverage! There are still a few things you need to use the Azure Portal to configure, but those are rapidly disappearing. Unfortunately, there's one more thing we'll need to use the Portal for, and that's for creating our initial Azure Virtual Network (VNet).

Connect to an Azure account

The first thing we need to do with Azure PowerShell is connect to our Azure account and select the subscription we're going to work with. Many users have multiple subscriptions they use for Microsoft Azure, and that's OK, but when you work with the Azure PowerShell cmdlets, you can only work with one subscription at a time.

There are multiple ways to connect to your Azure subscription, and each has advantages and disadvantages. The two most popular methods are the certificate method (which uses the Azure PublishSettings file) and the Azure AD method. We'll use the Azure AD method, but if you want to use certificates, use the AzurePublishSettingsFile cmdlets to get and import the certificates you'll need.

Authenticate to your Azure account

To use the Azure AD method of connecting to your Azure account, use the following steps:

1. Open a new Windows PowerShell console. This is important, because the $ENV:PSModulePath environment variable was updated as part of the installation of Azure PowerShell, as shown here.

```
# Environment before installing Azure PowerShell
$ENV:PSModulePath
```

```
D:\Charlie\WindowsPowerShell\Modules;C:\Program Files\WindowsPowerShell
\Modules;C:\Windows\system32\WindowsPowerShell\v1.0\Modules\;C:\Program
Files\Microsoft Azure Recovery Services Agent\bin\Modules\
```

```
# Environment after installing Azure PowerShell
$ENV:PSModulePath
```

```
D:\Charlie\WindowsPowerShell\Modules;C:\Program Files\WindowsPowerShell
\Modules;C:\Windows\system32\WindowsPowerShell\v1.0\Modules\;C:\Program
Files\Microsoft Azure Recovery Services Agent\bin\Modules\;C:\Program Files
(x86)\Microsoft SDKs\Azure\PowerShell\ServiceManagement
```

2. From the Windows PowerShell console, explicitly load the Azure module by using the following command.

```
Import-Module Azure –PassThru
```

```
ModuleType Version Name ExportedCommands
---------- ------- ---- ----------------
Manifest   0.9.1   Azure {Add-AzureAccount, Add-AzureApplicationGatewaySsl
```

3. Log on to your Azure account by using the following command.

```
Add-AzureAccount
```

This opens a window to allow you to interactively authenticate to Azure, as shown in Figure 10-3.

FIGURE 10-3 Signing in to Azure PowerShell

4. Enter the email address of the account you use for Azure, and click Continue. At this point, your path might diverge from these steps slightly, depending on which kind of account you have (personal, work or school, or both).

5. If you have both kinds of accounts and they have the same email address, you need to specify which kind of account you want to use, as shown in Figure 10-4.

FIGURE 10-4 Choosing which kind of account to use for authentication

6. If you're signing in with a Microsoft account, you'll be redirected to the Microsoft Account Sign In page, as shown in Figure 10-5. Enter your sign-in credentials.

FIGURE 10-5 The Sign In To Your Microsoft Account dialog box

The command finishes and returns the results of the accounts it found that are associated with the account you used, as shown here.

```
Id                    Type Subscriptions           Tenants
--                    ---- -------------           -------
charlie@contoso.com   User d7c39575-9148-4571-...  836a6638-ca7c-46ab-b0f8-...
                           efbd43b3-da98-4a7d-...
```

7. My account has two subscriptions associated with it. I could also run the command again to add additional accounts that are associated with different email addresses.

Set the current subscription

Even if you only have one subscription, you still need to set that subscription as the current subscription. First, get all your Microsoft Azure accounts by using the following.

```
Get-AzureAccount
```

Then, get a list of your current subscriptions by using the following.

```
Get-AzureSubscription
```

This returns a list of all the subscriptions associated with your account. In this chapter, I'm going to work with the first subscription that was returned, by using the following.

```
$myAzSub = (Get-AzureSubscription)[0]
```

We'll use the $myAzSub variable whenever we need to reference a subscription.

Create a VPN

Before we create our first Microsoft Azure virtual machine, we need to create the virtual networking environment that it will reside in. This will include critical networking information that will allow us to create a virtual private network between our domain controller, mvps-dc-02 in the msmvps.ca domain, and the new domain controller we're going to create in Azure. To configure connectivity, we'll use self-signed certificates.

> **NOTE** In this section, we are creating a point-to-site VPN, which is perfectly appropriate for a lab environment. However, for a true hybrid enterprise environment where multiple resources are distributed across both local datacenters and Azure, you can create a site-to-site VPN. For details on the supported devices, go to *https://msdn.microsoft.com/library /azure/jj156075.aspx*.

Create self-signed certificates

Before we start creating our virtual network on Azure, we need to create a couple of self-signed certificates: a root certificate that we upload to our subscription, and a client certificate that we generate to use for connecting clients (in this case, our mvps-dc-02 domain controller) to our VNet on Azure.

Create a self-signed root certificate

There are many ways to create a root certificate, including using the New-SelfSignedCertificate cmdlet, but the tried-and-true method, and one that is documented and supported by Azure, is using the makecert.exe tool. This is not part of Windows but is available as a feature of the free Microsoft Visual Studio Express 2013 with Update 4 for Windows Desktop, available directly from Microsoft at *go.microsoft.com/?linkid=9832280*. You'll need to sign in to a Microsoft account, but you can choose to download a disk image (.iso file) or an installer.

I've already got Visual Studio installed on my lab, so now we can open a Developer Command Prompt for VS 2013 window. This is available from a shortcut in the Visual Studio Tools folder that is in the Visual Studio 2013 folder on the Start Menu. At the command prompt, we'll change to a directory where we have write privileges, such as C:\Temp, and then issue the following command.

```
makecert -sky exchange -r -n "CN=MsMVPsCaRoot" -pe -a sha1 -len 2048 -ss My
"MsMVPsCaRoot.cer"
```

This command creates a self-signed root certificate that we can upload to Azure. It will place a copy of the certificate in our personal X.509 certificate store. You can view the certificate, and get the thumbprint for it, by using the Windows PowerShell Certificate provider, as shown here.

```
dir Cert:\CurrentUser\My
```

```
Thumbprint                                Subject
----------                                -------
772AF9E5316CE4416C2EA214AAB77528DA33B8E2  CN=794A113D-A20B-4F11-9C36-...
4D4089DF6A901E2E5836A9AD3D68BA02160FC79C  CN=MsMVPsCaRoot
```

That second certificate is the one we just created. This certificate will be uploaded to Azure when we create our virtual network.

Create a self-signed client certificate

We're also going to need self-signed client certificates to allow clients to create a VPN connection to our VNet in Azure. While we have that Developer Command Prompt For VS 2013 window open, we'll also create a client certificate, as shown here.

```
makecert.exe -n "CN=mvps-dc-02" -pe -sky exchange -m 96 -ss My -in "MsMVPsCaRoot" -is my
-a sha1
```

This creates a client certificate in our personal X.509 certificate store. You can view the certificate, and get the thumbprint for it, by using the Windows PowerShell Certificate provider, as shown here.

```
Get-ChildItem Cert:\CurrentUser\My
```

```
Thumbprint                                Subject
----------                                -------
772AF9E5316CE4416C2EA214AAB77528DA33B8E2  CN=794A113D-A20B-4F11-9C36-...
4D4089DF6A901E2E5836A9AD3D68BA02160FC79C  CN=MsMVPsCaRoot
C56AAEDE3002259D8BD8D4C67FA111EF853D6DFA  CN=mvps-dc-02
```

Because we're running this on a workstation and are not logged on to the mvps-dc-02 domain controller that we're going to use as the VPN endpoint inside our lab environment, we need to export the certificate as a .pfx file. To export the CN=mvps-dc-02 client certificate, along with the entire chain supporting it, with a password of "P@ssw0rd!", use the following commands, which use the thumbprint of the certificate to identify it.

```
$myPW = ConvertTo-SecureString -String "P@ssw0rd!" -AsPlainText -Force
Get-ChildItem -Path cert:\CurrentUser\my\C56AAEDE3002259D8BD8D4C67FA111EF853D6DFA `
             | Export-PfxCertificate -FilePath C:\Temp\myPfx.pfx `
               -Password $myPW
```

Now, move the .pfx file to mvps-dc-02 and then import it there by using the following commands.

```
$myPW = ConvertTo-SecureString -String "P@ssw0rd!" -AsPlainText -Force
Import-PfxCertificate -FilePath C:\myPfx.pfx cert:\CurrentUser\my -Password $myPW
```

These commands need to be run from an elevated Windows PowerShell prompt on the mvps-dc-02 computer, and the password used must match the password used to encrypt the .pfx file with Export-PfxCertificate.

Create a point-to-site VPN

Now that we have our certificates sorted, we need to actually create the virtual network we'll use for our cloud AD DS environment. Unfortunately, this is something you can't really do with Windows PowerShell, at least not for the first one. Before we start, though, let's make sure we know what values we're going to need for the VNet and the VPN. The VNet will need an address space, as will the VPN connection, and they can't overlap, nor should they overlap internal network address spaces in our internal network, to avoid routing issues. We use 192.168.10.0/24 for our internal lab network, so we'll want to avoid any 192.168 addresses for this virtual network.

> **NOTE** All addresses used for creating this virtual network must be RFC 1918 compliant private addresses. This means the addresses must be taken from the 10.0.0.0/8, 172.16.0.0/16, or 192.168.0.0/16 subnets. Only IPv4 addresses are supported at this time.

The VPN will have an address space for the actual VPN connections. This can be a maximum of 254 addresses, which are assigned dynamically. It will also have an overall address space that is used for the virtual machines and applications running in this VNet. We'll have a single subnet in the VNet, plus a Gateway subnet. The Gateway subnet can be no smaller than a /29 subnet. Finally we'll need to define at least two DNS servers, one for each domain controller. Table 10-1 shows the settings we'll use to create the VNet.

TABLE 10-1 Network settings for mvps-VirtualNetwork

Name	IP Address	Comment
mvps-dc-02	172.168.10.1	On-premises domain controller, dynamic VPN address.
mvps-dc-03	10.10.10.3	Azure virtual machine domain controller.
Point-to-site connectivity	172.168.10.0/24	Useable address range 172.16.10.1–172.16.10.254. These are addresses assigned to VPN clients.
Virtual network address spaces	10.0.0.0/8	The overall address space available to virtual machines, applications, and websites in this VNet.
Subnet-1	10.0.0.0/11	Useable address range of 10.0.0.1–10.31.255.254. The subnet that VPN clients can connect to.
Gateway subnet	10.32.0.0/29	Dynamic routing gateway network. Required to provide connectivity between the VNet and clients.

> **IMPORTANT** Do not attempt to create an Azure virtual network until you have fully thought out the network architecture you will use, and what addresses you will use. Address ranges cannot overlap each other, and any RFC 1918 addresses that you use internally should not be part of any of the address ranges used in this VNet.

Now, if you have your own version of Table 10-1 fully filled out and you're ready to start creating your Azure virtual network, log on to the Azure Portal and follow these steps:

1. Log on to *http://manage.windowsazure.com* with the same account you used for Add-AzureAccount.

2. Click Networks in the left pane of the Azure Portal to view the networks you have. We have no networks, as shown in Figure 10-6.

FIGURE 10-6 The Azure Portal

3. Click Create A Virtual Network to open the Create A Virtual Network Wizard.

4. Enter a name for the network, and select a location from the Location list, as shown in Figure 10-7.

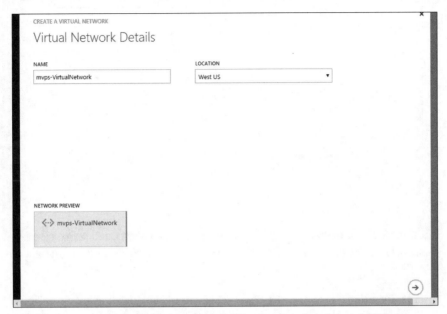

FIGURE 10-7 The Virtual Network Details page of the Create A Virtual Network Wizard

5. Click the right-pointing arrow in the lower-right corner of the page to open the DNS Servers And VPN Connectivity page.

6. Select the Configure A Point-To-Site VPN check box, and enter two DNS servers. The first of these should have the IP address that you expect the mvps-dc-02 domain controller to have when the VPN is active (see Figure 10-8).

7. Click the right-pointing arrow in the lower-right corner of the DNS Servers And VPN Connectivity page to open the Point-to-Site Connectivity page.

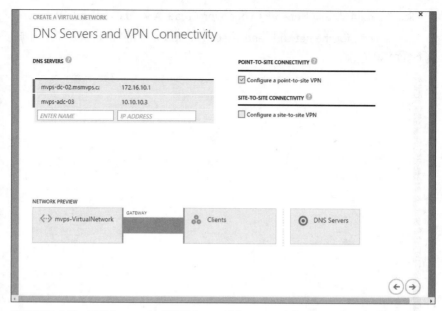

FIGURE 10-8 The DNS Servers And VPN Connectivity page of the Create A Virtual Network Wizard

8. Enter the value for Point-to-Site connectivity from Table 10-1, as shown in Figure 10-9. These are the available IP addresses for clients connecting to this VPN endpoint. The maximum is 254 clients (a /24 address space).

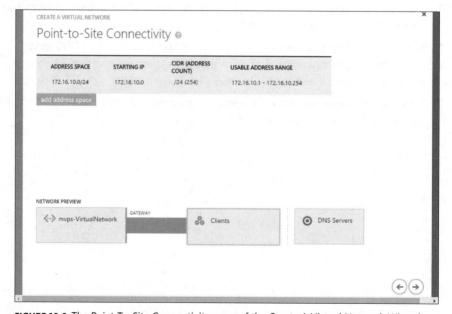

FIGURE 10-9 The Point-To-Site Connectivity page of the Create A Virtual Network Wizard

9. Click the right-pointing arrow in the lower-right corner of the page to open the Virtual Network Address Spaces page of the Create A Virtual Network Wizard.

10. Fill in the fields of the Virtual Network Address Spaces page according to the values in your version of Table 10-1, as shown in Figure 10-10.

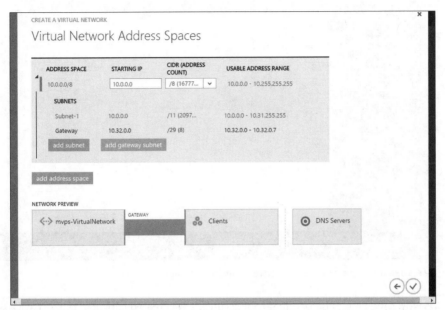

FIGURE 10-10 The Virtual Network Address Spaces page of the Create A Virtual Network Wizard

11. Click the check mark in the lower-right corner of the page to create the virtual network. Be patient, and when the network is created, you'll get the notice shown in Figure 10-11.

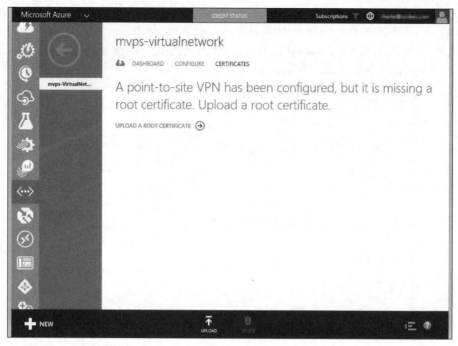

FIGURE 10-11 The mvps-virtualnetwork Certificates page

12. Now's the time to upload that root certificate we created earlier, in the "Create a self-signed root certificate" section. Click Upload to open the Upload Certificate dialog box shown in Figure 10-12.

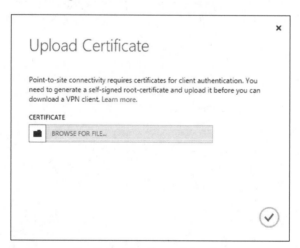

FIGURE 10-12 The Upload Certificate dialog box

13. After uploading the certificate, return to the main page for the VNet, where you'll find the status of the VNet creation and the certificate upload, as shown in Figure 10-13.

FIGURE 10-13 The mvps-virtualnetwork page of the Azure Portal

Download a VPN client

When the configuration and deployment of the virtual network is complete, you can download a VPN client to those computers that need to connect to Azure through this VPN. To download the VPN client for this network, use the following steps:

1. Navigate to the Networks page of the Azure Portal, and click mvps-VirtualNetwork in the details pane.

2. Click the dashboard tab to bring up the virtual network dashboard, as shown in Figure 10-14.

FIGURE 10-14 The virtual network dashboard

3. Click Download The 64-bit Client VPN Package to download a VPN package for mvps-dc-02.

4. Download the very long-named .exe file, and save it to the hard disk of mvps-dc-02.

   The file name is the GUID virtual network ID shown in the Quick Glance pane on the right side of the virtual network dashboard.

5. On the client computer (mvps-dc-02 for us), double-click the file to install the VPN client.

> **NOTE** In some environments, Windows SmartScreen might prevent the file from executing. Change the properties of the downloaded file to unlock it.

6. Click Yes when asked whether you want to install the VPN client. The new mvps-VirtualNetwork client is installed, as shown in Figure 10-15.

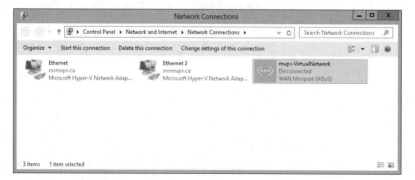

FIGURE 10-15 The Network Connections dialog box on mvps-dc-02

7. Double-click the mvps-VirtualNetwork icon in the Network Connections dialog box (ncpa.cpl) to open the Windows Azure Virtual Network dialog box shown in Figure 10-16.

FIGURE 10-16 The mvps-VirtualNetwork Windows Azure Virtual Network dialog box

8. Click Connect. You'll be prompted to update your routing table, which requires elevated privileges.

9. Click Continue. If you've done your certificates correctly, you'll soon be connected to the VNet.

Save the virtual network configuration

After you've confirmed that everything is working as expected, you can save the current configuration to a netcfg file (XML format). The netcfg file can be used to re-create the network if it gets removed, or you can manually edit the file to reconfigure the network. Use the following command to export the network configuration and save it to a file.

```
Get-AzureVNetConfig -ExportToFile T:\Chapter10\SampleVNetConfig.netcfg
```

XMLConfiguration	OperationDescription	OperationId	OperationStatus
<?xml version="1.0" encodi...	Get-AzureVNetConfig	325e9760-cb5e-abb3-8a22-eb...	Succeeded

You can remove a VNet by using the Remove-AzureVNConfig cmdlet. The network can't be in use when you remove it or the operation will fail.

Create a virtual machine

Now that we have networking set up and sorted out, we can leave the GUI of the Azure Portal behind and create our new virtual machine in Azure and configure it to be the domain controller in our new Azure-West site.

The process for creating a virtual machine in Azure is somewhat different than that used for creating a virtual machine in Hyper-V, though the result is quite similar. When you create a virtual machine on a computer running Windows Server and Hyper-V, you already know where your virtual machine resides, and the storage for it is the physical disks used to host the virtual hard disks (VHDs). But in Azure, you need to:

- **Connect to a subscription**   This is the Azure equivalent of connecting to the Hyper-V host in your datacenter that will host the virtual machine.
- **Set a location**   This is the Azure equivalent of deciding which datacenter your new virtual machine should reside in. The Azure location must be the same as the one the VNet was provisioned in.
- **Create a service**   This doesn't have an equivalent in the traditional local on-premises virtual machine deployment.
- **Provision a storage account**   This is the Azure equivalent of selecting the RAID array where your virtual machine's VHDs will be. You need to either select existing storage or create a new storage account for this set of virtual machines.
- **Create the virtual machine configuration object**   This is the equivalent of New-VM when working with a Hyper-V environment.
- **Deploy the virtual machine**   This is the Azure equivalent of starting a virtual machine.

Connect to the subscription

Before we can create an Azure virtual machine, we need to have an Azure subscription and connect to that subscription. (Follow the steps in the "Connect to an Azure account" section earlier in this chapter to connect to your Azure account if you haven't already done so on your current computer.) To set your active subscription to the first subscription in your account, use the following.

```
$AzSubs = Get-AzureSubscription
Select-AzureSubscription -SubscriptionName $AzSubs[0].SubscriptionName
```

Set a location

We need to decide where our Azure virtual machine will be hosted. If our virtual machine is going to be part of the VNet we just created and provisioned, we know it needs to be in West US. We could just enter that where we need to, but I prefer to let Windows PowerShell do the work. To get a list of Azure locations, use the following.

```
$Index = -1
Get-AzureLocation | Format-Table -Auto `
                        @{Label="Count"; `
                          Expression={($Global:Index+=1) } }, `
                        @{Label="Location Name"; `
                          Expression={$_.Name}}
```

```
Count Location Name
----- -------------
    1 Central US
    2 South Central US
    3 West US
    4 East US
    5 East US 2
    6 North Europe
    7 West Europe
    8 Southeast Asia
    9 East Asia
   10 Japan West
   11 Japan East
```

From this, we can tell that West US is the third location returned by Get-AzureLocation. We'll create an array of Azure locations, and then we can easily reference West US as the third in the array.

```
$azLocs = Get-AzureLocation
$azLocs[2]
```

```
DisplayName          : West US
Name                 : West US
AvailableServices    : {Compute, Storage, PersistentVMRole, HighMemory}
WebWorkerRoleSizes   : {A10, A11, A5, A6, A7, A8, A9, ExtraLarge, ExtraSmall,
                       Large, Medium, Small, Standard_D1, Standard_D11,
                       Standard_D12, Standard_D13, Standard_D14, Standard_D2,
                       Standard_D3, Standard_D4}
```

```
VirtualMachineRoleSizes : {A10, A11, A5, A6, A7, A8, A9, Basic_A0, Basic_A1,
                           Basic_A2, Basic_A3, Basic_A4, ExtraLarge, ExtraSmall,
                           Large, Medium, Small, Standard_D1, Standard_D11,
                           Standard_D12, Standard_D13, Standard_D14, Standard_D2,
                           Standard_D3, Standard_D4, Standard_DS1, Standard_DS11,
                           Standard_DS12, Standard_DS13, Standard_DS14,
                           Standard_DS2, Standard_DS3, Standard_DS4, Standard_G1,
                           Standard_G2, Standard_G3, Standard_G4, Standard_G5}
StorageAccountTypes      : {Standard_LRS, Standard_ZRS, Standard_GRS,
                           Standard_RAGRS, Premium_LRS}
OperationDescription     : Get-AzureLocation
OperationId              : 42fb23f6-5b3a-a0df-88e1-96edf9067170
OperationStatus          : Succeeded
```

Provision a service

This Azure account hasn't been used for anything recently, so I de-provisioned all the storage, virtual machines, services, and networking months ago. Therefore, before we can create a virtual machine, we have to create an Azure cloud service to host the virtual machine. We can create a cloud service that can host our mvps-adc-03 virtual machine by using the New-AzureService cmdlet. To create the new cloud service, use the following command.

```
New-AzureService -ServiceName "msMVPsService" `
                 -Location $azLocs[2].Name `
                 -Label "mvps-ca-cloud-site" `
                 -Description "AD DS Site for msmvps.ca in Azure"
```

```
OperationDescription    OperationId                            OperationStatus
--------------------    -----------                            ---------------
New-AzureService        3fdaa58b-06b1-a9e3-83ea-348ab9a0de0d   Succeeded
```

Provision a storage account

Next, we need to provision a storage account to host our virtual machines. Azure storage is infinitely expandable (if you have the money to pay for it) and can be provisioned with only high-speed solid-state drives (SSDs), only hard disk drives (HDDs), or a mixture of the two, as dictated by the needs of your virtual machines, applications, and websites. You don't make the determination of what kind of storage you want until you actually need the storage, and you don't pay for it until it's actually being used. The storage account just creates the framework that will hold the storage. Our storage account needs to be in the same Azure location as the VNet we're joining the new VM to.

To create a new storage account in the West US Azure datacenter, use the following command.

```
New-AzureStorageAccount -StorageAccountName "mvpvmstorage" -Location $azLocs[2].Name
```

OperationDescription	OperationId	OperationStatus
New-AzureStorageAccount	b22b5e74-e85b-a51a-acb4-41636e14502c	Succeeded

To assign this storage account as the current storage account for the subscription we selected earlier as our current subscription, use the following commands.

```
$subscrNam  = $AzSubs[0].SubscriptionName
$storName = (Get-AzureStorageAccount).StorageAccountName
Set-AzureSubscription -SubscriptionName $subscrNam `
                      -CurrentStorageAccountName $storname
```

The setting of $storName is valid only because we know that we have only one storage account, the one we just created. If we had multiple storage accounts in this Azure subscription, we would need to do as we did when using the $AzLocs variable—use the index value to select the one we want from the array of locations.

Create a virtual machine

The process of creating and deploying an Azure virtual machine is both simpler and more complex than that of deploying a virtual machine on a Hyper-V server. It is simpler because you don't have to worry about whether you have enough memory or disk space to deploy another virtual machine. You also don't have to worry that you might be overloading the available CPUs in the host or have too many virtual machines feeding through a single network card. For all intents and purposes, Azure has an infinite amount of disk, CPU, memory, and networking resources available, and you can use as much as you need and can pay for.

The process is more complicated because there are more and different parts to building a virtual machine configuration object before we can actually deploy the virtual machine. We *could* build a virtual machine in a single command line, but when we do that, we have to accept certain limitations. For our use, one of those limitations is critical—we can't configure the virtual machine with a fixed IP address. This is not good, so we'll do it the long way. For your future reference, the single-line command to create an Azure virtual machine is New-AzureQuickVM. It can even create the required cloud service if it doesn't already exist. The syntax for New-AzureQuickVM is as follows.

```
New-AzureQuickVM -Windows -ServiceName <string> -ImageName <string>
[-Name <string>] [-Password <string>][-ReverseDnsFqdn <string>]
[-Location <string>] [-AffinityGroup <string>] [-AdminUsername <string>]
[-Certificates <CertificateSettingList>] [-WaitForBoot] [-DisableWinRMHttps]
[-EnableWinRMHttp] [-WinRMCertificate <X509Certificate2>]
```

```
[-X509Certificates <X509Certificate2[]>] [-NoExportPrivateKey]
[-NoWinRMEndpoint] [-VNetName <string>] [-SubnetNames <string[]>]
[-DnsSettings <DnsServer[]>] [-HostCaching <string>]
[-AvailabilitySetName <string>] [-InstanceSize <string>] [-MediaLocation <string>]
[-DisableGuestAgent] [-CustomDataFile <string>] [-ReservedIPName <string>]
[-Profile <AzureProfile>] [<CommonParameters>]

New-AzureQuickVM -Linux -ServiceName <string> -ImageName <string> [-Name <string>]
[-Password <string>] [-ReverseDnsFqdn <string>] [-Location <string>]
[-AffinityGroup <string>] [-LinuxUser <string>] [-WaitForBoot]
[-SSHPublicKeys <LinuxProvisioningConfigurationSet+SSHPublicKeyList>]
[-SSHKeyPairs <LinuxProvisioningConfigurationSet+SSHKeyPairList>]
[-VNetName <string>] [-SubnetNames <string[]>] [-DnsSettings <DnsServer[]>]
[-HostCaching <string>] [-AvailabilitySetName <string>] [-InstanceSize <string>]
[-MediaLocation <string>] [-DisableGuestAgent] [-CustomDataFile <string>]
[-ReservedIPName <string>] [-Profile <AzureProfile>] [<CommonParameters>]
```

Build the virtual machine configuration object

The process of building a virtual machine configuration object is not quite like anything you do when you're deploying servers in a typical Hyper-V environment. I suspect that at some point, as Azure and Windows Server come closer together, the process of deploying virtual machines will become quite similar in both. I even suspect, without any direct knowledge, that the Windows PowerShell Desired State Configuration could be the vehicle that both adopt.

To start building our virtual machine configuration object, we need to decide what base image we're going to use, what size our virtual machine should be, and what the name of the virtual machine will be. First, let's figure out what images are available.

```
(Get-AzureVMImage).count
```

```
544
```

Wow. When I was writing the original Get-Help files for Azure PowerShell, there were no more than a couple of dozen or so images. Well, let's narrow that down a bit. We know we want to use Windows Server 2012 R2 for our cloud domain controller, so let's filter that result a bit, knowing that there's an ImageFamily property that should do what we need to filter down to a more reasonable number.

```
$ImgFamily = "Windows Server 2012 R2 Datacenter"
(Get-AzureVMImage | Where {$_.ImageFamily -eq $ImgFamily }).count
```

```
3
```

That's more like it. Let's just use the most recent of these images.

```
$imgFamily = "Windows Server 2012 R2 Datacenter"
$img = Get-AzureVMImage `
          | Where {$_.ImageFamily -eq $imgFamily } `
          | sort PublishedDate -Descending `
          | select -ExpandPropert ImageName -First 1
$img
```

```
a699494373c04fc0bc8f2bb1389d6106__Windows-Server-2012-R2-201504.01-en.us-127GB.vhd
```

Now that we've got the image, we need to decide on a virtual machine size. For our test lab, a virtual machine size of "small" will be more than sufficient. That equates to a single CPU, with 1.75 gigabytes (GB) of RAM and up to two data disks. Actually, we could easily use an A0 or ExtraSmall virtual machine for this scenario, because we're not authenticating thousands of users in our little lab. And the name for the virtual machine will be "mvps-adc-03".

```
$vmName = "mvps-adc-03"
$vmSize = "Small"
```

> **MORE INFO** For a complete list of virtual machine sizes and their names for use in Azure PowerShell cmdlets, go to *https://msdn.microsoft.com/library/azure/dn197896.aspx*.

That's all we need for the first step in the process, so let's create the virtual machine configuration object by using New-AzureVMConfig.

```
$mvpsVM1 = New-AzureVMConfig -Name $vmName -InstanceSize $vmSize -ImageName $img
```

Next, we need to modify $mvpsVM1 to add in local and domain credentials, and build in the domain and DNS name it will belong to, by using the following commands.

```
#Local Credentials
$lcred=Get-Credential -Message "Type the name and pwd of the local admin account."

#Domain Credentials
$dcred = Get-Credential -Message "Enter the name and pwd for the Domain Account"
$domDNS = "msmvps.ca"
$domain = "msmvps"
$mvpsVM1 | Add-AzureProvisioningConfig -WindowsDomain `
          -AdminUsername $lcred.GetNetworkCredential().Username `
          -Password $lcred.GetNetworkCredential().Password `
          -Domain $domain `
          -DomainUserName $dcred.GetNetworkCredential().UserName `
          -DomainPassword $dcred.GetNetworkCredential().Password `
          -JoinDomain $domDNS
```

```
AvailabilitySetName            :
ConfigurationSets              : {mvps-adc-03,Microsoft.WindowsAzure.Commands.
                                 ServiceManagement.Model.
                                 NetworkConfigurationSet}
DataVirtualHardDisks           : {}
Label                          : mvps-adc-03
OSVirtualHardDisk              : Microsoft.WindowsAzure.Commands.
                                 ServiceManagement.Model.OSVirtualHardDisk
RoleName                       : mvps-adc-03
RoleSize                       : Small
RoleType                       : PersistentVMRole
WinRMCertificate               :
X509Certificates               : {}
NoExportPrivateKey             : False
NoRDPEndpoint                  : False
NoSSHEndpoint                  : False
DefaultWinRmCertificateThumbprint :
ProvisionGuestAgent            : True
ResourceExtensionReferences    : {BGInfo}
DataVirtualHardDisksToBeDeleted :
VMImageInput                   :
```

Finally, as the last step in this particular configuration, we need to add the networking configuration for the virtual machine. If this were a production server, we would also want to configure the data disks, but we're not going to need them for this virtual machine. To add the static networking to our virtual machine configuration object, we'll use the following commands.

```
#Set fixed IP (static DIP)
$mvpsVM1 | Set-AzureStaticVnetIP -IPAddress 10.10.10.3
$mvpsVM1 | Set-AzureSubnet -SubnetNames "Subnet-1"
```

Deploy the VM

Now that we have the virtual machine configuration object complete, we're ready to create the virtual machine and assign it to a cloud service name and a VNet. We actually create the virtual machine by using the following commands.

```
$mvpSvc = "msMVPsService"
$vnet = "mvps-VirtualNetwork"
New-AzureVM -ServiceName $mvpSvc -VMs $mvpsVM1 -VNetName $vnet
```

```
OperationDescription    OperationId                              OperationStatus
--------------------    -----------                              ---------------
New-AzureVM             f94bcb6d-cd83-ab32-b935-79f19a97f7b8     Succeeded
```

Let's find out what we've created, by using Get-AzureVM.

```
Get-AzureVM -ServiceName $mvpSvc
```

```
DeploymentName            : msMVPsService
Name                      : mvps-adc-03
Label                     :
VM                        : Microsoft.WindowsAzure.Commands.ServiceManagement.
                            Model.PersistentVM
InstanceStatus            : Provisioning
IpAddress                 : 10.10.10.3
InstanceStateDetails      : Windows is preparing your computer for first use...
PowerState                : Started
InstanceErrorCode         :
InstanceFaultDomain       : 0
InstanceName              : mvps-adc-03
InstanceUpgradeDomain     : 0
InstanceSize              : Small
HostName                  : EMPLOYE-03N0OIO
AvailabilitySetName       :
DNSName                   : http://msmvpsservice.cloudapp.net/
Status                    : Provisioning
GuestAgentStatus          : Microsoft.WindowsAzure.Commands.ServiceManagement.
                            Model.GuestAgentStatus
ResourceExtensionStatusList : {}
PublicIPAddress           :
PublicIPName              :
PublicIPDomainNameLabel   :
PublicIPFqdns             : {}
NetworkInterfaces         : {}
VirtualNetworkName        : mvps-VirtualNetwork
ServiceName               : msMVPsService
OperationDescription      : Get-AzureVM
OperationId               : d0f7a02f4e24a8ac86cbc84a2cb991e6
OperationStatus           : OK
```

After a few minutes, the virtual machine status will change from Provisioning to Running, at which point, we can download a remote desktop connection (.rdp) file to connect to the server by using the following command.

```
Get-AzureRemoteDesktopFile -Name mvps-adc-03 `
                           -ServiceName $mvpSvc `
                           -LocalPath c:\temp\mvps-adc-03.rdp
```

OperationDescription	OperationId	OperationStatus
Get-AzureRemoteDesktopFile	54af77dc-727b-a697-aacb-7d9ebcd77424	Succeeded

We can open an RDP session to our new server by using the following command.

```
Mstsc c:\temp\mvps-adc-03.rdp
```

We're now ready to start configuring the new server and promoting it to be a domain controller in the msmvps.ca domain.

Configure the domain controller

Now that we have our new server up and running in Azure, we can configure it to be a domain controller just like any other domain controller at a remote site. This was covered in the other nine chapters of this book, so I'm not going to repeat it all over again. The steps we need to perform on the remote server are those covered in Chapter 4, "Deploy additional domain controllers." If the deployment of the Azure virtual machine went as planned, the mvps-adc-03 virtual machine is already joined to the msmvps.ca domain. Therefore, all we need to do is install the AD-Domain-Services role and promote the server to be a domain controller. To install the AD-Domain-Services role and update the Windows PowerShell Help, we use the following commands.

```
Install-WindowsFeature -Name AD-Domain-Services -IncludeManagementTools
Update-Help -Force
```

Before we promote the server to domain controller, we should create a new AD DS site and AD DS subnet. That's easy enough; we just did all that in Chapter 9, "Manage sites and replication." We can create a new site and subnet by using the following commands.

```
New-ADReplicationSite -Name Azure-West `
                      -Description "Cloud site in Microsoft Azure"
New-ADReplicationSubnet -Name "10.0.0.0/11" `
                        -Site "Azure-West" `
                        -Location "Microsoft Azure West-US"
```

Now we can promote the server by using the following command.

```
Install-ADDSDomainController `
     -NoGlobalCatalog:$false `
     -CreateDnsDelegation:$false `
     -CriticalReplicationOnly:$false `
     -DatabasePath "C:\Windows\NTDS" `
```

```
    -DomainName "msmvps.ca" `
    -InstallDns:$true `
    -LogPath "C:\Windows\NTDS" `
    -NoRebootOnCompletion:$false `
    -SiteName "Azure-West" `
    -SysvolPath "C:\Windows\SYSVOL" `
    -Force:$true
```

And when replication has completed, the server reboots and is a new domain controller in our msmvps.ca domain, as shown in Figure 10-17.

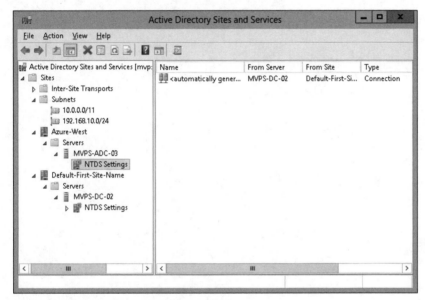

FIGURE 10-17 Active Directory Sites And Services

Summary

In this final chapter, you learned how to install the Windows PowerShell Azure module and how to connect to your Azure account. You created an Azure virtual network and configured it to support a point-to-site VPN, including creating the necessary root and client certificates.

You then learned how to create a virtual machine in Azure by first connecting to your subscription, provisioning a new cloud server and a new storage account, and then building the virtual machine configuration object and deploying the new virtual machine. Finally, you configured the new server in Azure as a domain controller in a new site and subnet to create a complete hybrid cloud solution.

Index

A

A resource records
   creating 28
   described 26
AAAA resource records
   creating 28
   described 26
account policies 135–142
AccountExpirationDate parameter 131
AccountNotDelegated parameter 131
AccountPassword parameter 131
Active Directory
   See also Active Directory Domain Services (AD DS)
   authoritative restores 157–162
   Azure AD 185
   backup methods 144
   cloud, types in 185
   non-authoritative restores 155–157
   offline media backup, creating 152
   restore methods 155
   role, installing on servers 67
   snapshots 153, 154
   Windows Server Backup 144–151
Active Directory Administrative Center (ADAC) 137, 138
Active Directory Domain Services (AD DS)
   See also Active Directory; DNS; sites
   Active Directory Recycle Bin 162–164
   authoritative restores 157–162
   Azure AD 185
   database, installing from media 92–94
   DHCP, activating in 38
   functional levels 10
   supported groups 51–54
   installing 6
   members, adding to groups 53
   non-authoritative restores 155–157

Active Directory Domain Services (AD DS) *(continued)*
   replication 178–180
   restore methods 155
   role, installing 105, 111
   schema, updating 79
   sites, configuring 168–174
Active Directory Domain Services role 105, 111
Active Directory Recycle Bin
   enabling 153, 162
   restoring objects, using 162–164
Active Directory Services Interface (ADSI) 122
Active Directory snapshots
   configuring 153
   restoring objects, using 164–166
AD DS (Active Directory Domain Services) *See* Active Directory Domain Services (AD DS)
ActiveDirectory module 6
ADAC (Active Directory Administrative Center) 137, 138
Add noun 7
Add-ADDSReadOnlyDomainControllerAccount cmdlet 88, 93
Add-ADGroupMember cmdlet 52
Add-ADPrincipalGroupMembership cmdlet 56
Add-AzureAccount cmdlet 198
Add-AzureProvisioningConfig cmdlet 215
Add-Computer cmdlet 68, 96
Add-DhcpServerInDC cmdlet 38
Add-DhcpServerv4ExclusionRange cmdlet 39
Add-DhcpServerv4Scope cmdlet 39
Add-DhcpServerv6ExclusionRange cmdlet 40
Add-DhcpServerv6Scope cmdlet 40
Add-DnsServerConditionalForwarderZone cmdlet 25
Add-DnsServerPrimaryZone cmdlet 17
Add-DnsServerResourceRecord cmdlet 27
Add-DnsServerResourceRecordA cmdlet 27, 28
Add-DnsServerResourceRecordAAAA cmdlet 27
Add-DnsServerResourceRecordCName cmdlet 27

D

Z

About the author

Charlie Russel has been a Microsoft MVP for Windows XP, Security, Windows Server, and now Windows PowerShell. He's a chemist by education, an electrician by trade, a UNIX and Windows sysadmin and Oracle DBA because he raised his hand when he should have known better, and an IT Manager for a major international software and security company by choice.

Charlie is the author of more than three dozen books about operating systems and enterprise environments and is the original author of the Get-Help pages for the Windows PowerShell Azure module. His recent books include *Exam Ref 70-411: Administering Windows Server 2012 R2* (Microsoft Press, 2014), *Working with Windows Small Business Server 2011 Essentials* (Microsoft Press, 2011), *Windows Small Business Server 2011 Administrator's Companion* (Microsoft Press, 2011), *Windows Server 2008 Administrator's Companion* (Microsoft Press, 2008), and *Oracle DBA Automation Quick Reference* (Prentice Hall PTR, 2004).

From technical overviews to drilldowns on special topics, get
free ebooks from Microsoft Press at:

www.microsoftvirtualacademy.com/ebooks

Download your free ebooks in PDF, EPUB, and/or Mobi for
Kindle formats.

Look for other great resources at Microsoft Virtual Academy,
where you can learn new skills and help advance your career
with free Microsoft training delivered by experts.

Now that you've read the book...

Tell us what you think!

Was it useful?
Did it teach you what you wanted to learn?
Was there room for improvement?

Let us know at http://aka.ms/tellpress

Your feedback goes directly to the staff at Microsoft Press,
and we read every one of your responses. Thanks in advance!